sewing happiness

a year of simple projects for living well

SANAE ISHIDA

SASQUATCH BOOKS
SEATTLE

Printed in China

Published by Sasquatch Books
20 19 18 17 16 9 8 7 6 5 4 3 2 1

Editor: Hannah Elnan
Production editor: Emma Reh
Design: Anna Goldstein
Copyeditor: Nancy W. Cortelyou

Front cover and page 71 • Photographs: Michelle Porter, Styling: Tristan Brando
Pages ii, 2, 80, 84, 89, 90, 92, 97, 110 • Photographs: Sanae Ishida, Styling: Rachel Grunig
Pages vi, 51, 86, 91 • Photographs: Sanae Ishida, Styling: Allegra Hsiao
Pages 18, 19, 35, 42, 43, 228 • Photographs and styling: Sanae Ishida
Page 24 • Photograph and styling: Michelle Porter
All other photos • Photographs: George Barberis, Styling: Rachel Grunig

Library of Congress Cataloging-in-Publication Data is available.

ISBN: 978-1-57061-995-3

Sasquatch Books
1904 Third Avenue, Suite 710
Seattle, WA 98101
(206) 467-4300
www.sasquatchbooks.com
custserv@sasquatchbooks.com

for my mom and koko

PEERLESS CARD INDEX No. 1

contents

author's note

I'D LIKE TO THINK THIS ISN'T your typical sewing book. It's part cautionary tale; part practical collection of simple sewing projects; part entreaty for gentler, less perfection-oriented ideals in life. At its heart, it's a personal story about unexpected transformations.

I want to start with a promise: if *I* can sew, anyone can sew.

I can't promise that the results will be flawless, or that you'll learn everything there is to know about sewing from the pages that follow—since I still can't get through a project without at least one mistake even after years of sewing. Still, if you take it one step at a time, one small task at a time, and just stick with it, you'll be surprised by how quickly your skills improve and how beautiful your final creations will be.

If you've picked up this book and you're new to sewing, or if you are coming back to it after an intermission, I think you'll find the projects completely doable. As with any new or rusty skill, you'll need to do some preparation up front and get your gear ready, and there might be a bit of a learning curve, but ultimately, all you need is a touch of inspiration, some basic tools, and the willingness to try. If you're anything like me, you might be tempted to go crazy and invest in every gadget and shiny accoutrement, but I've learned that not a lot is required to get started.

If you're more seasoned in the craftwork of sewing, my hope is that you will find the projects refreshing in their simplicity, and will consider them launching pads for more advanced variations to your liking. Of note is a small section I've included with my loose interpretation of Japanese-style embroidery called *Sashiko*, which is a charming detail to add to a plethora of items.

Simple sewing is my favorite kind. I did my best to streamline the projects so that they are straightforward and easy—my aim was to make them easy enough for my nine-year-old daughter to confidently give them a shot. To that end, there are no complex pattern sheets to cut or trace or tape together. All the elements for the projects can be whipped up with a few measurements and possibly an existing garment for reference. Fudging is allowed and encouraged. Mistakes are part and parcel of the process, and the seam ripper will become your best friend.

Speaking of my daughter, she will pop up quite a bit throughout the book. We've chosen to keep her name private, but I will refer to her as "KoKo," a nickname she's selected for herself. The word means "here" in Japanese, which evokes a sense of mindfulness for me, as in the *here and now*. I like it. KoKo is also the name of a female lowland gorilla that has mastered an impressive amount of sign language, and this too makes me inexplicably happy.

I try to dwell, like Emily Dickinson, in possibilities. With that in mind, I've attempted to make the projects in this book modifiable and customizable. There's a variety to choose from, including garments for kids and adults and home decor and gifts. All are full of possibilities.

PART I:

ESSAYS + LOOKBOOKS

Deep Chrome 9

introduction

IT WOULDN'T BE AN EXAGGERATION TO say that sewing saved my life and altered it forever. That's a pretty big claim, and I'm ready to back it up.

In late spring 2012, I was in a sorry state: I was severely ill, overworked, undernourished, overweight, disconnected from family and friends. It didn't start out that way, though. Just six months prior, I was at the top of my game. Or at least I thought I was at the top of my game.

I'd been welcomed into the fold of a large high-profile company, tasked to help shepherd what one manager called the "new crown jewel" product. It was a breathlessly fast-paced start-up environment, and the air was abuzz with the thrill of the unknown. "Scrappy," we called ourselves, cobbling together procedures, assembling teams from scratch, making it all up as we went along. I reported to a sweet woman with a great sense of humor, and I remember feeling important as I tugged at the elastic attached to my employee keycard to swipe open the glass sliding doors. It felt like a grand reentry into the corporate world after years as a stay-at-home mom.

Then shortly after I started working full-time, my boss abruptly left for an earlier-than-planned maternity leave, and at first, things kept chugging along in the same exciting vein. I took on a lot more work to cover for her absence, and I was revved by the added responsibilities. This felt like Significant Work requiring brainpower, unlike the schlep of potty training or planning playdates for my daughter, KoKo, that had previously occupied my hours.

As the team grew, the mood shifted. Suddenly, eighty-hour workweeks and all-nighters were the norm. I opened my laptop first thing in the morning, before brushing my teeth, just in case a crisis had developed since the 11 p.m. conference call with India I'd just had the night before. Unlike the initial phase of the project, which was filled with ebullient plans described with lingo along the lines of "synergy" and "mold-breaking," now my in-box filled up with bullet points that addressed problem after increasing problem.

But I'm a problem solver, and despite the lack of sleep, the nonexistent exercise regimen, and the horrific eating habits I was cultivating (a.k.a. the vending machine diet), I powered through. The higher-ups caressed my ego as they bandied about phrases like "rising star," and they offered me an office with an ergonomic chair. More money. Public accolades. A 20 percent discount to an opulent gym that looked more like a nightclub, complete with a DJ and velvet lounge sofas.

Driven by newfound ambition and a sense of validation, I didn't have much of a life outside of my job. One evening, as my family assembled around the kitchen table for a quick meal, my daughter exclaimed, "Mommy! We never have dinner together anymore. This is so weird!" I looked at my six year old with bleary eyes. My husband said nothing. Intellectually, I could clearly see that I was turning into someone else, someone I didn't particularly like. The kind of person who chose Excel reports over family mealtimes. More often than not, I was a distracted and irritable mother and wife. My daughter's words stung, and I fumbled an apology, but the next morning, I opened my laptop first thing again.

I was so caught up in my workaholic mayhem that I didn't think it was outrageously odd when a pregnant coworker said, "I just hope the baby comes after the product launch date." And when the stress became too much, I rushed over to the nearest mall during my short breaks to buy overpriced clothing with abandon. Pretty clothes gave me momentary relief, although my vending machine diet was forcing me to size up several times over, which then upped my stress. And so the cycle continued.

Just before I'd started my job, I'd gone to get my first routine mammogram and I was relieved to find out that I was clear of any cancer indicators. However, the doctor suggested that I go see a specialist because my thyroid hormone levels seemed a touch high. I hunted down a chipper, Harvard-educated endocrinologist who confirmed that I definitely had slightly elevated numbers. "But it's nothing to worry about. Let's just keep an eye on it and I'll see you in three months," she said cheerfully.

Three months later, I was back in her office and she knitted her brows with concern. My hormone levels had shot up to alarming levels. "Graves' disease," she pronounced, and prescribed medication. Thyroid abnormalities, which result in autoimmune disorders, affect a shockingly large number of people—women mostly—but my doctor said that no one really knows why. Stress seems to be a huge factor. This was very bad news for me, since I subsisted purely on stress. In fact, as soon as I returned to work, I forgot to take my meds in the whirlwind of other seemingly more important to-dos.

Sure enough, by that point, I exhibited disturbing health symptoms. I'd developed a chronic, body-wracking cough, and every time KoKo came home with a little cold from school, I would catch it and it would evolve into a state akin to pneumonia. Each time, my coughing worsened. I sounded strikingly like a seal in a torture chamber.

Still, I refused to stop working. I kept making mistakes, got mired in office politics, missed appointments and deadlines. The worst was when I would suddenly jolt upright during a stultifying meeting because I realized I'd forgotten one of KoKo's school performances. Every day was a minefield at the office, and my workload increased as I produced less and worse. Panicked by my poor showing, I doubled down by virtually eliminating sleep and drinking about fifteen cups of coffee a day. This was a bad move. On several occasions, I shrunk in humiliation as I was publicly reprimanded and criticized in all-team meetings. At home, things weren't any better. My star had fizzled out with a whimper.

My body kept deteriorating. One time, a coworker took me aside and asked in worried sotto voice if someone had punched me because my eye looked terribly bruised. It was an odd side effect of my condition, but what was odder was that when I went to look at myself in the bathroom, I couldn't see it. I tilted my head this way and that, trying to get a glimpse of the black eye but with no luck. Whether this meant I was losing a grip on reality or whether I'd just gotten used to my beat-up appearance, I have no idea. I was a big, fat, sick mess.

And then, in May 2012, I got fired.

Initially I couldn't comprehend what was happening. Two people sat me down, squirmed a little, and informed me that my services were no longer needed. I am Asian—overachievement is baked into my DNA. My first job was at the age of twelve (I bussed tables at a restaurant), and I had never truly stopped working from that point on. In over twenty-five years, I'd held jobs in vastly wide-ranging fields and industries, and believed that my singular strength was in being an excellent worker. Getting fired was unthinkable! I sputtered. I cried. And then I left, fully shamed.

It would take over a year for me to understand it, but it turned out to be the best thing that ever happened to me.

This book is about how—over the course of many, many months—I redefined my priorities, reversed my illness, and rediscovered my love of sewing and creating in general. How I learned to live better, on my own terms. I didn't do it all at once though, it hasn't been easy, and my life is far from picture-perfect now.

As a kid, I remember a woman who lived up the hill from my family, in the *really* nice part of the neighborhood. She was the mother of my brother's friend, and she had this spectacular, airy house with gargantuan windows built by a famous architect. She wore cream-colored "ensembles" and everything surrounding her looked polished, spotless, and ready for a tea party (or so my twelve-year-old self thought). She was slim and fit and seemed like a devoted mother, but she also worked full-time at a glamorous design-y job; she represented the ideal for me. I don't recall ever meeting her husband, but I imagined they had a lovely relationship centered around romantic candlelit dinners on their majestic balcony (I don't actually know if they had a balcony since I only saw a portion of their house once). But I did know I wanted *that*.

For most of my adult working life, I'd been striving for the promise of the cream-colored ensemble, and for a couple of weeks at the beginning of the job that ultimately went all wrong, I felt like that woman with the magazine-worthy existence. I've since learned that the cream-colored ensemble promise is an empty one. Actually, I've learned that lesson a million times over, but like with most vital lessons, I seem to need to keep relearning it. The reality is that our house is ramshackle with windows that really ought to get washed more often. I wear almost exclusively gray, navy, and black clothing because it hides paint stains, and conversely shows stray threads from my myriad sewing projects—the darker colors make it easier to pluck them off. My days are messy, my relationships full of ups and downs, and from the outside looking in, my daily routines probably seem utterly boring.

But I'll tell you this: nowadays how I spend my every day feels real, joyful, unpolished yet meaningful—and it is a privilege to be able to share my story and these projects with you.

summer

summer: health

THE FIRST THING I NOTICED AFTER I got canned, besides the coughing and never-ending fatigue, was the abundance of time. I'd become so accustomed to scheduling my days down to the second, I wasn't sure what to do with an empty calendar. I'd already booked KoKo into multiple summer camps with the assumption that I would be working full-time, and my husband was busy at a new job. *What to do?*

Of course, I couldn't do much those first few weeks of my newly minted status in the ranks of the unemployed. Graves' disease is an autoimmune condition. Manifested through overactive thyroid hormone production, a.k.a. hyperthyroidism, it elicits a host of scary symptoms: bulging eyes, goiters, excessive heart palpitations, and constant tremors, to name a few. Insomnia and high levels of anxiety are common. It's a lot like choking down a handful of amphetamines, and in the worst-case scenario, the heart can jackhammer into oblivion. According to the endocrinologist, my hormone levels were "off the charts" by May 2012, and she urged me to seriously consider surgery to remove my thyroid.

Strangely, I didn't exhibit any of the expected signs of hyperthyroidism. I obsessively checked my eyes for any indications of bugginess and my throat for unsightly lumps, but except for a passing comment from my mom that my pupils looked weird, I showed no external physical abnormalities other than the mystery black eye. Expected symptoms or not, I was very, very sick. Sometimes, when I would be tossing and turning in a half-awake state and hacking up a lung, KoKo would sit at the edge of my bed and pat my foot. In a small and shaky voice, she would ask me over and over, "Mama? Are you OK? Are you going to die?" All I could do was hold her hand because I didn't know the answer.

I was also out of shape. In one of the cruelest jokes for someone who has battled with body image issues since preteen years, I had managed to gain nearly twenty pounds despite the fact that significant weight loss is one of the hallmarks of Graves' disease. I'd also aged about fifteen years in the six months since I'd developed my condition, and I was no spring chicken to begin with. I would stare at myself in the mirror and wonder, *Who is that crone?*

I slept a lot that first month, which was the smartest thing I'd done in ages. When I wasn't sleeping, I read voraciously, and I found particular comfort in dystopian young adult novels. I enjoyed being transported to futuristic, steampunk, or fantasy worlds in which good prevailed over evil and innocent romances blossomed. Immersing myself in desolate and ravaged terrains with dwindling food supplies and supernatural conflicts made my own circumstances feel less bizarre.

After a few weeks of almost nonstop slumber, my cough subsided. I was starting to look less like the undead, even if I was still weak. I'd been thinking a lot about my body and my health in general and had read a slew of books about well-being in addition to the dystopian YA novels. After unscientific yet copious research, I deeply evaluated my situation. Although it wasn't conscious or deliberate, from the moment I was diagnosed with the illness, some part of me had consistently rebelled against the idea of infusing my body with chemicals as a means of healing. This explained why I kept "forgetting" to take my meds. Armed with a lot of book knowledge and contemplation time, I tried to listen intently to my body. I kept asking myself, *What does my body want? What does it need?* The response took some time and was faint, but it was also clear. It wanted to rest and feel nourished and move. Against doctor's orders, I decided not to take any medication and to instead focus on the basics: sleep, food, and exercise. Though it sounded so commonsensical, this decision felt strange and unfamiliar to me. The overdeveloped people-pleaser in me balked at the thought of disobeying my endocrinologist, but I had a hunch that I was heading in the right direction.

I felt pretty confident that I'd established a good sleep routine as I was getting at least eight hours a night on a regular basis. So I turned my attention to food.

My diet was still atrocious. My family had developed a take-out habit and we'd frequently order from the local pho, Thai, or pizza joint. Green leafy vegetables scarcely passed our lips. And on days we didn't eat take-out, I stumbled around the kitchen trying to assemble quick meals. I'm a decent but not particularly adventurous cook, and I found myself making the same cheese-laden pasta dishes relentlessly because they required little effort and were popular with the members of my family. My stomach felt distended after these meals, and I retreated to my bed feeling sluggish and tired.

I'll start with adding more vegetables, I resolved. A salad with every dinner. That seemed manageable. Chopping vegetables was therapeutic and meditative, and after a while, I looked forward to evening meals. Soon, since I was cutting up so many vegetables anyway, I began experimenting with green smoothies and juices. For the next month, I slept and chopped. And read.

It was working. I had more energy and didn't need to crawl back into bed after small exertions. And my skin looked brighter, the wrinkles less prominent—what an unexpected bonus!

With this increased energy, I knew it was time to start exercising. But oh, how I *loathe* exercise. I can't even recount how many gyms I've joined for which I've let memberships lapse, how many yoga studios I enthusiastically patronized, only to guiltily ask for a refund after a week or two. Some time around middle school I convinced myself that I'm not a runner, and I've upheld that belief religiously for decades.

But my research was unequivocal about the benefits of exercise. If there ever was a magic pill, exercise is it. To prevent my tendency for burnout, I started small: a ten-minute walk. Even with my renewed vigor, that was pretty much all I could handle, and it would be ten minutes more than I was moving at the time. I usually didn't even bother to change into workout gear. I just slipped on my clogs and circled the block slowly. Every day. Over the course of several weeks, I gradually increased the duration of my walks, and I even dug out tennis shoes that were buried in the back of our hall closet.

Sleep. Chop. Walk. I led a quiet and routinized existence all through the beginning of summer, and my health was improving every single day. Eventually, riddled with guilt from previous months of neglect, I promised KoKo that I would paint her bedroom pink for her birthday. I moved the furniture (that nearly did me in), covered every square inch of the floor with plastic, and primed and rollered her room into a rose-colored wonderland while she was at gymnastic camp. Who knew that painting was such good exercise? Motivated, I then painted over the neon yellow in the master bedroom with a soft silvery gray hue while she was at cooking camp. During zoo camp, I hauled plywood sheets from Home Depot, stained them, and built a shelf in the basement, only to have it come crashing down. At my shame-faced request, my handy neighbor came to the rescue (my husband's not so handy, and apparently, neither am I). In late July, I covered one side of the kitchen with chalkboard paint and my husband wrote in gigantic letters "I love KoKo."

I was on a roll. In the utility room as I was putting away the painting supplies, I found my old sewing machine I had used when KoKo was a baby. I couldn't remember how long it had been since I'd sewn anything. I filed that thought away for later.

"OK, what are you doing? Your blood test results are *amazing*." I was sitting across from my endocrinologist, holding out my hands for the tremor test (where I extend my hands in front of me, palms down, and try to hold them steady). My hands stayed firm, and my doctor gushed about how much better my thyroid hormone levels looked. She had been unsettled by my refusal to take medication, but now she stared at her charts in disbelief. She confided that she'd never seen anyone go through such startling improvements without meds. I told her about my lifestyle changes, about the sleeping and chopping and walking/painting. I told her that I'd been doing everything I could to reduce stress and that I'd been thinking about picking up hobbies I'd let drift years ago. "Whatever you're doing, keep doing it!" she endorsed with her signature exuberance. It's what I needed to hear, and I was ready for the next step: creating.

For the summer projects, I've tried to include fun and practical projects to encourage the trifecta I found so helpful: better sleep, kitchen time, and physical activity. I incorporated origami elements into many of the projects, because aside from the fact that this traditional Japanese craft has been a lifelong staple of mine, it lets me experience the magic of taking a single sheet of paper (or fabric) and transforming it entirely with a fold here, a tuck there, a simple twist-a-roo. My summertime rehabilitation period felt very much like that: taking simple steps to transform my health.

ORIGAMI PILLOW

SLEEP. I'VE ALWAYS UNDERESTIMATED THE POWER of sleep, and I have no doubt that it was the summer of slumber that jump-started the rehabilitation process for me. During those hazy, drowsy days, I spent more time than I care to remember with my pillows and realized how a small indulgence like a stylish object on which to rest my head can add so much joy. These deceptively complicated–looking pillows that echo the folds of origami shapes add panache to any bed, couch, or cozy reading spot. Instructions on page 124.

TOOTH FAIRY PILLOW

(variations: dwox + whale + penguin + butterfly)

WHEN MY DAUGHTER'S BABY TEETH STARTED falling out at an alarming rate that same summer, I made her a little hand-stitched tooth fairy pillow. It was an understated thing, circular with a subtle pocket. Each time, she would reverently place her newly extracted tooth and a note in the pocket. Then she slipped the small pillow under her bigger, plushier one and spent the last moments awake wondering out loud what the tooth fairy might leave behind. Once I heard her deep breathing, I would sneak into her room, clutching the standard issue dollar bill. The most memorable note was the one that read: "I'd like $100 please." The tooth fairy did not oblige, but I marveled at KoKo's chutzpah.

My original pillow was very simple but I wanted to add more origami flair to the pillows included here, complete with some Sashiko embellishment and a stealth pocket. I tried a variety of fauna shapes and settled on a penguin, a whale, and a butterfly—and I meant to create a wolf, but it ended up looking like a combination of a dog + wolf + fox, which is OK with me. We'll call it a *dwox*. Instructions on page 128.

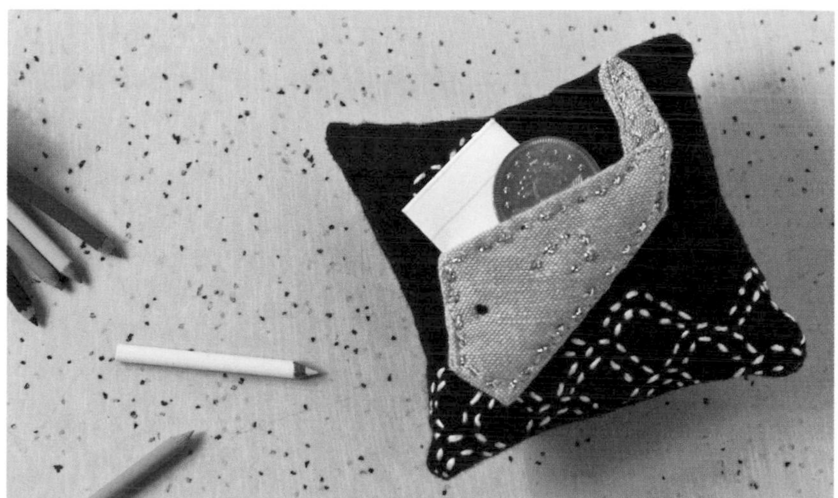

TRIANGLE ECO BAG

IN ADDITION TO THE AMPLE SLEEP, my salad days (in the literal sense) propelled me toward increased vitality. Spending so much time preparing healthy foods requires frequent visits to the grocery store. A rainbow of produce looks oh-so-chic and dare I say more appetizing in this cleverly designed bag. Toss in a freshly baked artisanal baguette and dinner is more than half ready. Not only is it environmentally friendly to bring your own grocery bags, once you've cottoned onto the ninja-style folding of the fabric, these are thoroughly enjoyable to make. Instructions on page 136.

CROSS-BACK APRON

(variation: kid)

COOKING HAS NEVER BEEN MY FORTE, but I've learned a thing or two in the kitchen since I vowed to incorporate more vegetables into my diet: (a) cooking can get messy, (b) dishwashing can get soggy (we don't have a dishwasher), and (c) large front pockets are always handy, mainly for tossing in random objects that my child seems to endlessly stuff into my palms. This traditional Japanese-style apron addresses all three issues and is a winsome addition to the kitchen for kids and grown-ups alike. Instructions on page 140.

YOGA PANTS

THE ONLY TIME I LASTED MORE than two weeks at a yoga studio was when I took prenatal yoga and this was driven by a desperate, hormonally charged desire to have a healthy pregnancy for my unborn babe. I can't say that I enjoyed the yogic experience, but that might have been because of the morning sickness. Similarly driven by a desire toward health while stymied by thyroid hormones, I snail-paced my way toward physical fitness with great determination. I had visions of sun salutations and eventually snaking my ankle behind my ear, but reality didn't catch up with my visions. I did learn to enjoy walking long distances and jogging though. I also found ways to work in small amounts of vigorous movements into my days (vacuuming with gusto counts!) and began to wear yoga pants on a regular basis. It's surprising how simple and gratifying these are to make. Instructions on page 147.

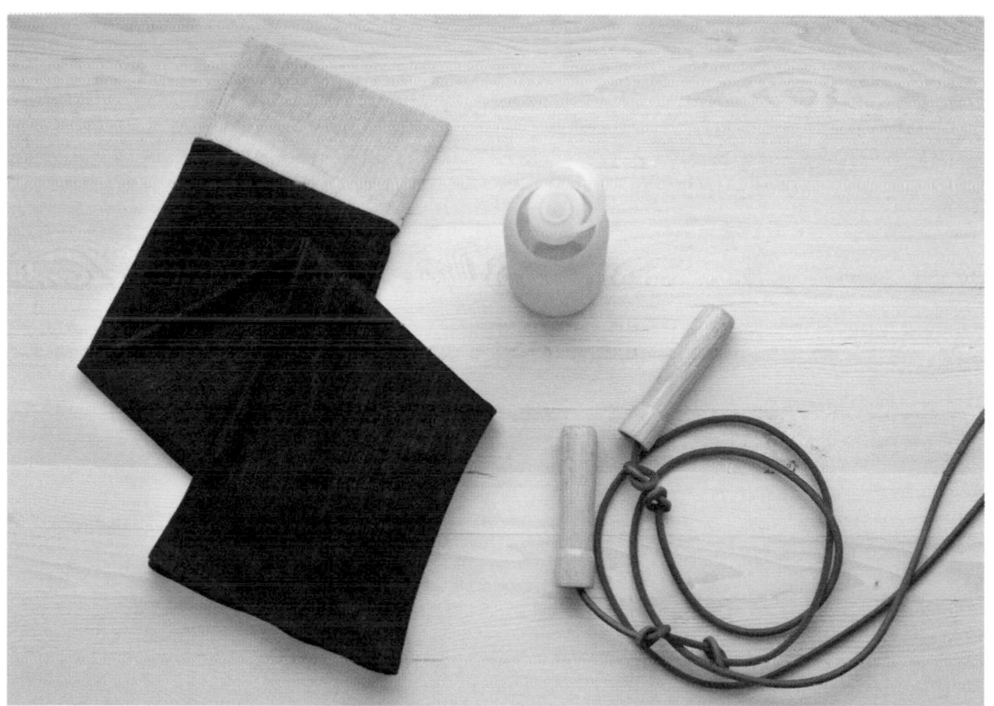

fall

fall: creativity

I'VE KEPT A DAILY JOURNAL FOR over twenty years. It started in college, fall quarter of my freshman year. I was in line to pay for my textbooks when I saw a small blue spiral-bound notebook emblazoned with the school logo. On a whim, I decided to buy the notebook and wandered over to the campus café. I was eighteen and felt so grown-up ordering a cup of coffee and a croissant. Balancing my drink and pastry and books and shiny new notebook, I settled into a seat. The murmurs of other students and the lilt of background music felt . . . *just right*.

I opened the notebook. It was too early in the school year to start studying and I wasn't sure what to do. I doodled a bit and without thinking too much about it, I started writing. I don't own that notebook anymore and I don't know what I wrote that first day, but I continue to write in small notebooks in coffee shops, occasionally doodling along the margins. Many are spiral-bound, some are not; all are crammed with my teeny tiny writing. And almost always, there is a cup of coffee and croissant beside my notebook. I feel lucky that I now live in Seattle, where coffee shops are plentiful and welcoming.

Because this journaling habit is so ingrained, it was the one creative and emotional outlet I continued even while I worked at the job that undid me. I would steal pockets of time to scrawl quick thoughts at the closest café (sometimes even in the company cafeteria). And while I recuperated,

I still scribbled away tucked under the blankets, surrounded by pillows until I could trudge to the nearest coffee shop.

I spent an inordinate amount of time journaling that summer after I got fired, analyzing and rehashing how things could have gone so wrong. There was a lot of feeling sorry for myself. There was a lot of self-doubt, with a sense of my identity breached somehow—if I wasn't an excellent worker, a stellar corporate minion, what was I? I filled several journals obsessing about my shame. But as my health improved, my self-flagellations gave way to more curious inquiries.

What was I excellent at?

I didn't know.

What do I love to do?

I made a list:

Write
Illustrate
Sew
Photograph
Design

Then I added a few more things . . .

Am I great at any of these?

No.

But could I be?

Maybe.

I studied the list, and sewing seemed like something I could excel at. There's less subjectivity to it, since it's fairly easy to ascertain a well-made sewing project from one that's not. I was attracted to the idea of measurable progress, the notion of practicing how to produce satisfyingly even seams. So straightforward! Yet, there's plenty of creativity involved.

It had been a long time since I'd dusted off my Bernina sewing machine, and I still required much schooling in the art and craft of sewing. I needed to give myself a challenge of sorts to motivate myself to practice regularly. Then the image of my very first sewing project came to mind: the ladybug Halloween costume I made for KoKo when she was two years old. I'd wrangled a massive piece of cheap red felt and somehow fashioned it into puffy wings, and then hand-stitched black felt circles all over. It took me three full days with very little sleep, and I remembered how she squealed like a monkey tossed into a banana tree when she wriggled herself into it. I carried on making tiny outfits before I lost steam and got caught up with the minutiae of life by the time KoKo was about three and a half.

That was it! I would sew all of KoKo's clothes. In fact, starting with the school year, for the entire twelve months I wouldn't buy any ready-to-wear (except underwear and socks). I would pour my creative energies into crafting a handmade wardrobe for her. To stay accountable, I called my mom—who lives in Los Angeles—and told her about my newfangled idea. I promised to post weekly outfits on a blog I'd just created so she could see what I made. I was excited. It was just the right kind of crazy to get me inspired.

I selected a summery dress for my first foray into the handmade wardrobe project. I deciphered instructions from a Japanese sewing book, and slaved over it for an entire afternoon while KoKo played with the neighbors in the yard. I completely botched the yoke and the pockets were placed unevenly, but when I whisked it out of the sewing machine after the last stitch, it was with triumphant flourish. Made out of a soft gray-and-blue-striped cotton, what I held in my hands looked decidedly like a dress. Sewn by me! I wiped the sweat from my forehead and dashed outside, demanding that my daughter put it on immediately, and just like when she was two, she squealed delightedly.

Every week, I sewed something new. Another dress. Pants. Tunics. A blouse. A jacket. A wool coat! I worked my way through the many Japanese sewing books I had accumulated over the years and I was having a blast. Pretty soon, the pieces were looking better, and I became so fast at sewing I was pumping out entire outfits, then two outfits per week. I loved it. And so did KoKo.

At the same time, I was practicing with gouache paints to improve my illustrations and trying my hand at photography. I continued to write both in my journal and on my blog, and one day KoKo hugged me and said, "Mama, you seem so happy lately!"

I was. I was happier than I'd ever been. I derived so much pleasure from the crafting of the blog posts, which combined all the elements I loved: writing, illustrations, photography, sewing, design. Every day, I would get out of bed, excited about what I would make. Should I sew something? Or maybe draw an elephant? Perhaps I could try a different way of photographing an interesting DIY project I found online and tried? Since my mom was my only regular blog reader, I felt so incognito, and it was incredibly freeing. The stakes were super low. I laughed at some of the things I made (failed scratch-and-sniff cards! felt bunny dolls with diapers!)—I was having *so* much fun.

It also didn't matter that I wasn't "pro" at any of my endeavors. I could see incremental progress and improvements and that propelled me to keep trying. I wasn't keen on making any of it into a career, and in many ways, I was afraid to go that route since I still felt raw from my last job failure. And gradually a handful of people formed into a small community through my blog. Warm and kind and talented women started to find me online, and to encourage me. It started with a comment or two on the blog that buoyed me with supportive words. A trickle of friendly emails followed, and we exchanged ideas, which then led to collaborations on sewing ventures and other creative projects. My world kept expanding, and I continued to meet extraordinary women who shared my interests and commiserated with my struggles. I felt like someone had accidentally signed me up for the most charming craft camp with the best counselors and fellow campers. It embodied all the goodness of summer camp without any of the snark or homesickness. I even had the opportunity to meet up with quite a few women in person, and they were just as wonderful as I'd anticipated *and* became dear friends—all of this motivated me to persevere and stretch myself.

By the end of fall, handmade clothes filled KoKo's closet. I looked at the array of apparel lined up neatly on small white plastic hangers, and I shook my head in wonder. Every single one of them came from my hands. My iron-singed, needle-pricked, roughened hands.

There's an overarching sense of terror about creating something that didn't exist before and putting it out into the world for judgment, but when you do it repeatedly (whether that world is a child or the interwebs), the confidence muscle strengthens. It's inarguable that proper nutrition, sleep, and exercise are critical for one's well-being, but what I hadn't expected was how health boosting it was to simply make time to create. My physical condition remained steady from my summer rehab, and with this new phase of creative output, I felt even more robust mentally and emotionally, and experienced a new kind of confidence. It was quieter, like a soothing whisper. It wasn't the brittle bravado that depended so much upon the external validations of a big paycheck and job titles. Making things, I realized, is *very* good for me. I started to develop a kind of self-trust, the ability to listen to a voice within. I call it my instinct or intuition, but it's hard to define. The closest I can get is that it's a blend of a pixie and Sherpa, an unassuming yet wise guide, so demure and easily overwhelmed, it needs ample space and silence and time and gentle play to be heard above the din of "should." That fall, I finally had the space, silence, time, and freedom to play.

In the United States, fall signals a fresh beginning, and every autumn, I feel a wellspring of renewed vigor to develop new skills and embark on adventures. The following projects invite you to explore a variety of creative pursuits. May they spark some mojo to experiment with words, paints, images, and all manners of textiles.

JOURNAL/BOOK COVER

AS A LONGTIME JOURNAL KEEPER, I'VE filled hundreds of notebooks with my scrawls over the years. After extensive trial and error, I've landed on spiral-bound notebooks as my default choice, but I'm also smitten with the hardcover Moleskine notebooks that come with the little elastic to keep the book firmly closed. I also like getting the more economical hardbound sketchbooks from the local art store; and creating a custom cover is a great way of adding the elastic and your own personality. With or without elastic, the cover can elevate wedding guest books, scrapbooks—really, any kind of book. Instructions on page 151.

QUICK DIY SKETCHBOOK

DOODLING HAS ALWAYS BEEN AN ESSENTIAL part of the journal-writing ritual for me, but my journal pages are often lined. Sometimes, the lines feel inhibiting. I came up with this easy-peasy project to specifically feed that part of me that longs to be greeted by blank, unlined pages that allow me to freely think with visual renderings. These are compact and convenient to carry around for those inspired moments and for when little kids get antsy for an activity. Presto: instant engrossment. Instructions on page 155.

CAMERA STRAP

DESPITE SPENDING MUCH OF MY CAREER in the photography field, I was always intimidated to get behind the camera and instead stuck to managing photographers or photo shoots or image editors. It wasn't until the autumn season when I started earnestly sewing KoKo's clothes and snapping photos of them that I caught the photography bug. I suddenly wanted to understand aperture and shutter speed and ISO and that badge of the real aficionado of photography: *manual mode*. I had a starter DSLR camera and trained myself by taking hundreds of photos of each garment. I loved looking through them all to find *the one*. As much as I appreciated my camera, I'm a visual person hugely affected by product design, and continuously lamented the lack of pretty camera straps that appealed to my own aesthetics. Then I thought, *why not make my own?* Instructions on page 157.

FELT FLORAL CROWN

WHENEVER I HANDLE FELT FABRIC, I invariably think about that ladybug costume I made in 2007, the one that sent KoKo into fits of zealous squeals. It was that very first sewing project that instilled a new kind of obsession in me. I suddenly saw the world with brand-new, superpower contact lenses, knowing that I could make whatever I wanted, the *way* I wanted. Remembering that feeling was what roused me to give sewing another go. As homage to that sweet ladybird, which is another name for ladybug, I created this miniature flower garden on a crown—it's sure to become a dress-up box staple that will transport the wearer to flights of fancy. Instructions on page 160.

THE STARTER DRESS

(variation: tiered)

IT WAS SO FAR-FETCHED, THIS IDEA to sew all of KoKo's clothes for one year, but the most logical starting point seemed like a simple dress. Part of me thought I could pull it off, but a bigger part of me suspected that I would quit or lose steam or somehow fall short. It was this just-out-of-reach-ness that appealed to me and kept me going, and what cemented my resolve was starting small and building slowly. I had very little expectations for myself and that helped too. The first dress I made was similar to this summery number. I sweated copiously and felt confused much of the time, but simultaneously, a thrill surged through me as I watched the dress take form. That wonky little frock will stand out in my memory forevermore. Instructions on page 164.

winter

winter: relationships

THE RELATIONSHIP THAT SUFFERED THE MOST during my short stint as a stay-at-home mom turned full-time employee was the one with my husband. At the lowest point, he broached the possibility of finding his own place to live, and I was so far gone in my illness and in my attempt to stay in the corporate rat race, his words didn't fully register. His mouth moved, words came out, but all I heard was a jumbled, incoherent mass of slow-motion sounds. We were unhappy with each other, that much was clear. Ours wasn't some star-crossed pairing from the get-go, but after fifteen years, we had a finely tuned secret weapon to carry us through even the harshest of moments: we could always laugh together.

But for the first time, we weren't able to joke our way out of the discomfort and problems. I didn't know why. To me, it seemed like we'd gone through worse in years past and survived. Yet something had severed and cracked, and I felt broken. We are natural contradictions: his extroversion to my introversion; his ability to see the big picture to my detail-orientation; his unreserved machine-gun wit to my reticent straight man. At the core, I believe we have the same values about loyalty and honesty and integrity and all the lofty ideals. I often think of us as paddling a two-person kayak, piloting a rickety craft together. In order to keep the kayak afloat and moving ahead, we need to paddle with our synchronous values. But to turn, tandem kayakers need to paddle in opposite directions, and this requires some finessing to effectively negotiate the turns—sometimes our extreme innate differences cause us to spin in circles.

It seemed as if our imaginary kayak had split in two, and we now passed each other in stony silence, mirthless. There were moments when we managed a strained smile.

A close second in terms of damaged relationships was the one with KoKo. But with her, as soon as I was back in stay-at-home-mom mode, albeit bedridden for a good while, she quickly forgave me and rejoiced in my return, showering me with endless hugs and kisses.

Some reparations were in order. With the holidays around the corner, I was determined to make this one extra special. I didn't grow up in a religious household though my parents dabbled a little bit in both Buddhism and Christianity. I have vague memories from when I was very small of a Los Angeles temple with a lot of Japanese folks eating mochi and noodles, and of my dad joining a Bible study group for a spell. But the thing I remember most about those early holidays was that my mother always gave my brothers and me those dollar store Advent calendars with chocolates nestled behind numbered cardboard doors that flipped up. I looked forward to them every Christmas, and my mother still adores them to this day. In the hopes of establishing a similar tradition for KoKo, I decided to flex my crafting biceps for my own version of an Advent calendar that winter. A quick search yielded instructions for a lovely set of gem-shaped boxes, so I cut and folded and glued twenty-five gems in gold, silver, and sparkly white paper. I filled them with treats and strung each on baker's twine, then glowed in my Martha moment. KoKo did a happy dance when she saw the Advent calendar, of course, and we started off the holidays with a bang.

I also busied myself sewing up gifts for my friends, whom I'd sorely neglected. They had been patient with my repeated cancellations, the constant e-mail checking in their presence, and my despairing requests for last-minute childcare. For several friends, I made pouches filled with tea and other relaxing goodies; and for others, I whipped up tea towels made out of the highest quality linen I could find. Over several evenings, I industriously decorated the tea towels with tiny understated Sashiko stitches.

Batches of homemade caramels wafted their sharp sweet scent throughout the house as I packaged them into small waxed paper bags for neighbors. I was grateful to be reconnecting with the small groups of people who had unfailingly supported me, despite the distance I'd created.

But with the husband, I knew that he wouldn't be easily won over by paper crafts or handmade goods, so I didn't even try. Instead, I waited. The quotidian punctuated our days, and the currents of trivialities smoothed over the crags and shards of disappointments. I found solace in those seemingly boring, unglamorous moments when it felt like we weren't on the offensive or defensive. We resumed our weekly Saturday brunches. We took turns to kiss our daughter good night. We created new routines now that our roles had shifted yet again. It took a long time for us to navigate to a place that looked sort of like peace, or at least détente.

Matters weren't helped by an unexpected relapse on my part; my health had started to decline again. Perhaps it was the stress of the season and the high expectations that come with it. I'd also become lax about my daily exercise and diet routines, which definitely had an impact. A profusion of sweets filled our cupboards, and I snacked on them mindlessly. And as the temperatures dipped, I was spending more and more time loafing about and avoiding physical activity. I was still sleeping enough for the most part, but did sacrifice quite a few nights to get gifts done in time. It was so easy to slide back into a less than healthy lifestyle, I almost didn't notice.

Luckily, or not so luckily, my hyperthyroidism serves as a clanging alarm, and my body was now quick to react to mistreatment. As soon as I stopped taking care of myself, I started coughing and my energy levels depleted. *Oh*, I remembered, *the basics: sleep, walk, chop*. It was time to get back on the health wagon.

As I refocused on my physical fitness and nutritional needs, the short-lived days of December and January gave way to February. For Valentine's Day, I wrapped a handmade gift for my husband and proffered it to him tentatively. I had sewn a pair of boxer shorts out of turquoise cotton with small colorful circles that looked like abstract Japanese lanterns. He scrutinized them for a minute after clumsily tearing the paper apart. He immediately tried them on, but oh, they were too small! I was so used to sewing pint-sized outfits for KoKo and couldn't gauge adult male sizes properly—they got stuck mid-thigh, and he made an off-color joke and then he smiled. I laughed and laughed. I felt something give. A gust of tense air loosed. We just might be OK.

In Japan, gift-giving is prompted by *giri*, or obligation, and is a cultural imperative. One must never visit someone without a present in hand, and the Japanese have made the practice into a commercialized art form. Stunningly prewrapped gifts are available everywhere you look, and each prefecture and city has iconic items of renown. For a couple of years I lived in the city of Matsusaka in Mie Prefecture, and this particular region was known for beer-fed beef and indigo-dyed cotton. Cleverly packaged Matsusaka beef and indigo handkerchiefs graced the storefronts of many a train station vending area. For other regions, it might be buckwheat noodles. Or mandarin oranges. Usually, the iconic item is food. I grew up with this mentality and to this day still feel compelled to be at the ready with a gift.

But now, gift-giving is an act of love and compassion. I revel in thinking about what would make the recipient light up, and what would not only be aesthetically pleasing, but also useful. I kept these guidelines in mind when creating the following projects, which are quick to make (to avoid losing sleep as I am wont to do when ensconced in gift-making) and highly customizable.

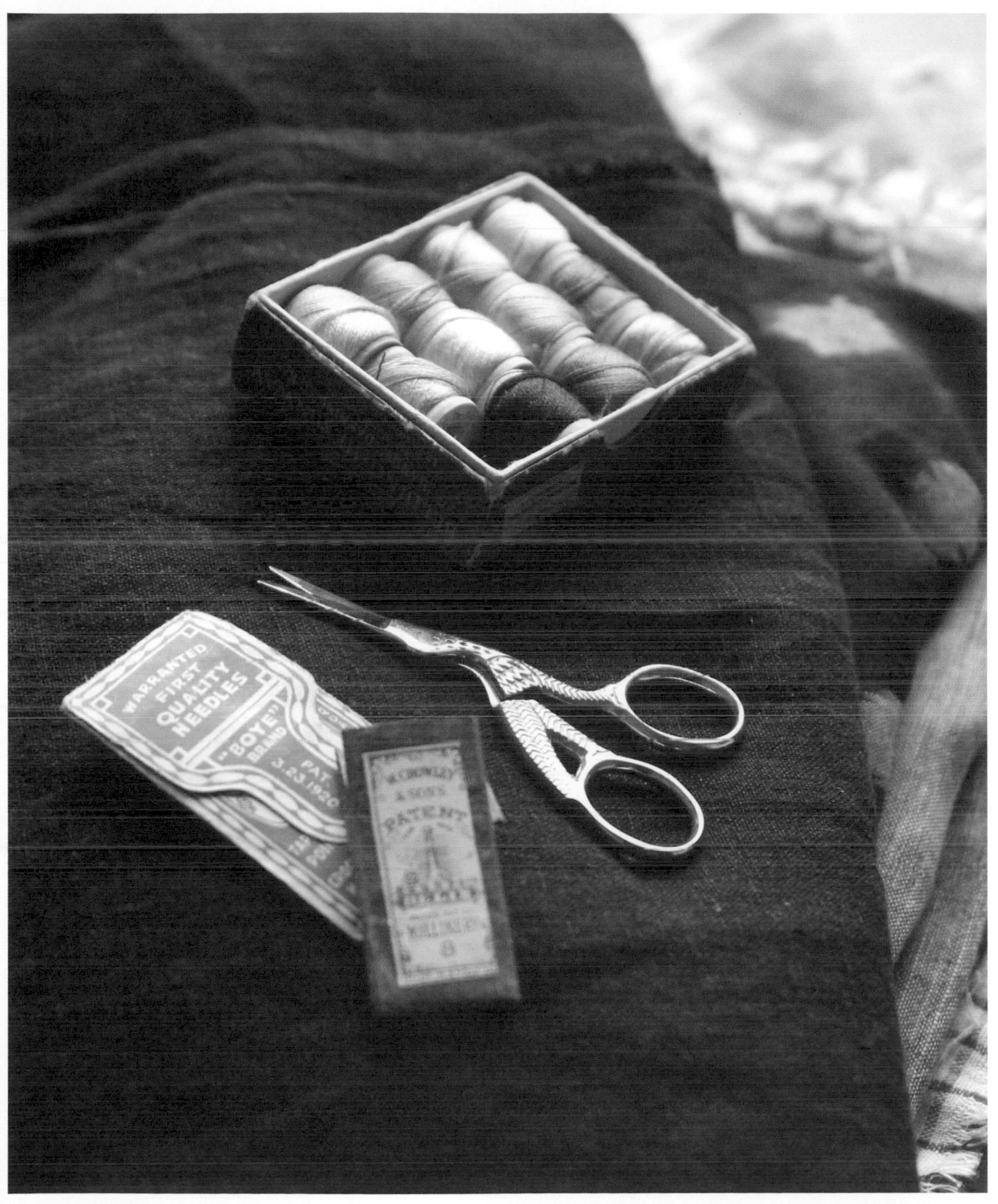
WARRANTED
FIRST
QUALITY
NEEDLES
"BOYE"
BRAND
PAT.
3.23.1920
PATENT

FORTUNE COOKIE ADVENT CALENDAR

IN OUR HOUSEHOLD, THE HOLIDAYS NOW officially start with a handmade Advent calendar. The tradition started when I crafted that paper gem version, and now I make a new calendar every December (yes, it's labor-intensive, and no, I wouldn't have it any other way). Watching KoKo leap out of bed to partake in the countdown fills our mornings with good cheer and hearty snuggles as she bounds back upstairs to share with us the message/treat/interesting tidbit she received. That's the part that makes me feel extra lucky. Instructions on page 173.

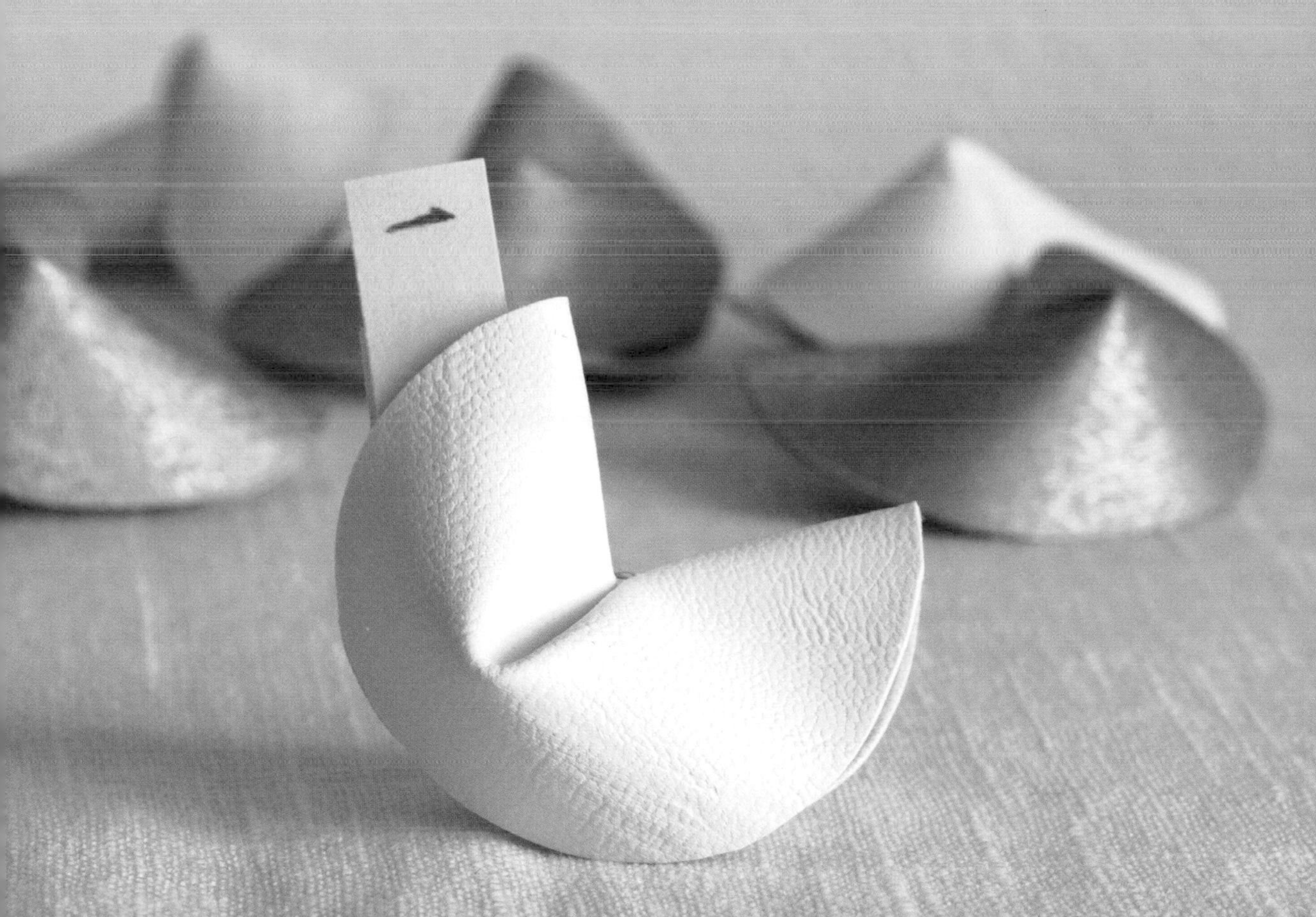

DOPP KIT

IT'S TOUGH TO SEW FOR MY MAN. He has surprisingly particular requirements (a certain western type of plaid shirt, cargo pants from Walmart), which seems like it would make it easier, but I can't help but try something different . . . maybe in the hopes that it will expand his horizons. The one shirt I've made for him in my sewing career has been an utter flop, tainting all future attempts. It might have been the slubby puke-y green silk that turned him off. It might have been the uneven collar and the unkempt placket that I didn't sew into place for some reason. And let's not forget the ill-fitting and underwhelming turquoise boxer shorts. At any rate, with the help of a friend, I've hit upon the ubiquitous yet universally appealing guy gift: the Dopp kit. Instructions on page 175.

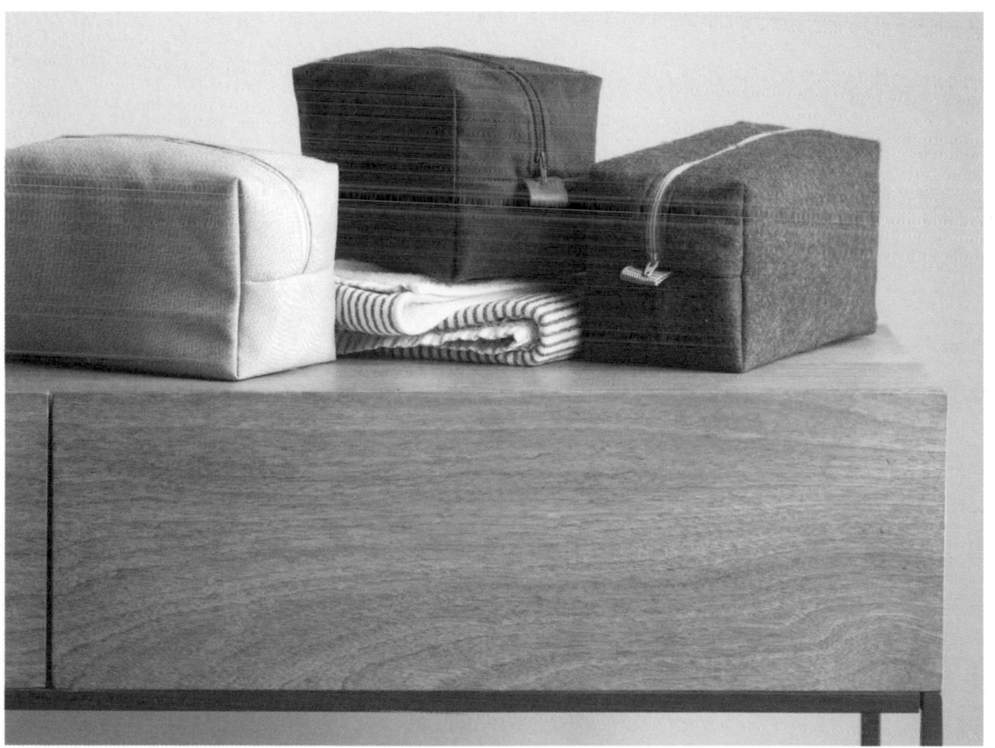

Bach
CHERRY PLUM
Bach
ASPEN
Bach

HEATING PAD

(variations: square + cloud + moon)

ONE OF THE SURPRISING HIT HOLIDAY gifts was a set of heating pads I gave KoKo. As temps dipped down to near-frigid, she initiated a nighttime ritual: once she stepped out of the bath—scrubbed clean, pajama clad, teeth brushed, and ready for bed—she zapped her heating pad in the microwave for a minute and a half and then tucked her feet underneath its warmth as she read herself to sleep. Adding a few drops of essential oil onto the heating pad before warming it up makes it extra soothing. You may even want to include a couple of pretty essential-oil bottles as part of a gift package. Instructions on page 179.

10

BABY KIMONO TOP + BLOOMERS

TOWARD THE END OF THE YEAR, I discovered a tiny fabric store tucked behind one of my favorite coffee shops. It was like finding a secret hideaway, my very own Narnian wardrobe. I slowly became friends with the lovely owner as I visited her store constantly to admire the beautiful selections she curated. She knew that I loved to sew, and before I knew it, she offered me the opportunity to teach a sewing workshop there. The baby outfit class I taught featured a more rudimentary version of these bloomers as well as a pinafore top. Instead of the pinafore, however, I've included a kimono top design that is much easier to construct from scratch. Instructions on page 181.

COLOR-BLOCK ZIP POUCH

MY FRIENDS HAVE EXQUISITE TASTE AND widely varying interests. It can become a full-time job trying to find a suitable gift for each and every one. The zip pouch rescues me repeatedly since I'm a firm believer that there's always a use for zip pouches. I derive a lot of satisfaction from filling the pouches with carefully chosen goodies tailored for the recipient. From glam clutch to diaper holders, by varying the size and fabric choices, the zip pouch will surely be a crowd-pleaser. Instructions on page 190.

spring

spring: letting go

SPRING! IN SEATTLE, FOR A BRIEF two-week period, cherry blossoms explode like cotton candy all over the city. The air is still crisp, with hints of caressing sunshine to whet the appetite for summer days. Nearly twelve months had passed since the launch of my "early retirement," as my husband likes to call it.

Every time I see my endocrinologist, her examination includes a goiter check. She gently presses her fingertips to my throat, where my thyroid glands reside. "Any soreness?" she asks, and I always say, no. Press, press, press. She declares my neck to be fabulous and we move on to my health experiment, as I've come to think of it. She grills me on whether I'm sleeping enough, how much I'm exercising, what I'm eating. We talk about the results of my blood tests. And then I give her an update on my latest crafting obsessions. After about ten minutes, I'm ushered out of the office with instructions to return in several months.

There was (and still is) a part of me that wants to eradicate this disease from my system. And I want to do it in the most natural way possible. I thought that if I sweated enough and ate all the right foods and slept like a normal human being, I would be able to pat the illness on the backside and yell "good riddance!" I believed that if I drank enough green juice and green tea and lived green and avoided green feelings, I would emerge a whole, undiseased person. I can certainly control much of it through a healthy lifestyle, but nothing is guaranteed and never will be. My best shot is to consistently continue with the various wellness-conscious regimens that I've built into my days since, as my doctor put it, "once you have Graves', it's forever."

That spring, I busied myself with cleaning and purging and thought a lot about letting go. Letting go of not just the physical detritus, but the mental, emotional, and spiritual stuff too. Of releasing expectations, which seems to be where I stumble the most.

As I tossed out old paint cans from the summer DIY bonanza and finally tackled the horror show that was our basement, I came across my meticulously organized binder of sewing patterns for women. Long, long ago, I'd hoped to start sewing my own clothes and prolifically acquired patterns at those fabric store mega-sales. I had over one hundred patterns, all in alphanumeric order from Burda to Vogue.

It seemed like a natural progression to start sewing for myself now that I'd become comfortable making clothes for KoKo. And unconsciously, I had stopped buying ready-to-wear for myself as well. Yet, I hesitated.

You see, one of the biggest obstacles I've struggled with all my life is my weight. I dreaded the thought of measuring myself and committing my actual dimensions to paper. We all know about the unrealistic expectations around appearance and the standards of beauty we receive via mass and social media. I've found that the expectations are even more brutal in the Asian culture. One time, when I was teaching English in Matsusaka, I visited family in the city of Himeji, which is about a three-hour train ride away. My aunt served a delicious and light lunch of rice, fish, and vegetables, and I noticed that one of my cousins had a red string tied to her pinky. When I asked her about it, she told me it was to remind her not to eat because she'd gained too much weight the week before. She was required to be at the table to entertain the guest (me), and every time she accidentally picked up her chopsticks, she would see the string and would put them down. Though she was in her early twenties, several years younger than I was at the time, my skinny cousin had the shrewdness and authority befitting a middle-aged personal trainer. She looked me up and down, and told me I should do the same. She also told me I should really use a chemical whitening cream because my tan made me look poor.

Asian culture aside, I actually blame most of my body dysmorphia on being born and bred in Los Angeles, the capital of shallow values, ruthlessly fed by the Hollywood machine. Because of the proximity of the studios to where I lived, even in those pre-Internet days, I felt acutely aware of how I stacked up against the actresses and models that I would often see around town. I continued the mental comparisons well into adulthood, especially after giving birth and watching my body morph. Battling with my own body image as a mother is one thing, but one day KoKo refused to wear one of the dresses I made.

"It makes me look fat," she said, "*I'm* fat." She was six years old. My heart stopped.

Suddenly, I was twelve again, in a bathroom stall in middle school. I was about to flush the toilet when I heard my name and stood stock still with my hand poised on the handle.

Girl 1: "Did you see Sanae?"

Girl 2: "Yeah, what about her?"

Girl 1: "Have you noticed that she's getting fat?"

Girl 2: "Totally. Her legs are getting *so* big!"

Then they laughed and left the bathroom. I'm pretty sure they knew I was in that stall. I wasn't certain who the girls were, but I was in a program for "advanced" students and teasing came with the territory. I believe that middle school can be a hormone-addled landscape of awkwardness and uncertainty and maybe even cruelty for most kids, but until that moment I had never thought about my weight, and it changed the way I saw myself completely. My self-esteem plummeted and from that day, the mirror reflected an ugly girl with elephantine legs.

What strikes me as especially heartbreaking about that incident is that I wasn't fat at all. When I've chanced upon pictures of my twelve-year-old self, I see a normal, healthy little preteen. But that conversation planted a seed, and ultimately it grew into a self-fulfilling prophecy. I believed fiercely and uncompromisingly that I was fat and therefore not good enough.

I yo-yo dieted endlessly. I compared myself to others, and always came up short because I stopped seeing myself as a whole person but in bulbous parts. *Oh, my legs are so much fatter than hers and we're the same height*, I would agonize. *No more desserts! Only beets!* I would vow to myself when a friend happened to mention a miracle beet cleanse. All this led me to eat worse and worse, and by my second year in college, I had gained far more than the Freshman Fifteen, though I was never bigger than a size 10. But when you're surrounded by size 0 aspiring actresses (which seemed to be the standard-size female in Los Angeles), size 10 is huge.

At a cognitive level, I'm aware that I'm not fat, just as I know that women in ads are Photoshopped into unrecognizable specimens. There is, however, a vast chasm between knowledge and down-to-the-marrow understanding. That day when my lovely and slender daughter tossed aside the dress I had hand-stitched, I realized that no words would ever suffice. Somehow I was transmitting all of my body issues onto her without realizing it, and I knew that I had to get over myself. *Now.* I needed to be proud of the way I am—just as I am—so that she too would learn through daily observation to be self-confident. To be healthy and strong and beautiful regardless of size. If I didn't show her what self-acceptance looks like as a girl, as a woman, as a human being, how could I expect her to recognize and grow into it? Soon I wouldn't be her main role model and she would turn exclusively to her peers. In this era of curated images of flawlessness, it's no wonder a six-year-old was worrying about her appearance. I might not be able to have an impact on how she views herself in the future, but I could plant the right seeds now and hope for the best.

So I had to begin with myself and question my beliefs about my body. I started by measuring my bust, waist, and hips. My thighs, my arms. I cringed at the numbers but wrote them down, and looked at them. *Really* looked at them. After a while, they sat on the paper innocuously, simply numbers and not judgments. Then I sifted through my patterns and plucked an asymmetrical knit tee that looked easy and somewhat flattering. I sewed it up, took awkward photos of myself sans makeup or styling—my hair was in a messy ponytail—and posted it on my blog. Cringed some more.

Just as I had decided to sew weekly for KoKo, I vowed to sew something for myself regularly and post it online for accountability—weekly, if possible. I wouldn't digitally alter anything, not even a zit. I would talk about the size I cut out, how I felt wearing the garment, whether it was something that belonged in my closet. It would be about progress and letting go of impressing people or looking a certain, acceptable way. I would find my style, not one dictated by trends or pundits. This style would be entirely of my own making based on what felts right for me.

"Mama, I love your legs, they're so cute!" KoKo said when I was trying on a dress I'd just sewn months into my mission to craft a handmade wardrobe for myself. "They look like giant squashes!" I paused, with the dress half-on. And then I laughed. And couldn't stop laughing, because it's so true. No amount of exercise will change the genetically determined shape of my legs, and after months of sewing for myself, I recognized that I had stopped worrying about them. I've come a long way from that day in the bathroom stall in the seventh grade. I took my daughter, the girl who so lovingly admired my strong and sturdy legs, into my arms, feeling proud and flattered.

I'm still exploring and I won't lie: I don't feel proud of my body all the time. I still have bouts of insecurities and many of my sewing attempts are failures. There are times when I feel bloated and PMS-y and just want to spend the whole day in my pajamas. But I do know that sewing clothes for myself has completely changed the relationship that I have with my body. I'm a lot less critical, and because I have so much more control over the fit of a garment, the angst associated with trying on clothes has dissipated. My approach is more analytical now, taking notes on how to improve construction and quality.

The process of ascertaining my style has been a fascinating one as well. I've discovered that I love dresses, which is something I'd avoided most of my life because of my hang-ups about my legs. That alone feels like a major victory. And despite the fact that architectural garments with bells and whistles made out of woven fabric are fun to make, they're not the clothes I reach for instinctively. I live in knits, but that doesn't mean I want to look sloppy. I'm constantly seeking the intersection of comfort and style. Slowly but surely, I think I'm getting there. What's changed most, though, is that instead of trying to create clothes that will make me look thinner, the *most* important question I ask for every completed handmade garment is this: *does this make me happy?*

Armed with an easy-peasy infinity scarf to hide my would-be goiters (and perhaps a pair of sunglasses just in case my eyes start to bug out), some fabric buckets to keep my life organized inside and out, a sweet trivet to rest my warm beverage during contemplative writing sessions, and let's not forget a comfortable yet stylish knit dress, I feel ready. Ready to be OK with myself, and I hope by being OK with myself I will communicate to my daughter and all the young women surrounding me the very message *I* wanted to hear: you're enough just as you are.

SINGER

INFINITY SCARF

HOW IS IT THAT A SIMPLE scarf can add so much stylistic oomph? What draws me to the loop shape in particular is that it makes wearing it virtually goofproof. Wind it around your neck once or twice, and done! Whereas with traditional scarves, you could drape it, knot it, let one end hang *just so* . . . the choices are almost too plentiful. Choices are wonderful sometimes, but the infinity scarf is just another example of how constraints can help free up much needed mental space that might otherwise get caught up in needless decision-making. And you'll still look smashing without the effort. Instructions on page 194.

S IS FOR SALMON
Little Kunoichi

EVERYTHING BUCKET

(variations: with handles + color-block)

CLEANING IS CHALLENGING FOR ME. SCRUBBING, vacuuming, dusting, and doing the laundry . . . I'd rather put them off for another day and sew instead. Organizing, however, is a whole different story. The act of creating systems and purging and sorting and improving efficiencies—now, *that's* where I shine. As I pondered how to let go of all the things that seemed to hold me back, I engaged in the obligatory spring cleaning and truly reveled in reorganizing my life. These fabric buckets are just the kind of receptacles that spark my love of systematizing and structuring. Instructions on page 197.

JASMINE
GREEN TEA
INGREDIENTS:

SASHIKO TRIVET

MY DAUGHTER HAS TWO DEAR FRIENDS she's known all her life. I met the moms when I was in my second trimester, and the three of us immediately clicked. As we waddled around with our big bellies, filled with anticipation of a new entity entering our lives, we started a tradition that we've continued for almost a decade.

We meet up every month, rotating hosting duties. We always brew up pots of tea for the grown-ups and serve treats for the kiddos. Even during the most hectic times, we've carved out time to get together, and this no-fuss trivet makes me think of our gatherings, of friendships and comforting rituals. Instructions on page 203.

VERSATILE KNIT DRESS

IT TOOK ME A WHILE TO work up the courage to start sewing for myself. But once I did, I was addicted. Through trial and error, I ascertained that I like clean, streamlined designs. No frills, frou-frou, or blinding bling for me. And when it comes to clothes, I'm all about comfort. I've tried a lot of different patterns since I started sewing, but the ones I wear over and over are the ones made out of knit with little fanfare. That's exactly what I've created here—a low-key dress made out of knit jersey. I've had to go through a myriad of iterations to figure out what style works best for my unique body type, and I'm not sure if I've completely nailed it yet, but I keep trying. The best part is in the practice and learning, and I hope you'll feel encouraged to do the same. Instructions on page 207.

LUDLOW-"TYPE A"
LUDLOW MANUFACTURING & SALES CO.
Ludlow Quality
BOSTON MASS.
50 3
2 OZ.
STITCHING THREAD
WINSTED SILK COMPANY
WEST WINSTED CONN.

epilogue

AS OF THIS WRITING, THREE YEARS have passed since I was fired. My life looks very different now. My thyroid condition is in remission, though I still have to be vigilant about my health practices daily. I work hard at nurturing my relationships, with family rituals and weekly dates to connect with friends. I create something every day. I don't succeed every day, but I get up and try anew each morning.

I have sewn over three hundred garments for myself and my daughter, and though I'm pleased about this accomplishment, I am reevaluating the direction I want to take with sewing so that it's more intentional and less about weekly production. What's funny is that because my daughter obviously has too many clothes, on the rare occasion when we cruise through a retail store to buy underwear or socks, she doesn't even glance at anything on the racks. And except for two T-shirts and a pair of capri knit pants that were purchased out of dire need on an unplanned trip (we didn't even have a toothbrush with us), I haven't bought a single item of clothing for either of us in over thirty-six months. This is quite possibly the most liberating change I've made as a former shopaholic.

The other day, KoKo said to me, "Mama, if nothing is perfect, why does the word exist?" It's a good question. I don't have the answer, but I love that she has somehow absorbed the belief that nothing is perfect—to me that seems like the healthiest attitude to have. It's something I have to remind myself to hold onto all the time.

Over the course of the many changes I've made with the help of innumerable supportive friends and family, I've come to the conclusion that it's all about habits. Willpower is limited and short-lived—when I relied on discipline alone, I constantly regressed, not just with my health but with everything else, and felt frustrated. But once I managed to make the activities I deemed important into habits one at a time, every day became more fulfilling. Not necessarily easier (though habits can make a lot of things easier), but richer.

It is with the deepest and ardent hope that I've created this book so that you too might make this age-old craft a habit. I find so many life lessons to be learned from sewing. It requires a commitment to start, which is always the hardest part. But once I grab a piece of fabric and start ironing, I almost always want to keep going to the next step of cutting out the pattern pieces. And I inevitably feel that resistance to thread my sewing machine, but as soon as I do, I can't wait to start sewing. I'm a master procrastinator and can spend all day coming up with excuses not to initiate the zillions of projects I want to try. I find that if I rely on waiting to *feel* like doing something, I'll never do it. As Little Richard croons, "A little bit of something, sure beats a whole lot of nothing, babe." My little bit of something has resulted in three-hundred-plus garments.

And a sequence must be followed—this is key. Sure, there are shortcuts and hacks, but to produce quality, you need to invest the time. There is inherent satisfaction in proceeding from one step to the next, building one element upon another. A flat, two-dimensional piece of woven thread becomes a three-dimensional bag, flower, dress—it's magical, really. Sewing is the ultimate teacher of patience, and worthwhile things, they take time. My mother's favorite Japanese saying is *Chiri mo tsumoreba, yama ni naru*, which roughly translates to "even specks of dust will eventually become great mountains."

And often—much more often than I'd like—mistakes will force me to pause and to redo. Mistakes are good. They are important. But they are good and important only when I learn from them. This is the part I struggle mightily with: mistakes teach me humility and limitations, and I don't like to be reminded of them. Yet, with enough redos and tinkering, I figure out my own way of doing things that feels more natural to me, and my confidence grows with every completed project. Practice, practice, practice.

What I love most about sewing is how it allows me to dial down the pace in this frenetic world and connect to myself. I take my fabric pieces and gently place them beneath the presser foot. I lower the presser foot and needle, position my right foot on the pedal. Fingers guiding the fabric, I let the weight of my foot depress the pedal, and the needle moves and the machine hums. My thoughts wander. I check the seam, clip threads, and repeat. I feel a deep sigh inside, a settling. I don't want to be anywhere else, do anything else. And just like life, I am slowly creating something beautiful and meaningful to me out of seemingly nothing, and I have an infinite amount of resources and inspiration at my disposal, if only I would accept them. And oftentimes, when the resources seem inaccessible, the very constraints are what result in the most cherished, if I would just let go of expectations and the need for perfection. To me, this is happiness.

I wish *you* sewing happiness.

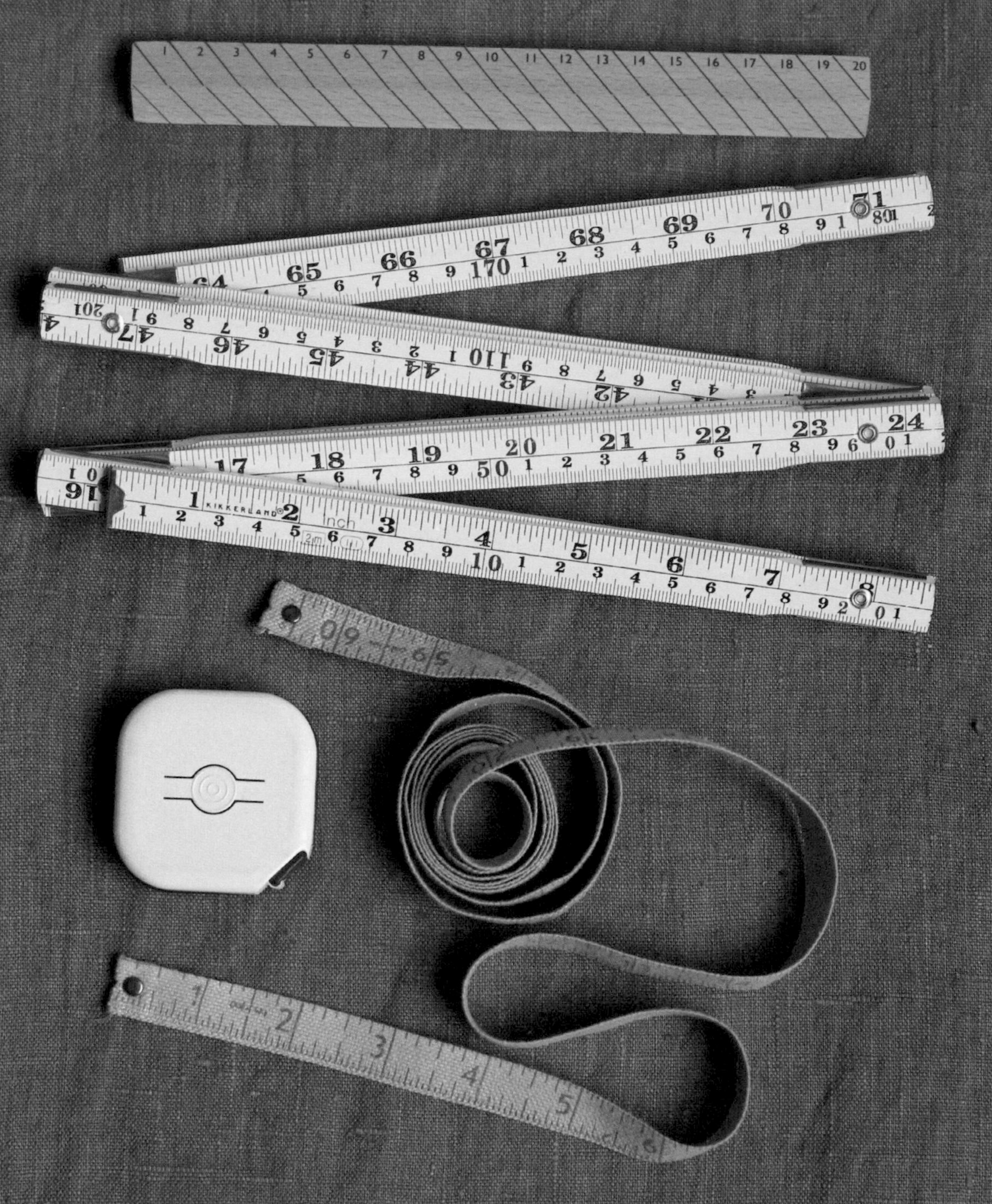
KIKKERLAND
inch

PART II:

INSTRUCTIONS

LUDLOW TYPE A
STITCHING THREAD
CLOVER

sewing basics

AS WITH ANY CRAFT, IT'S EASY to get lost in the allure of shiny baubles, pretty extras, and the latest gadgets, but sewing really only requires a few key tools and supplies. At first glance, the list may look long, but many items don't take up much space and once you're set up, the tools will become an integral and indispensable part of your sewing adventures. In my years of sewing, I've probably purchased every product available on the market, or at least it feels like it. At one point, I could have easily constructed a behemoth rivaling King Kong made entirely out of sewing supplies. But slowly, I've eliminated what felt extraneous or ineffective, and kept what made my sewing process easier. There are innumerable books on sewing tools for you to explore, but my list below is what works for me. Part of the fun is discovering what works for *you*.

A SEWING SPACE

A sewing space is necessary, naturally, but it can be anything from a dining room table to a dedicated sun-dappled loft studio. At one point, I sewed in a large-ish closet in one of the many tiny apartments we've rented. Here's my list of must-haves in my sewing space:

SEWING MACHINE: Almost all of the projects in this book will utilize a sewing machine, but you don't need anything fancy. As long as it sews a straight line and zigzag stitch, you're pretty much set. For the first couple of years, I sewed with a $50 Singer from Target, and it served me very well—and I still have it as backup.

P.S. I frequently reference a serger (overlockers for you outside of the United States) for sewing with knits, but you absolutely do not need one for any of the projects.

SEWING MACHINE FEET: Except for the occasional zipper insertion, which requires a **zipper foot** (although some will argue that you don't actually need one), the only presser foot you need is the default one often known as the **all-purpose foot.** *All-purpose*, you'll find, is the theme around here. For sticky or slippery fabric like leather, waxed canvas, and laminate, I've discovered the loveliness of a Teflon foot, but this is absolutely an extra and not necessary at all. If you decide to make the adjustable apron, you just might need to bust out with the **buttonhole foot.** Some machines also come with a special foot to create a mock-overlock stitch, which is a lot like the kind of stitches created by an overlocker/serger. This is also a nice-to-have but not required. All-purpose, zipper, and buttonhole—that should cover all the presser feet you really need.

SEWING MACHINE NEEDLES: Make sure you have two types in your arsenal: **all-purpose** and **knit-friendly.** Knit-friendly needles are labeled "ballpoint," "stretch," or "jersey"—take your pick. If you decide to add leather or leatherlike accents to the projects (as I have done), a leather needle, which is thicker and sturdier, can ease you through those tough layers.

HAND-SEWING NEEDLES: I like the eyes of my needles to be on the bigger side, because my vision is not what it used to be. There are a variety of hand-sewing needles, but I generally purchase the variety pack with multiple lengths. Nothing fancy.

KEY FOR PHOTO ON FACING PAGE: 1. TAPE MEASURE 2. HAND-SEWING NEEDLES 3. THREAD 4. CLIPPERS 5. MACHINE NEEDLES 6. CHALK PENCILS 7. SEAM RIPPER 8. FABRIC SHEARS 9. PINS 10. CHALK 11. ROTARY CUTTER 12. RULERS

1.
2.
3.
4.
5.
6.
7.
8.
9.
10.
11.
12.
SCHMETZ
JERSEY
CLOVER
PARVEEN

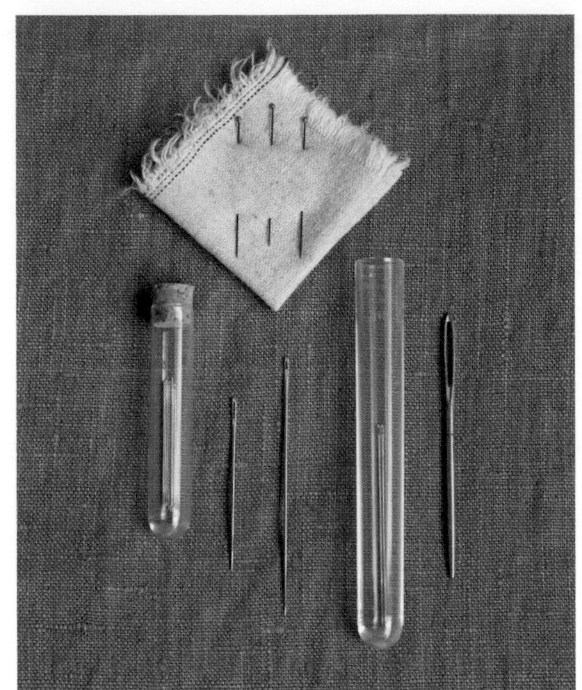

PINS: Metal-head, glass-head, flower-head . . . there are a bazillion types of pins, but invest in ones you find pleasing since you'll be using them a *lot* to hold fabric pieces together.

PINCUSHION/MAGNETIC PIN HOLDER: You'll need a place to house all the pretty pins you choose. The most effective way I've found to corral pins is with a magnetic pin holder, but I also have a few pincushions strewn about as well.

"WONDER" CLIPS: This product by Clover is another extraneous-but-helpful item that does the same work as a pin but is easier to use with items that tend to move, like zippers and bias tapes, or fabrics that don't like pin pricks, like knits, waxed canvas, and leather-esque textiles.

THREAD: I'm never very picky with my threads and focus more on the colors than the actual thread material. I generally get the all-purpose polyester kind.

SMALL SCISSORS: You'll be clipping a lot of thread as you sew, and having a sharp, small pair of scissors nearby is *de rigueur*.

SEAM RIPPER: A must.

POINT TURNER: You'll need a sharp (but not too sharp) tool to push out corners of garments and bags and such. I actually love to use the wrong end of a small paintbrush, but there's a plethora of point turner options, including chopsticks.

KEY FOR PHOTO ON FACING PAGE: 1. BUTTON HOLE MEASURING TOOL 2. AWL 3. BODKIN 4. SEAM GAUGE 5. BIAS TAPE MAKER

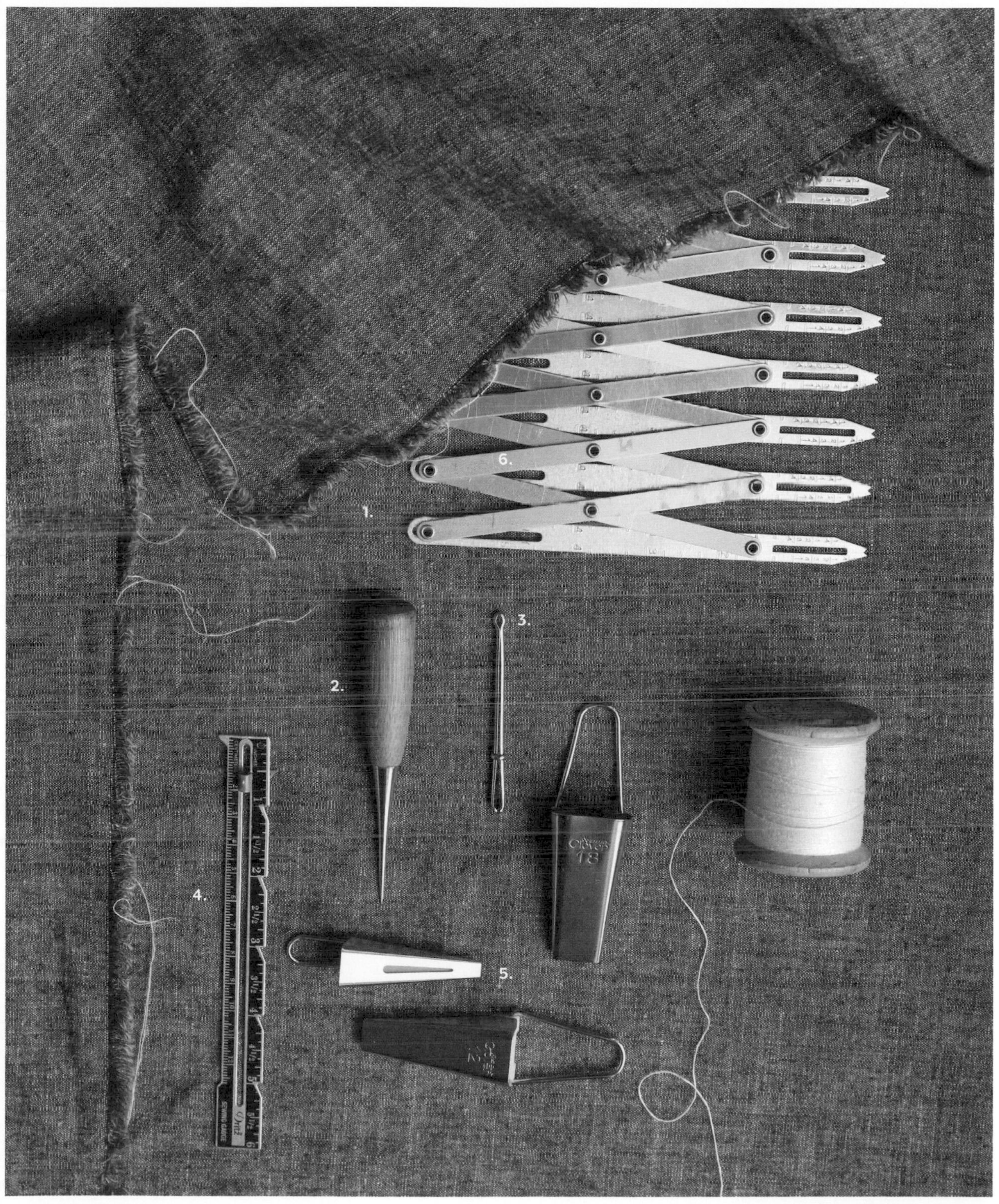
6.
1.
3.
2.
4.
5.

1.
2.
3.
4.
5.
PARVEEN
gingher
gingher

BODKIN/SAFETY PINS: A bodkin looks like a pair of tweezers and is used to thread elastic through casings. A safety pin will do just as well.

LOOP TURNER: Sometimes you'll need to turn smaller sewn pieces inside out, and this upside-down bubble-blower looking thing with a hook on one end makes the task less strenuous.

THE CUTTING ARENA

Over time, you'll become very familiar and comfortable with cutting fabric, and I'd venture to say this is the most important part of sewing. Don't scoff at the "measure twice, cut once" adage because nothing is more disheartening than wasting beautiful fabric because of a cutting mistake. You'll need a decent-sized surface to spread out fabric, and this may be the aforementioned dining table or a floor or a rickety cutting table like the one I have. Here are the tools that I keep on my cutting table:

FABRIC SHEARS: You'll want a bent-handle pair (I like what Gingher offers) to avoid crab hands at the end of each sewing session. Always make sure to cut *only* fabric with your shears, as paper will dull them in a lickety-split.

ROTARY CUTTER: I am actually not a huge user of rotary cutters. They work well for cutting straight lines (of which there are many in the following projects), but I mostly like to create bias tapes and knit bindings using these supersharp, rolling blades. Otherwise, I'm a shears girl.

PINKING SHEARS: These bring to mind a torture chamber device with jagged teeth, but are an easy way to "finish" a raw fabric edge to prevent future fraying. I recommend using this tool for the Dopp Kit (page 175).

KEY FOR PHOTO ON FACING PAGE: 1. VINTAGE JAPANESE-STYLE CLIPPERS 2. FABRIC SHEARS 3. JAPANESE-STYLE CLIPPERS 4. SMALL EMBROIDERY SCISSORS 5. ROTARY CUTTER

CUTTING MAT: Look for these self-healing mats in the largest size you can afford because they are so helpful. Not only are they vital when using your rotary cutter, they also help with measuring fabric (they're marked with measuring grids) and keeping the fabric from shifting around as well.

QUILTING RULER: You've probably seen these see-through (usually with yellow lines) plastic rulers. They make an excellent part of the drafting kit that I'll get into a little later, but for now note that they make cutting with a rotary blade a breeze.

MARKING TOOLS: My favorite brand is Clover for marking tools, but I have them from all sources in all shapes from wedge chalk to erasable markers to mechanical chalk pencils. Try out a few to see which type you like, and make sure to get a light color and a dark color.

PATTERN WEIGHTS: I hear there are pattern weights sold by sewing suppliers, but this is the one sewing tool I get from the hardware store. I stock up on the large metal washers to act as weights, individually or stacked. They work fabulously for holding pattern pieces in place on fabric while tracing around them.

THE IRONING STATION

I cannot stress enough the importance of ironing, or pressing, as we say in the sewing world. The proper application of a hot iron to your project can make or break the final outcome . . . OK that's an exaggeration, but for an optimal finish, pressing is paramount.

IRON: No need to shell out serious dough for an iron. Mine retailed well under $100 and it's a dream to use. A steam function is an added bonus, but not really crucial since you can always use a spray bottle filled with water.

It's important to point out that you are, in fact, pressing with the iron and not gliding it back and forth over the fabric. Firmly place your iron in the desired spot, hold for a few seconds, then slide to an adjacent spot and hold again.

IRONING BOARD: Ironing boards range from small, over-the-door types to the industrial size and weight of a dry cleaner's, but find what works for you and your space. I've heard that during photo shoots, prop stylists will sometimes just use large pieces of plywood with a little batting and canvas laid on top for a makeshift ironing board. The wider ironing board models are easier for me to use, but my favorite one was a built-in, vintage board at the same apartment where I sewed in the closet. It was from the 1930s, made out of wood, and was in excellent condition.

SEAM GAUGE: I use these small metal rulers to measure hems and folded edges of fabric. They're the kind with a little plastic slider to help you with various seam allowances too. They are so handy that I actually keep one near my sewing machine and another by the ironing station.

PRESS CLOTH: I like the synthetic mesh press cloths because I can see through them, but organza works just as well. Be careful with your heat setting with the mesh press cloth. It's meant to protect the fabric you are working with but it may melt itself.

TAILOR'S HAM AND SLEEVE ROLL: These are decidedly nice-to-haves. They help with ironing garments and curved seams.

THE DRAFTING KIT

Because pattern pieces are not provided in this book, some drafting will be part of each project. For the most part, you'll just need to plot out straight lines, and sometimes you'll add a few curves but have no fear! The following supplies will make drafting patterns less intimidating and simplify the task.

PATTERN PAPER: Throughout all the projects, I'll be referring to the "pattern paper." You can use my fave kind, called Swedish tracing paper—which is white, slightly sheer, durable, and sewable—or large rolls of brown kraft paper, or big pads of tracing paper that you can find at art stores that can be taped together. The rolls of white drawing paper found in IKEA's kid section also make excellent pattern paper.

PENCIL: Use whatever kind of pencil you have on hand. I usually use a mechanical pencil.

ERASER: You may end up erasing a lot of your lines, or you might be the type to leave your sketched lines intact. Either way, an eraser is a good thing to have in your kit.

PEN: All pattern pieces should be labeled and you can certainly use your pencil, but I like to use a pen to write out information about the pattern piece when I feel like it is ready to go (e.g. Kimono Top Front—cut 2). It's purely psychological.

RULER: Any ruler will do and one with both metric and imperial measurements tends to be my go-to.

TAPE MEASURE: Made from fabric or vinyl, this tool is for measuring bodies and other three-dimensional or curved objects.

KEY FOR PHOTO ON FACING PAGE: 1. CHALK PENCILS 2. TAILOR'S CHALK 3. CHACO LINER PEN STYLE

1.
CLOVERCHACOPEL
CLOVER
JAPAN
クロバーチャコペル「水溶性」
CLOVER JAPAN
2.
HANCOCK LONDON
3.
CLOVER

SCISSORS: You'll need a designated pair of scissors for cutting out paper pattern pieces. Make sure to *never* use your fabric shears when cutting paper, as this will dull the blades rapidly and tragically.

TAPE: I have an impressive stockpile of scotch tape, though I've tearfully used washi tape in a pinch (washi tape is easy on the eyes but not so much on the wallet). The tape is useful when modifying pattern pieces or when you need to tape together paper for a larger surface area to create patterns.

FEATURED FABRICS

These are my favorite types of fabric. You will see them featured repeatedly in the book:

COTTON: I've dubbed it the "all-purpose textile." The variety available is vast, and I gravitate toward cotton meant for apparel, like voile and lawn, rather than quilting cotton, which tends to have less drape. Of course, fabric choice is entirely dependent on the project.

DOUBLE-GAUZE: The fabric masterminds in Japan came up with this ingenious textile that is literally two layers of gauze attached together with invisible stitching. Breathable, comfortable, and—well—gauzy, it's wonderful stuff.

GENUINE LEATHER/FAUX LEATHER: I understand that political issues surround the usage of leather derived from animal hides, but from a purely aesthetic and practical point, leather accents are fantastic additions to the various projects included in this book. Because there is no fraying, they make sewing a snap, and once you get the hang of stitching leather pieces (which tend to stretch a little), they're surprisingly easy to handle. If you just can't stomach using real leather, try one of the excellent faux options on the market these days. For the purposes of this book, I will reference “leather” to mean genuine or faux leather throughout. Choose what makes you happy.

KNITS (A.K.A. STRETCH FABRICS): How did people function without T-shirts? I’ll never know, but like all fabrics, knits can range in drape, weight, texture, and substrate content. The main differentiator between wovens (such as linen, cotton, and double-gauze) is that knit fabrics stretch. And with stretchy fabric, it’s good to keep in mind something called “recovery,” which is the capacity for snapping back into their original dimensions after being stretched.

LINEN: This nubby woven cloth is made from the fibers of the flax plant and is the queen bee of fabrics as far as I’m concerned.

WAXED CANVAS: This currently on-trend textile is utilitarian and good-looking. Its provenance is cotton canvas treated with a coat of wax to render it water-resistant, making it a popular choice for outdoor wear.

WOOL FELT: Remember all the elementary school projects you made out of felt? The kind I recommend is the nicer version made entirely or partially out of wool. It is thicker, far more durable, and lovely to work with.

You can use any type of fabric you’d like for any of the projects, of course, and I highly encourage experimentation, which is part of what makes sewing so rewarding. I know that in the beginning I was intimidated by the thought of sewing with knit fabrics, but now I truly appreciate that I don’t need to be quite as precise, and still yield impressive results. With garment sewing, in particular, I love that I end up with a comfortable piece of clothing that gets worn over and over. In case some of you feel the same sort of trepidation about the stretchy stuff, I’ve included some tips and my own methods for sewing knits in the Handy Terms + Techniques on the following pages.

HANDY TERMS + TECHNIQUES

Here is some noteworthy information plus some of the more frequently used terminology and methods to which I refer throughout the book—but please bear in mind that this is not meant to be a comprehensive list.

BACKSTITCHING: I don't actually call this out in every project, but unless you are gathering a piece of fabric for a skirt, let's say, you will *always* backstitch at the beginning and end of every seam you sew. This means that you will sew a few stitches, then select your "back" button (or pull a lever or whatever functionality for reversing that your machine is equipped with) to sew backwards over the first few stitches you created (or the last few if indeed you are at the end). I backstitch about 4 or 5 stitches normally, and you can consider this step the equivalent of tying a knot in the thread to secure it. Otherwise, your stitches will unravel and your hard work will be for naught.

BASTE: A baste stitch holds pieces of fabric together temporarily. This can be done with a lengthened machine stitch or with a running stitch by hand.

BIAS TAPE: A bias tape is a thin strip of material cut at a 45-degree angle on the fabric. This allows the tape to stretch more, making it pliable and better suited to cover the raw edges of fabric on curves, like necklines and armholes. A bias tape maker is useful here, but you could simply press the fabric strip in half, toward the wrong side, then press the upper and lower edges toward the center crease (also toward the wrong side). Now you have a bias tape.

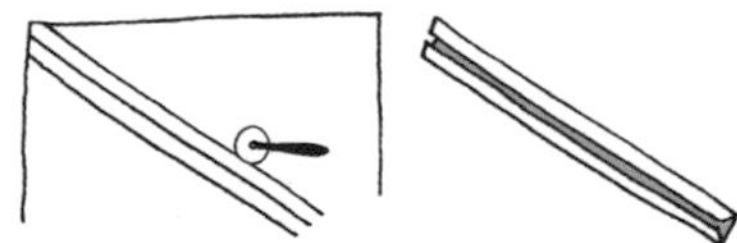

EDGESTITCH: Another term I use a lot in the book is "edgestitch." This type of stitching is at the very edge of the fold of a fabric, usually ⅛ inch or less from the edge. It is often considered decorative, but in the following projects, edgestitching is more often utilized as reinforcement or to finish sleeves and hems. In this way, I'm going a bit rogue since hemming is technically supposed to be done from the front of the garment so the stitches appear even (stitches created on the underside tend to look slightly less uniform—some jiggling with the tension can help make the underside stitches look more even), but I'm either inept at ironing evenly or can't sew straight, because I inevitably get wonky results when I try to sew from the right side of the garment to finish sleeves or to complete hemming. You're welcome to go rogue with me.

FABRIC PREPARATION: Make sure to prewash and dry all fabrics. You will also want to iron/press the fabric before you begin drafting or tracing patterns onto the fabric. The exception to this general rule of prepping fabric would be for textiles that fall into the waxed canvas, leather, and wool felt categories.

FINISHING: Fabrics such as cotton and linen will fray, and to prevent fabric edges from unraveling and turning into an unwieldy mass of threads, they will need to be "finished." This can be done in several different ways: with pinking shears, by zigzag stitching, by overlock stitching with a serger if you have one (my favorite method), or with a French seam. There are a few other ways, but I won't go into them in this book. Some textiles recommended in this book will not fray, e.g. knits, wool felt, and leather. You will not need to finish the raw edges for these unless you want to.

FRENCH SEAM: All you need to do to make a French seam is to start by sewing about ¼ inch (depending on the project) along the edge with the WRONG sides facing.

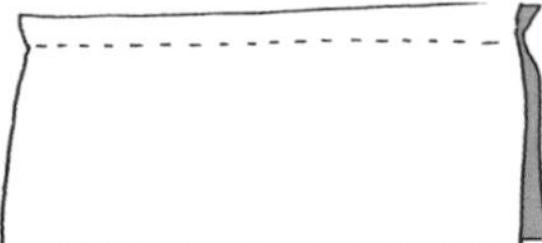

I like to trim this seam down to close to ⅛ inch because I always end up with little frayed edges showing through once I've finished stitching. This is optional, however.

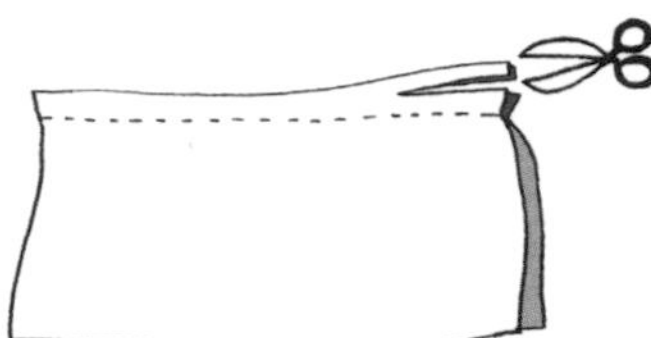

Then, press the seam to sandwich the raw edge between the RIGHT sides facing. Now sew ½ inch from the seam edge, and this will encase the raw, frayed bits.

Press, and that's it!

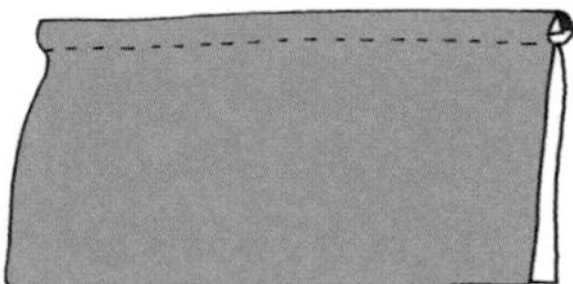

GATHERING: Some projects involve gathering portions of the fabric. The easiest way I've found is to lengthen the machine stitch to its maximum. Then, without backstitching at all, stitch two parallel rows on the fabric. I usually stitch about ¼ inch from the top edge of the fabric for the first row, and then sew another row ⅝ inch or so from the first one. Leave a tail of thread of about 3 inches on each side and pull these thread tails gently to gather the fabric.

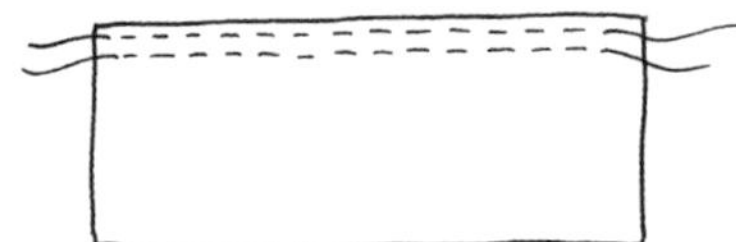

GRAIN LINE: The grain line will guide you when cutting out pattern pieces from fabric. The straight grain is parallel to the selvage (see below). The cross grain is perpendicular to the straight grain. And cutting on the bias grain means cutting diagonally, at a 45-degree angle. Think of it as a tic-tac-toe grid. The vertical lines are straight grain, the horizontal lines cross grain, and if you get three *x*'s in a diagonal row, it's a bias grain.

I determine the grain line by what I call the "pull test." I tug at a piece of fabric to see which side stretches more. If I pull up and down and it stretches more than side-to-side, then I know that the side-to-side is parallel to the selvage. And vice versa. So the side that stretches *less* is parallel to the selvage and stronger.

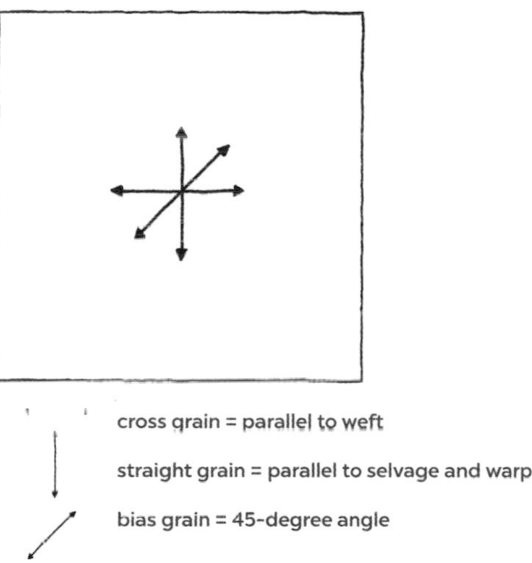

RIGHT SIDE/WRONG SIDE: In the instructions, you will see the words "RIGHT" and "WRONG" in all caps. These refer to the right, or the outer-facing, side of fabric and the wrong, or interior-facing, side of the fabric. Sometimes it's pretty obvious, but there are times when a fabric looks identical on both sides. In such cases, I recommend using your marking tool to indicate which side is the WRONG side to make assembling the pieces easier down the line.

SEAM ALLOWANCE: The seam allowance is the section of the fabric between the stitching line and the edge of the fabric when at least two pieces of material are sewn together. Although ⅜ inch is the predominant seam allowance I like to use, the seam allowance will vary depending on the project, so I've made sure to include the specific seam allowance information in each step. It is phrased as "sew ⅜ inch from the raw edge" or as "sew with a ⅜-inch seam allowance."

SELVAGE: Selvage is the morphing of the original sixteenth-century word "self-edge" and refers to the nonfraying edge of a piece of fabric that runs parallel to what's called the warp. When you buy fabric, it's the section of the fabric with the brand and designer information printed on a thin strip right at the edge. You can see that it doesn't unravel at all. The warp comprises threads that run longitudinally—in other words vertically or up and down—and the weft comprises the threads that are woven in and out between the warp threads. See the illustration under Grain Line on the previous page.

SLIP STITCH: Many of the projects reference slip stitching by hand to close openings in a seam. You will start by double-knotting the end of your thread and inserting your needle from the underside of one opening edge to hide the knot. Pull the needle all the way through and pick up a few threads directly across from where you pulled out your needle. Then pick up a few threads from the other side, inserting the needle from under the seam slightly away from the original stitch. Continue stitching this way until the opening is closed.

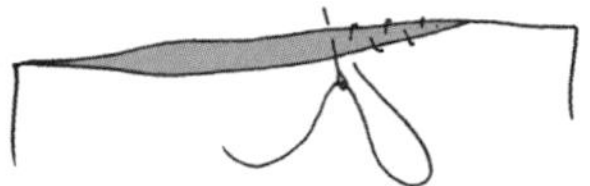

SEWING KNITS

I didn't have a great fear of knit fabric when I first started sewing because I didn't know any better. I whipped up a bat costume for my daughter for her third Halloween, not fazed in the least with the yards and yards of black jersey (though I did puzzle over how to finish the hems). Then I started to read sewing blogs and tutorials online and discovered that there was a veritable phobia when it came to sewing stretch fabrics. The phobia weaseled its way into my own brain, and pretty soon I was avoiding any type of fabric that was designed to stretch. It took a full year of sewing before I ventured tentatively back into the realm of sewing knits with abandon.

It turns out that my beginner's attitude was right: knits aren't all that bad. They're quite unfussy, really, and if you stick with blends that include a little spandex or nylon (in the 2 to 5 percent range), there's not a whole lot of difference between sewing knits versus wovens. Plus, you don't actually have to finish the raw edges because there's absolutely no fraying! I personally like to finish my raw edges with a serger, but again, this is just my own preference.

The two things to keep in mind with sewing knits are 1) the needle, and 2) the stitch type.

The Needle

For knit fabrics, make sure to change your sewing machine needle to a ballpoint, jersey, or stretch needle. You will be happier for it since these needles are specifically designed for knit fabrics. Some people recommend a walking foot, but I don't use one and have sewn dozens and dozens of knit projects successfully.

For hemming knits, some people swear by a double or twin needle. These needles require two thread spools and create two parallel straight lines on the top and a zigzag stitch on the underside. I've had mixed results with twin needles and tend to stick with zigzag stitching with a ballpoint needle to hem knit projects. Give it a whirl and see if you like it.

The Stitch Type

There are several stitch options for knit fabrics. A regular straight stitch isn't ideal because it doesn't have enough elasticity and stretch and will break easily.

STRETCH STITCH: Most modern machines come with a stretch stitch. I don't like mine because it takes forever to sew with this stitch, but it *is* extremely stretchy.

ZIGZAG STITCH: You can use your standard zigzag stitch, or do what I do: reduce to a width of about 1 and increase the length to 3. This looks a lot like the stretch stitch above, though not slanted, and sews much faster.

MOCK OVERLOCK STITCH: My machine comes with a mock overlook stitch but requires a special foot. It sort of looks like an overlock stitch; I like its decorative appearance. However, this stitch also takes longer than a zigzag stitch and the fabric gets caught in the needle plate or bunches up under the feed dogs sometimes (at least for me), so it's not my favorite.

OVERLOCK STITCH: This is the stitch you see on commercial knitwear. It requires an overlocker, which is a fantastic investment if you plan on sewing a lot of knits and is extremely fast, albeit scary. An overlocker, or serger as we call it here in the United States, is not at all necessary to sew knit fabrics, and I prefer to sew with my regular sewing machine because I feel like I have more control that way. But I do love to finish my raw edges with the overlocker.

TOPSTITCH: Topstitching is a straight stitch created from the right side of a piece of fabric, usually with thread that matches the fabric color. For the projects included in this book, topstitching is generally used for necklines to secure the seam allowance in place. When you don't stitch the seam allowance in place, sometimes it pops up and is visible from the neckline, which doesn't look that great.

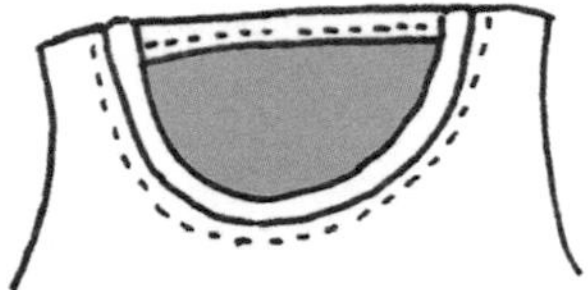

Once you've figured out which one of these stitches you prefer, you're off to the races!

the mini sashiko primer

I GREW UP SURROUNDED BY *SASHIKO* stitching. My mother has been collecting kimonos and Japanese textiles for as long as I can remember, stuffing them into closets and boxes and occasionally taking them out to lingeringly admire each piece. As a transplant to sunny Los Angeles, she must have found memories and solace in handling those inky blue cotton pieces painstakingly decorated with white or red embroidery.

Sashiko has a long history and humble origins dating all the way back to the 1600s. In Japan, wives of fishermen would mend tattered clothing using simple running stitches, reinforcing the seams over and over. It's often translated as "little stabs," and though that's not inaccurate, I've always thought of the word "pierce" in translating the word "sasu" from which "sashi" is derived. "Little pierces" has a nicer ring to it, don't you think?

Over time, Sashiko developed into a decorative craft—an embellishment rather than a necessity.

I'm drawn to how easy it is, how down-to-earth. You don't even need a hoop. Yet, through the accumulation of little pierces with an extra-long needle, complex arrays of shapes and stories can emerge.

TOOLS

- Sashiko or extra-long needles
- Sashiko thread or cotton embroidery floss
- Scissors
- Fabric (cotton and medium-weight linen; linen-cotton blends work best for me, as they merge the best of both worlds)
- Thimble (optional)

1.
OLYMPUS
刺し子糸
綿 100% 40m
2.
OLYMPUS
刺し子糸
綿 100% 40m
OLYMPUS
刺し子糸
綿 100% 40m
3.
4.
5.

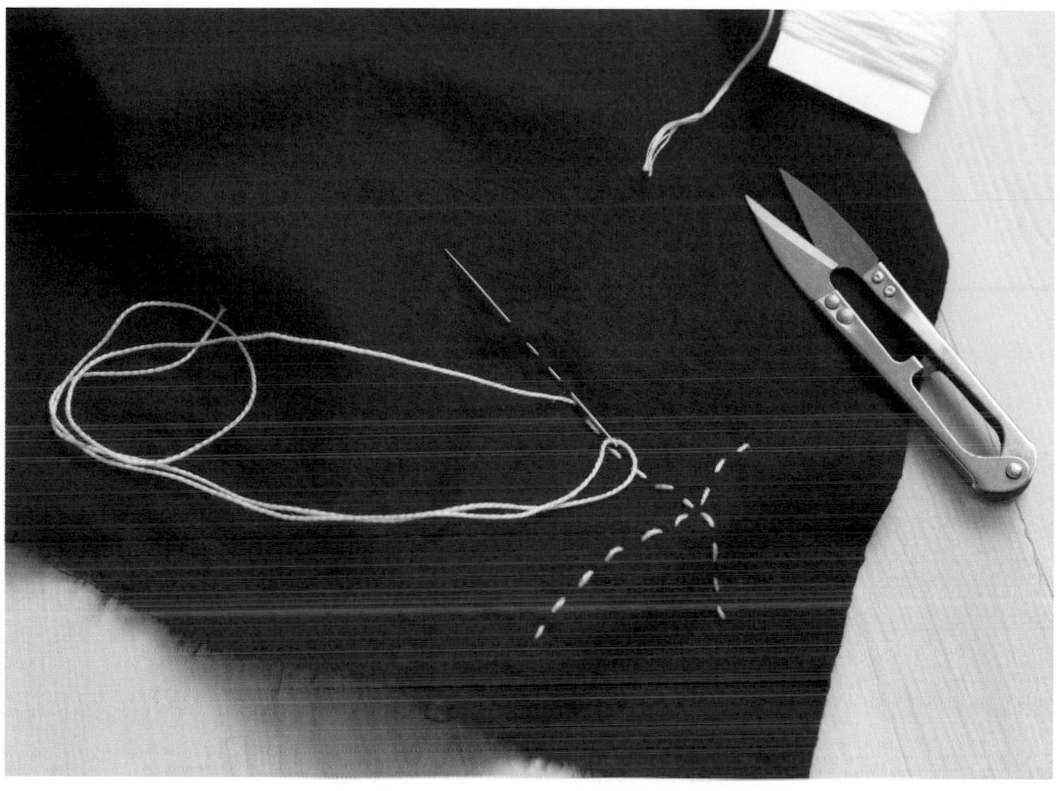

This section is a basic overview of the traditional Sashiko methods and common designs. However, I've never been a stickler for following designated patterns. My stitches are always a little crooked, somewhat uneven. I consider it endearing, though, of course, I also appreciate and admire the workmanship of machine-like precision. Whether you are a traditionalist or more interpretive like I am, I think you'll find Sashiko stitching thoroughly enjoyable. The only project that intentionally incorporates Sashiko is the Sashiko Trivet on page 203, but these little stitches can be applied to virtually any of the projects.

Sashiko needles and thread can be found at many independent fabric stores, and are also available online. If you choose embroidery floss instead, you may only be able to use three or four threads of it if the eye of the needle is not large enough. See Resources on page 215 for a list of select stores that carry Sashiko-specific supplies.

KEY FOR PHOTO ON FACING PAGE: 1. CARBON OR CHACOPY PAPER 2. SASHIKO OR EMBROIDERY THREAD 3. BOW SCISSORS 4. SASHIKO NEEDLES 5. CLIPPERS

BASIC STITCHES

Traditionally, Sashiko stitching starts without a knot. The illustrations below show how to secure the thread without a knot; however, since the back of the fabric will not show up in any of the projects included in this book, feel free to use a knot to get things started.

1. On the wrong side of the fabric, pluck two or three threads with the needle.
2. Without pulling the thread all the way through, insert the needle into the exact same place you started.
3. Continue to pull the thread until a small loop forms, then insert the needle through the loop.
4. Keep tugging to tighten the stitch, and now you're ready to start!

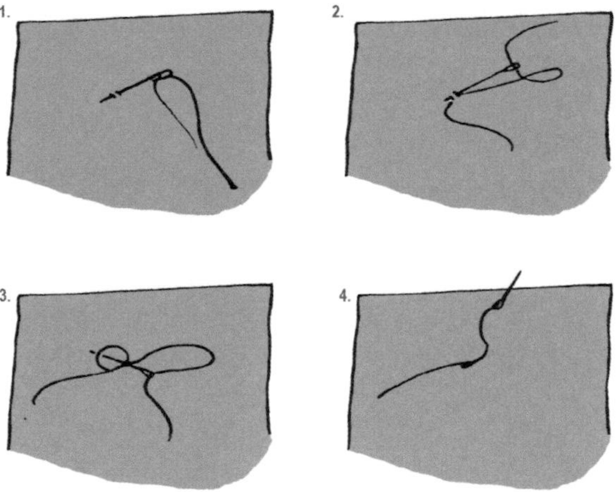

5. The Sashiko stitch is a running stitch with a 3:2 ratio; this means that the stitches on the visible side are longer than they are on the bottom, like so:

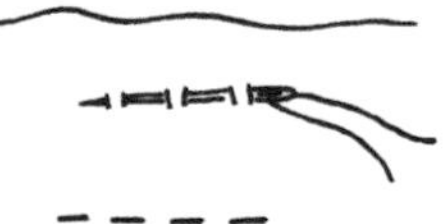

STITCH SPACING

Sashiko typically maintains certain amounts of spacing where stitches meet at a corner or right angle.

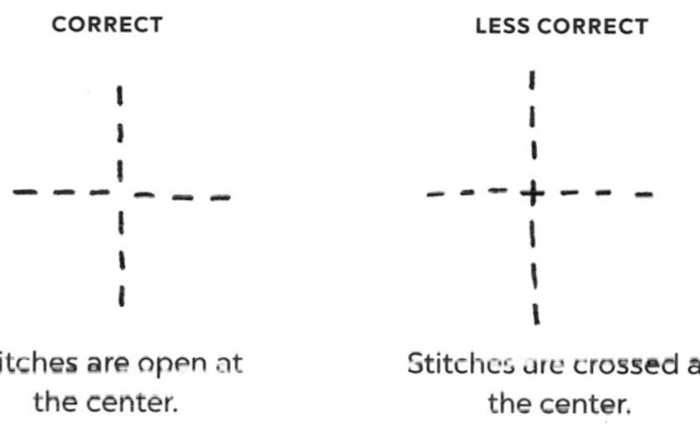

CORRECT

Stitches create a sharply defined angle.

LESS CORRECT

Too much space at the corner makes for a less well-defined angle.

CORRECT | **LESS CORRECT**

When stitching a corner, a small slack in thread on the wrong side will help prevent excessive pulling when viewed from the right side.

CORRECT | **LESS CORRECT**

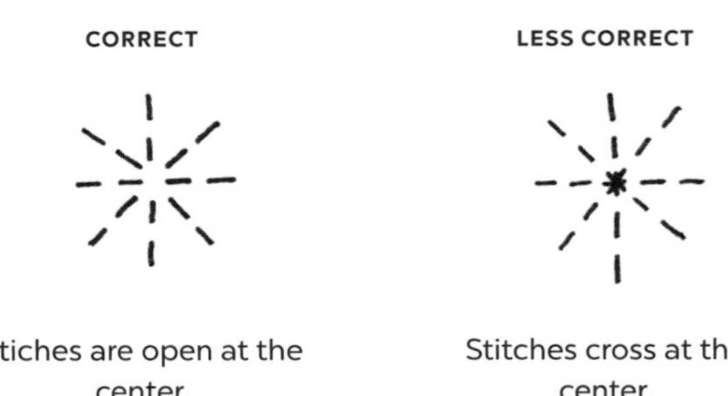

Stiches are open at the center.

Stitches cross at the center.

Note: Stitches crossing at the center is considered less ideal than open stitching; however, some designs are meant to have crossing lines, so it really depends.

STITCH ORDER

Tradition dictates that you stitch the horizontal and vertical lines first, then the diagonals, then fill in any other smaller shapes—but feel free to stitch in any order that feels comfortable to you. If there are other, more intricate elements in your design, you may need to try out a few directions to see what works best.

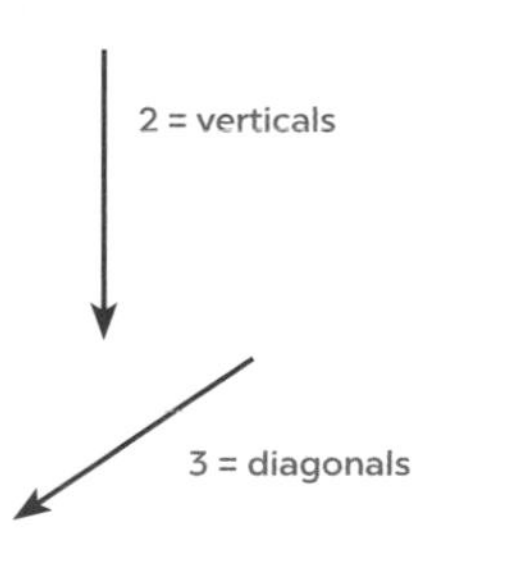

COMMON DESIGNS

Sashiko designs were originally inspired by nature and are typically based on a grid structure. Below are illustrations of some of the more prevalent designs. I've also included some templates to get you started.

Shippo Tsunagi (linked seven treasures)

Yabane (arrow)

Hishi Moyo (diamond pattern)

Asanoha (hemp leaf)

HOW TO TRANSFER SASHIKO DESIGNS ONTO FABRIC

There are several ways to transfer the designs onto fabric.

1. Trace the pattern onto fusible interfacing using a pencil or marker. Iron the interfacing on the WRONG side of the fabric. Remember you will be stitching from the back side, so you will want to keep the stitches shorter on the wrong side and longer on the front side. It may feel counter-intuitive to stitch this way, but it will become second nature quickly.
2. Use a transfer or carbon paper such as Chacopy, which is available in lighter colors (white, yellow, pink) so that the markings are easily visible on dark colored fabric. Place the Chacopy paper with the carbon side facing down on the RIGHT side of the fabric and trace/draw the design. Because the lines will fade quickly, trace over the design with iron-away marker after you've transferred the design.
3. Mark directly on the fabric using tailor's chalk or marker. Drawing lines with a quilter's ruler is helpful.

And if all of this seems like a lot more work than you've bargained for, simply play around with some running stitches and see what emerges!

Templates that correspond to the illustrations on the facing page are included on the following pages. Give the templates a whirl or come up with your own inspired designs.

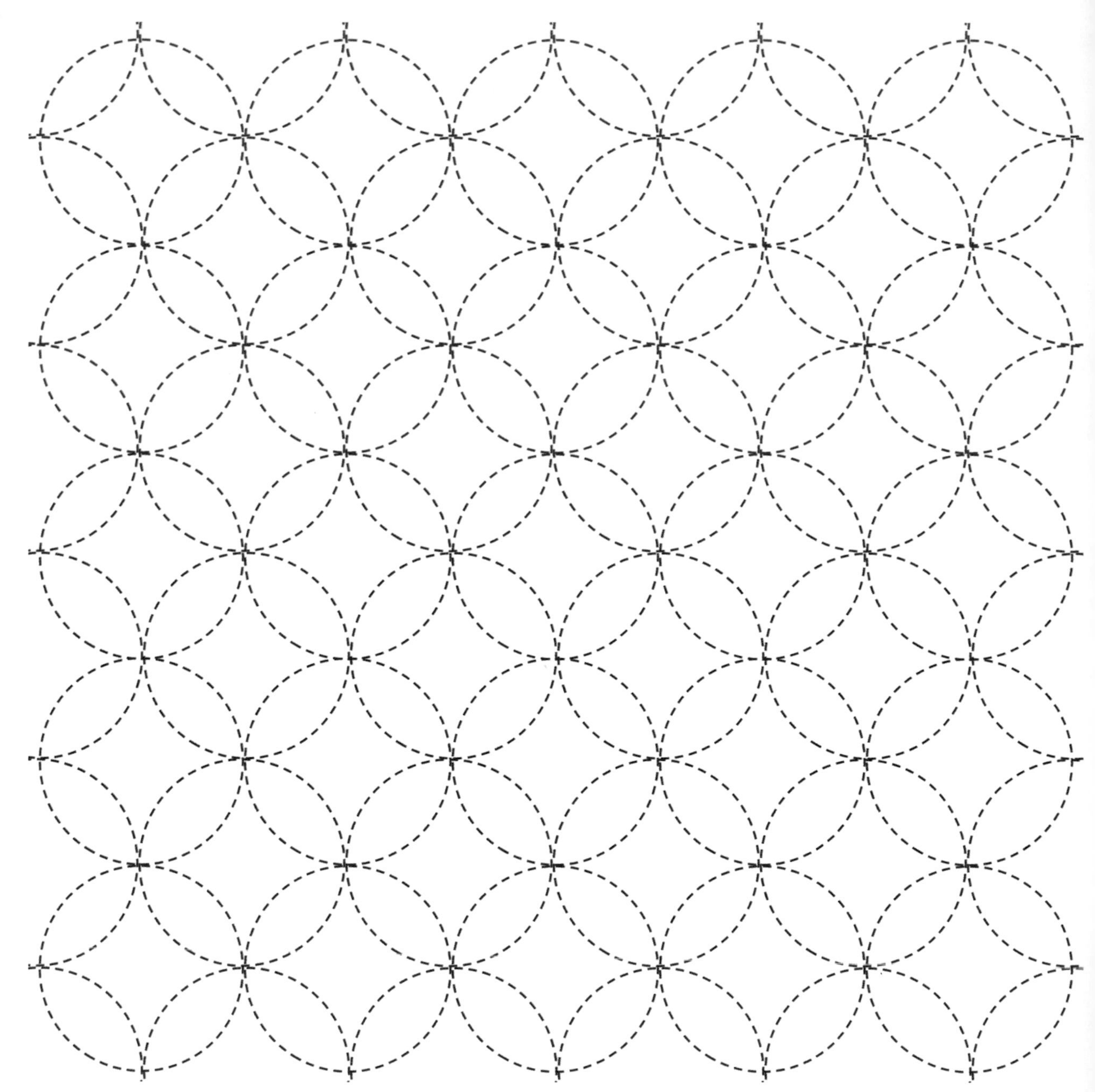

Shippo Tsunagi (linked seven treasures)

Yabane (arrow)

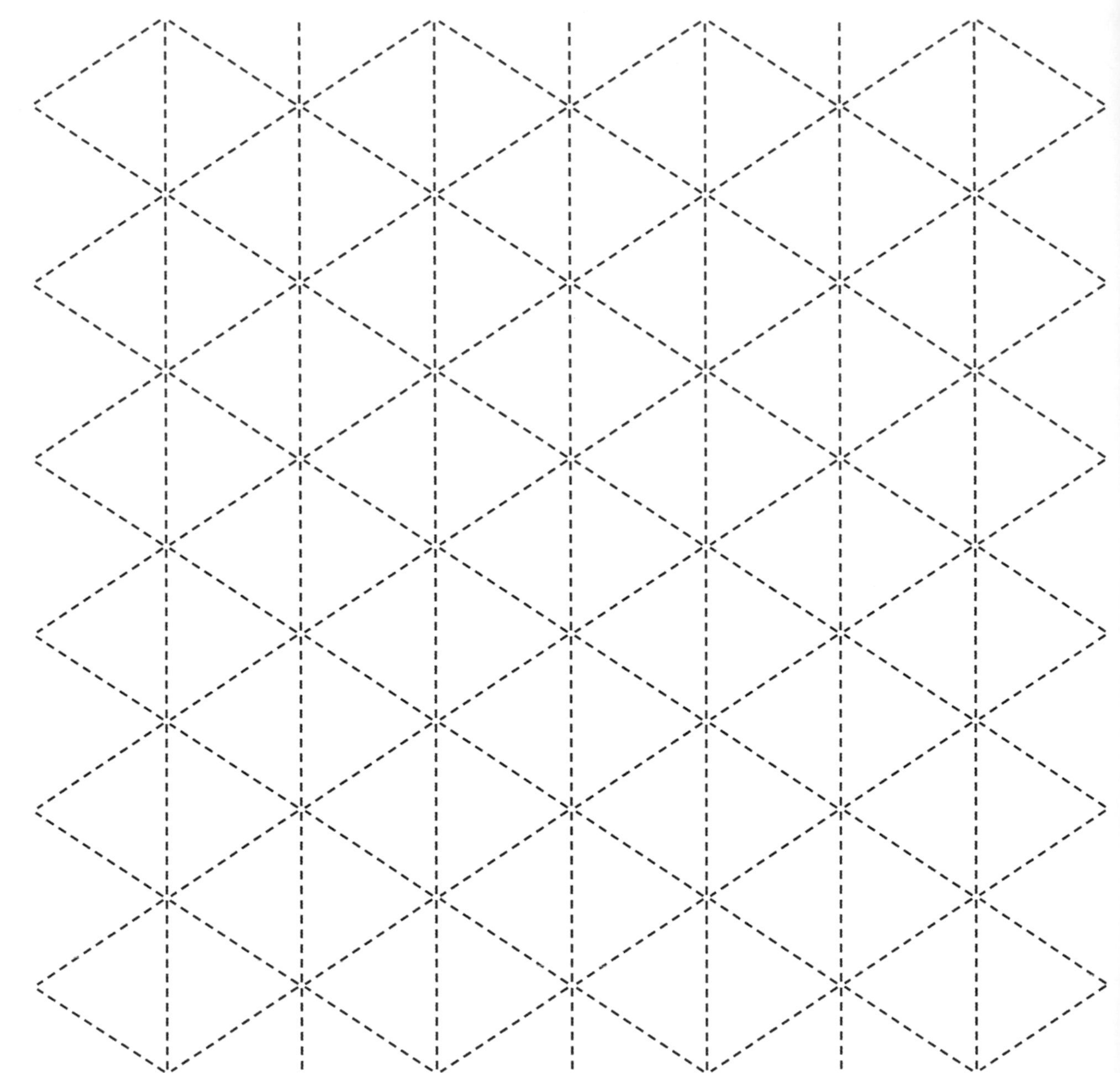

Hishi Moyo (diamond pattern)

Asanoha (hemp leaf)

instructions

ORIGAMI PILLOW

I LOVE FOLDING ORIGAMI CRANES; even restaurant napkins are prone to becoming little birds. These pillows have geometric shapes reminiscent of the Japanese craft, but are much easier to make than cranes since they don't involve any intricate or complicated folds, just a few straight stitches. I provided instructions for my favorite design that mimics origami, but the possibilities are infinite.

The graphic and streamlined design of the pillow makes it versatile for all types of decor. I constructed all of my pillows out of linen, and I highly recommend using solid colors to let the folds stand out. If you're not a fan of the raised seams, the underside is just as pretty and can be used as the front. Not only is this a superfast project, but it's a great way to improve your edgestitching skills as well. There's a tiny little bit of math involved, but it's not too painful, I promise. I recommend using a square pillow for this project, although you can of course apply the steps to a rectangular-shaped pillow. Keep in mind that for a rectangular shape, the folds will appear elongated if you follow the instructions below. Photos on pages 16 and 17.

SUPPLIES + MATERIALS

1½ yards woven fabric

Coordinating thread

Rotary cutter and metal ruler (optional)

Pillow insert

FABRIC RECOMMENDATIONS

Linen and slightly slubby textiles work wonderfully for these pillows. Quilting cotton and lighter weight canvas are great too. Make sure to prep the fabric by washing, drying, and pressing.

FINISHED DIMENSIONS

About 20 by 20 inches

FABRIC PIECES: Front (1), Back (2)

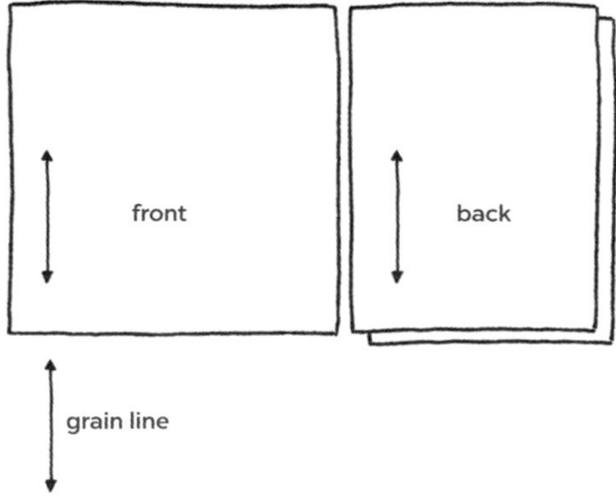

CONSTRUCTION STEPS

1. Calculate the size of the front piece by adding 1 inch to the actual pillow insert dimensions, and cut the fabric. For my 20-by-20-inch pillow insert, I cut a 21-by-21-inch piece.

2. You need two pieces for the back. The height is the exact same measurement as the pillow insert height. For the width, multiply the insert width by ¾. So for a 20-by-20-inch insert, each back piece will be 15 by 20 inches.

3. Fold the front (square) piece diagonally to form a triangle with the WRONG sides facing. Press the fold, and sew a ⅛-inch seam from the folded edge.

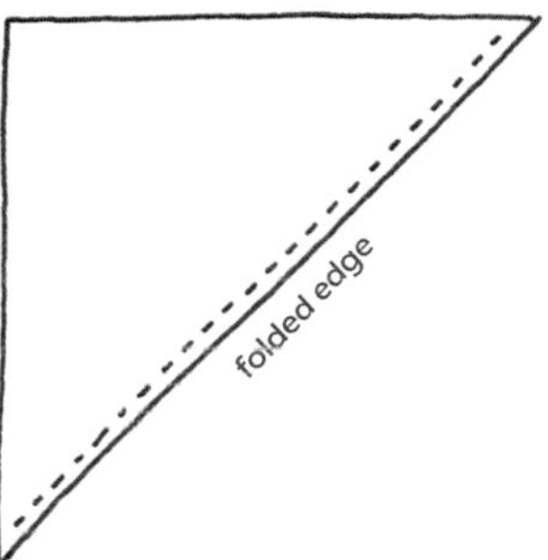

4. Open up the square and press the entire length of the seam from the WRONG side first. Then, still working from the wrong side, press the fold down to one side. (It will look like a pintuck and it doesn't really matter which way you press it.)

   Repeat step 3 with the diagonal fold going the other way.

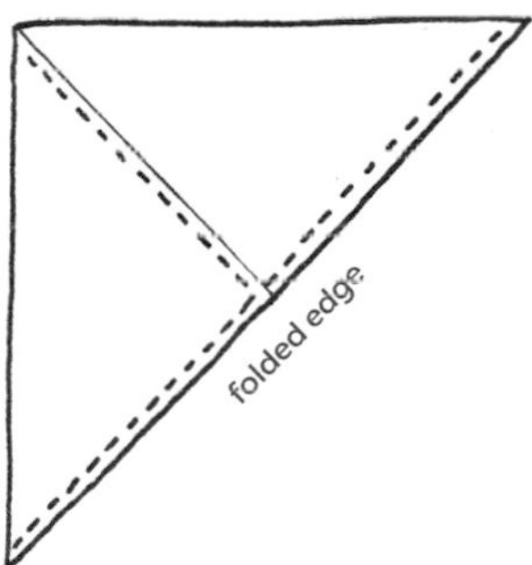

5 To sew the horizontal and vertical lines, fold in half, the WRONG sides facing, press, and sew ⅛ inch from the folded edge.

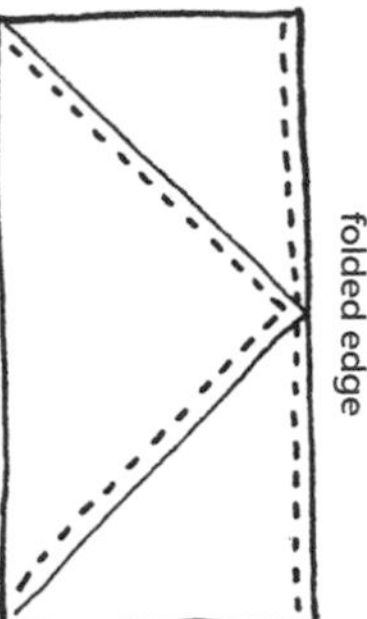

6 Open and press the pintuck to one side. Repeat the steps to create the other perpendicular line.

As the folds start to overlap, your sewing machine may have trouble smoothly gliding over the bumps. Gently pull the fabric from behind as you stitch; you may need to manually crank the hand wheel as you pull if the needle seems especially resistant.

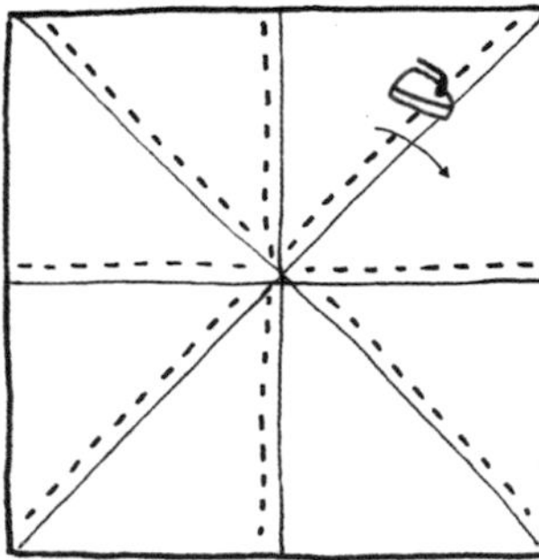

7 Flip the square over so that the pintucks/raised folds are face down and the WRONG side is facing up. Using the horizontal and vertical folds as guides, fold and press each corner toward the center, the WRONG sides facing. This will create a diamond shape. Working from the front side, sew ⅛ inch from each folded edge. Once all four sides are sewn, flatten out the piece by unfolding all the corners. Press each fold to one side. As you rotate the square to press the folds, try to press them in the same direction.

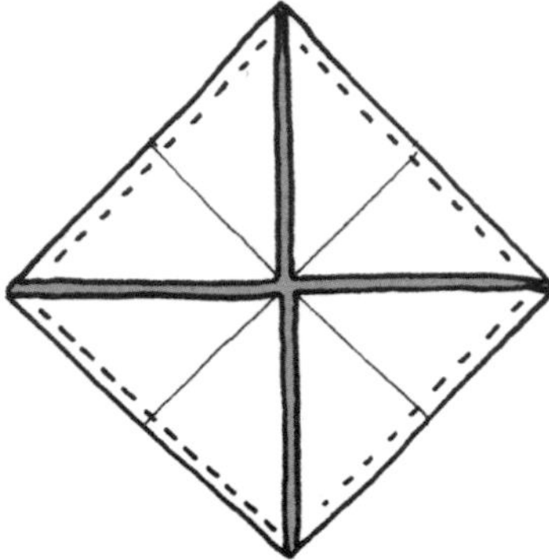

8 For one of the back pieces, fold the long edge (the one that is the same measurement as the pillow insert height) ⅜ inch toward the WRONG side and press. Fold this piece another ⅜ inch, and press again. Edgestitch along the inner folded edge. Repeat with the other back piece. These two pieces will form an envelope closure.

9 Align the back pieces with the front piece, RIGHT sides facing. Trim the edges if the front and back pieces don't exactly match up; the fabric pieces should form a square. A rotary cutter and metal ruler are handy to use for this. You may end up with a size that's a little smaller than the pillow insert, and that's fine. The pillow will actually be fluffier this way. For reference, my back pieces overlapped about 6 inches, but this number will depend on your pillow size.

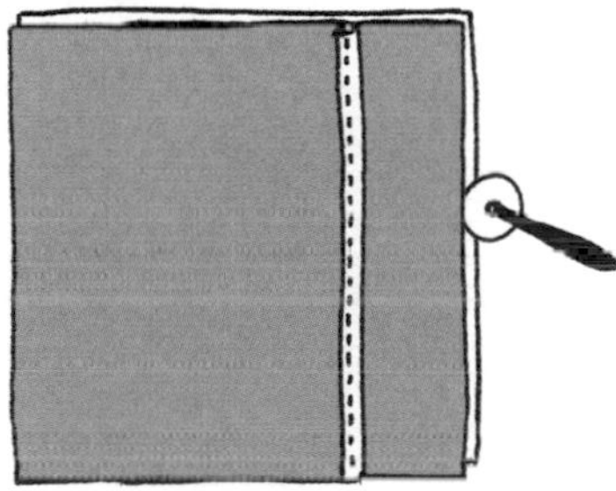

10 Pin and stitch along the perimeter of the pillow ⅜ inch from the raw edge. Keep the needle in the fabric as you pivot at the corners to get sharp, clean right angles. Since the raw edges will be hidden within the pillow, there's no need to finish them, but if your fabric is especially prone to fraying, it's a good idea to finish the edges with your preferred method: pinking shears, zigzag stitching, or overlock stitching.

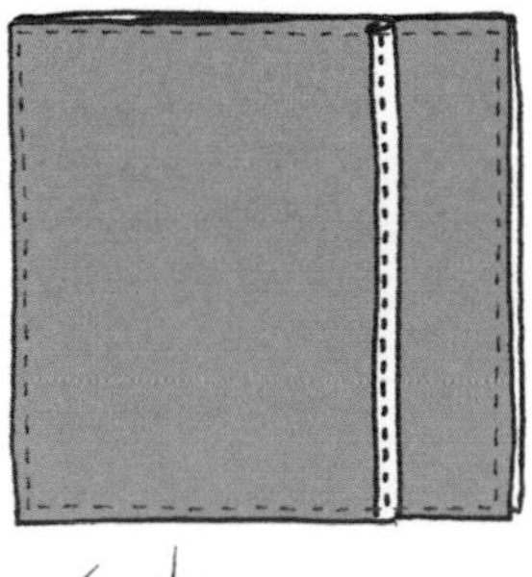

11 Clip the corners, being careful not to cut into the seam or get too close to the seam because that will weaken it. Turn the pillow RIGHT side out, and use a point turner to poke out the corners. Be careful not to poke holes through the seam.

12 Place the pillow insert inside the cover, and you're all set!

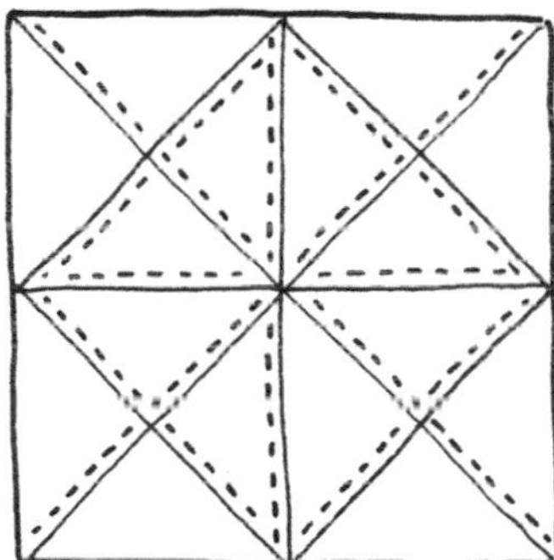

TOOTH FAIRY PILLOWS

LIKE THE ORIGAMI PILLOW, THESE look a lot more complicated than they really are, and you could even use scraps from the Origami Pillow to construct this kid-friendly project. Note that currency sizes—especially for coins—may vary depending on where you're based, so plan accordingly as you leave the opening for the stealth pockets. The Sashiko embroidery is absolutely optional, but you could get creative with all sorts of designs should the muse whisper in your ear.

When the need for a tooth fairy pillow passes (or if you don't need one to begin with), keep in mind these make excellent pincushions too! Photos on pages 18 and 19.

SUPPLIES + MATERIALS

Scraps of very thin linen or cotton

Coordinating thread

Polyfill or cotton batting/stuffing

Hand-sewing needles

Sashiko or embroidery thread (optional)

FABRIC RECOMMENDATIONS

Try to use very thin linen or cotton (such as lawn) for the origami shapes to reduce bulk when folding. It's a good idea to prep the fabrics by washing and drying, but it's not entirely necessary for these small pillows. Do make sure to press your fabrics before cutting them out, since you want to start with accurately measured and flat pieces for the origami steps.

FINISHED DIMENSIONS

About 3¼ by 3¼ inches

CONSTRUCTION STEPS FOR THE PILLOW

1. Make the origami shape of your choice (see Construction Steps for the Origami Shapes, page 130).

2. For the pillow, cut two 4½-by-4½-inch squares.

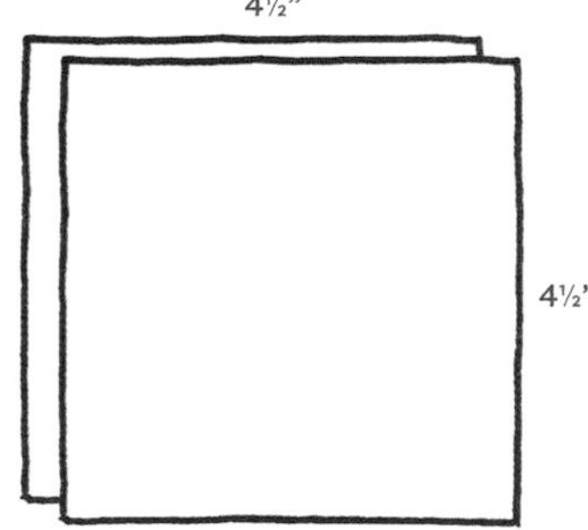

3. Pin the origami shape to the center on the RIGHT side of one of the squares. It's faster to machine stitch, but I find I have more control when I slip stitch the shape on by hand. Make sure to leave the following parts (indicated by the green line) unstitched for each shape to create a pocket.

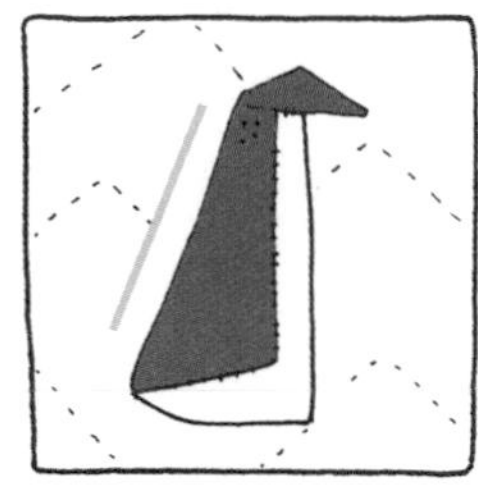

4. If desired, add Sashiko stitches for decorative elements right onto the origami shape or on the pillow background.

5. With RIGHT sides facing, pin and stitch around the pillow with a ⅜-inch seam allowance, leaving about a 2½-inch opening on the bottom.

6. Clip the corners and trim the seam allowances down to about ¼ inch. Turn the pillow RIGHT side out and use a point turner to poke out the corners. Be careful not to poke holes through the seam.

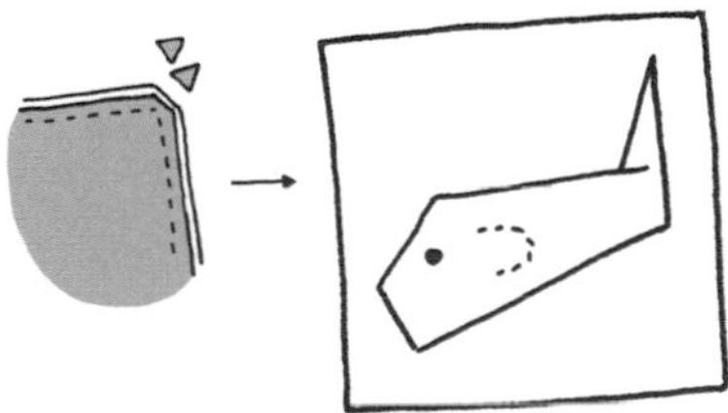

7. Fill the pillow with your choice of stuffing. Slip stitch the opening closed.

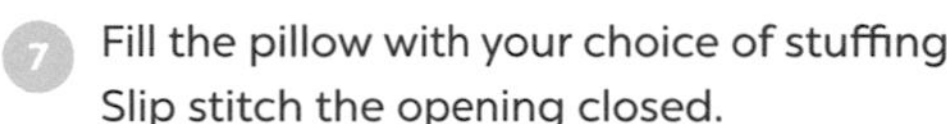

8. Let your child roll or fold up his or her note to the tooth fairy and place it, along with the tooth, into the hidden pocket. Let the anticipation begin!

DWOX *(a.k.a. a creature of a vague dog-wolf-fox origin)*

1. Cut a 3½-by-3½-inch piece of fabric. Fold at the center with the RIGHT sides facing to form a triangle, and press. Stitch along the raw-edge sides with a ¼-inch seam allowance, leaving about a 2-inch opening on one side.

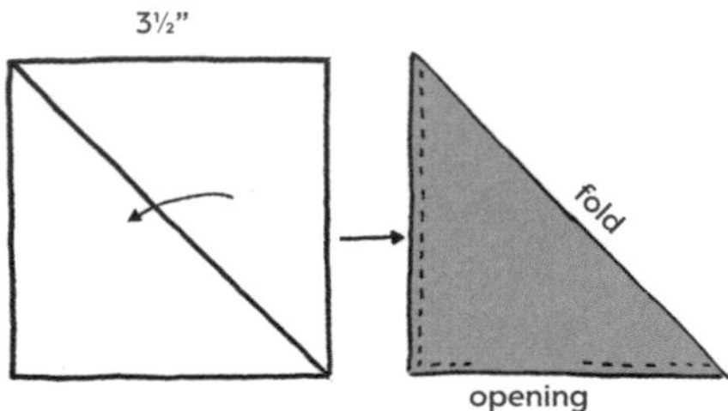

2. Clip the corners and turn RIGHT side out, pushing out the corners with a point turner. Be careful not to poke holes through the seam. Press, making sure to tuck in the seam allowance at the opening so that it is flush with the rest of the seam. Topstitch with coordinating thread, if desired (I didn't).

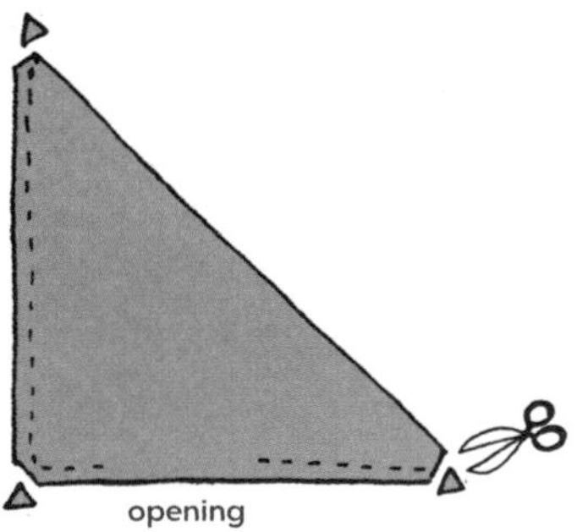

3. Determine which side you want as the front side and arrange the triangle so that the longest straight side is on top. Fold the top two corners toward the back to form ears, and press.

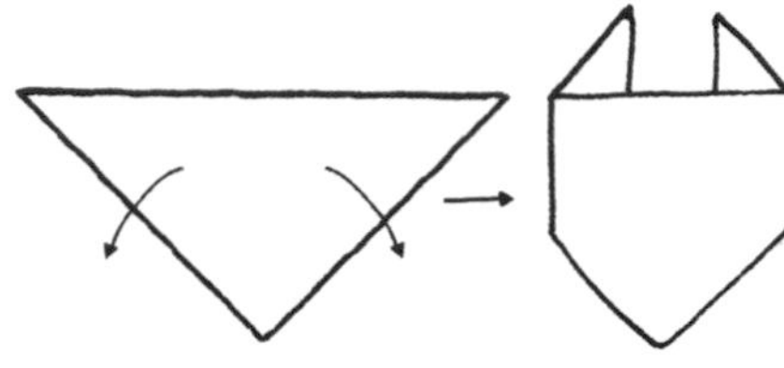

4. Using coordinating thread, slip stitch the ears to top of head. Switch to Sashiko or embroidery thread, and create eyes and a nose. Sew on the whiskers after you've attached the dwox to the pillow. Proceed to the Construction Steps for the Pillow on page 128.

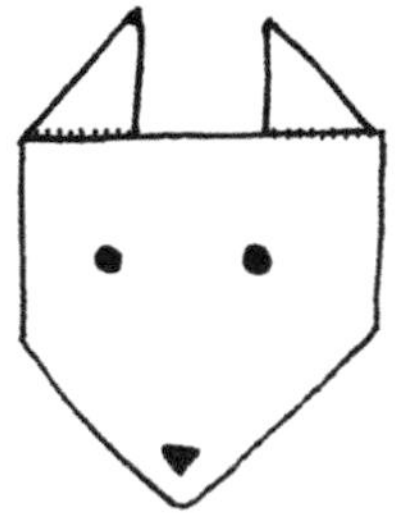

WHALE

1. Cut two 4-by-4-inch pieces of fabric. With the RIGHT sides facing, stitch around the edge with a ¼-inch seam allowance and leave about a 2-inch opening on the bottom.

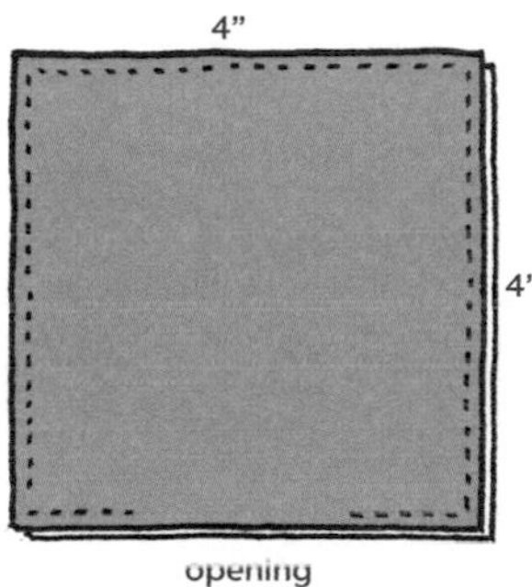

2. Clip the corners and turn RIGHT side out, pushing out the corners with a point turner. Be careful not to poke holes through the seam. Press, making sure to tuck in the seam allowance at the opening so that it is flush with the rest of the seam. You now have a slightly smaller square. Press and topstitch with coordinating thread, if desired.

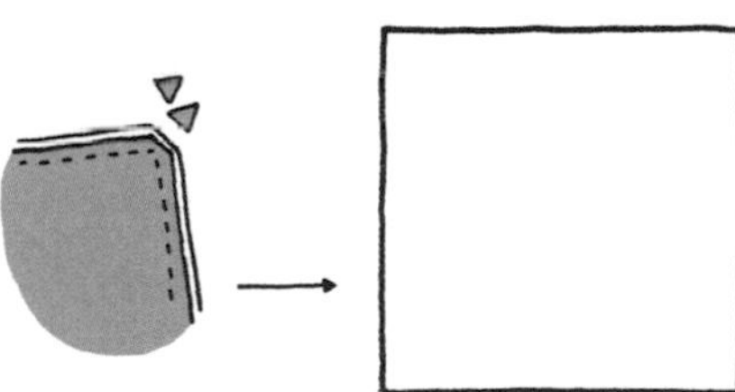

3. Determine which side will be the front side, and place the square piece so that the back side is facing up. Fold along center diagonal line so that it forms a triangle and press. Note: In the steps that follow, the back side will be indicated by the gray shading to differentiate it from the front, and this doesn't mean the fabric is showing the WRONG side as in steps 1 and 2.

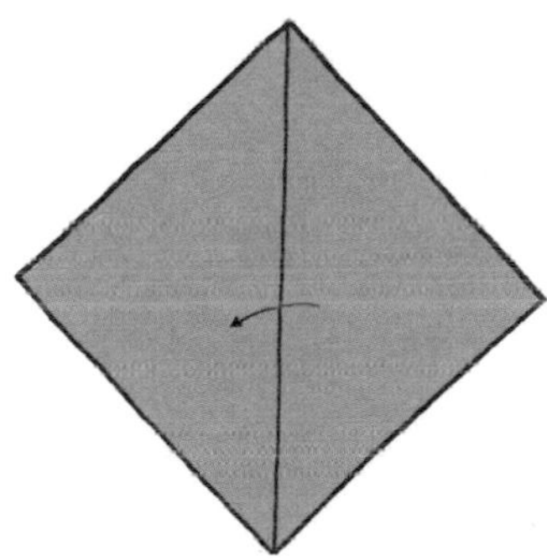

4. Open the triangle and fold each side toward the creased line, which will form a kite shape. Press.

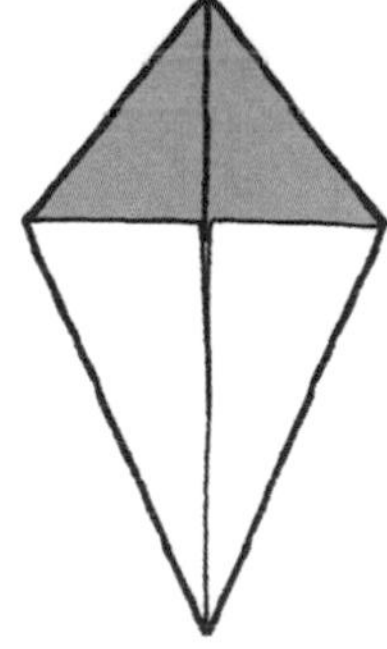

5. Fold down the top tip to meet the center of the folded sides. Press. Fold in half with all folds tucked inside, and press again.

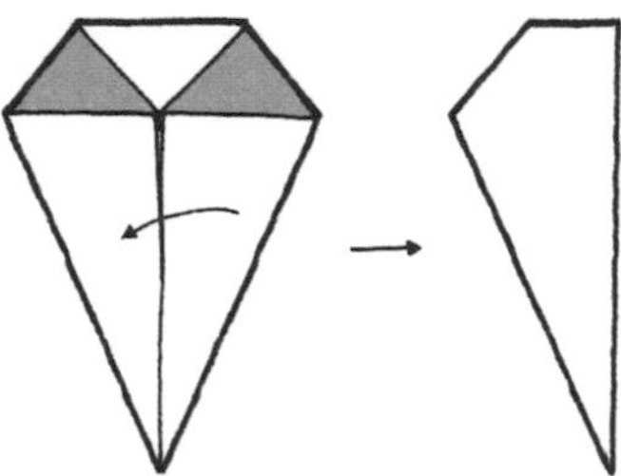

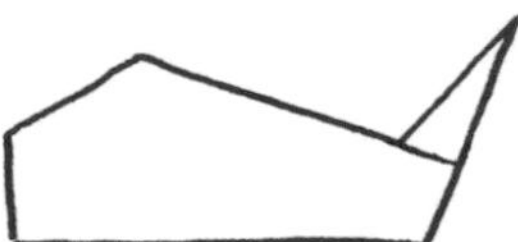

6. Place shape with long, flat side as the base, then fold the pointier end toward the back and up to form the tail. Press.

7. Using coordinating thread, slip stitch the tail to the body. Switch to Sashiko or embroidery thread, and create the eye, fin, and any other embellishment you'd like. Proceed to the Construction Steps for the Pillow on page 128.

PENGUIN

1. Cut two 4-by-4-inch pieces of fabric. One piece should be light and the other dark. With the RIGHT sides facing, stitch around the edge with a ¼-inch seam allowance and leave about a 2-inch opening on the bottom.

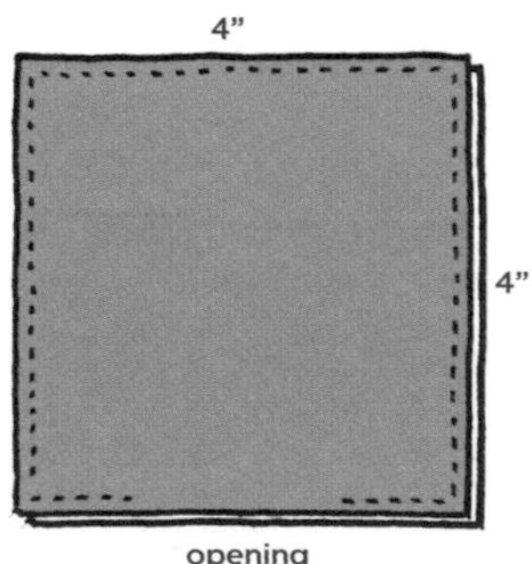

2. Clip the corners and turn RIGHT side out, pushing out the corners with a point turner. Be careful not to poke holes through the seam. Press, making sure to tuck in the seam allowance at the opening so that it is flush with the rest of the seam. You now have a slightly smaller square. Press.

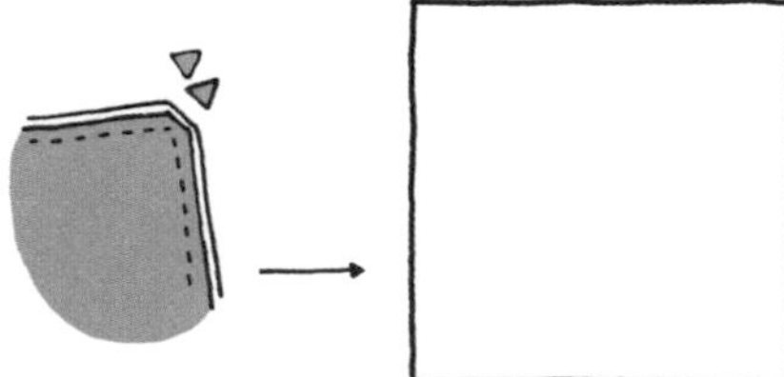

3. Lay the square so that the dark side is facing up. Fold along the center line so that it forms a triangle and press.

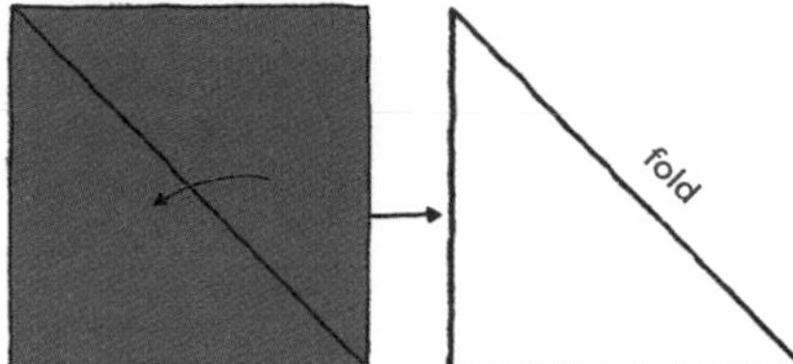

4. Open the triangle and fold one corner up to the center along the crease. Press.

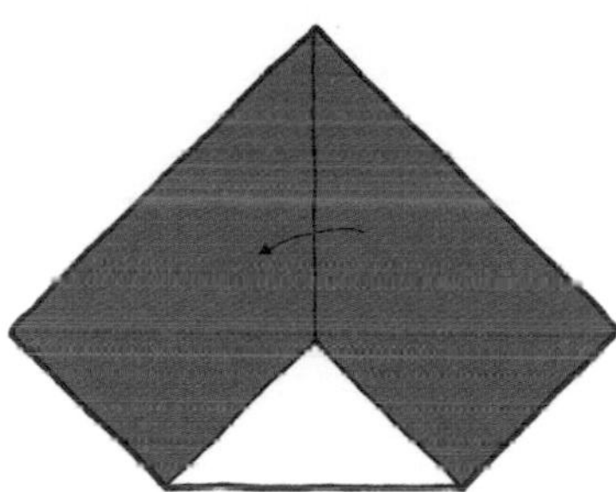

5. Following the crease line, fold in half with the dark sides together. Press.

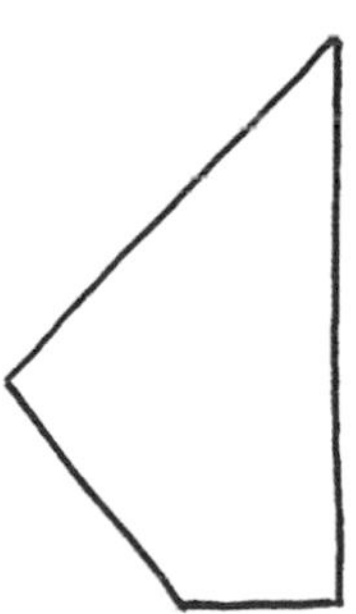

6. Fold each dark side back toward the light side to form wings about halfway in. Press.

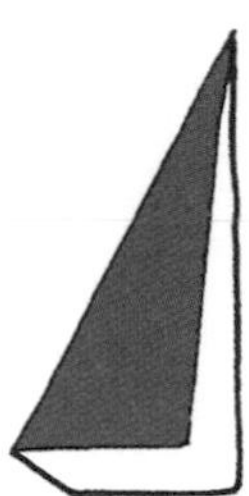

7. Flip the tip of triangle down to create the head and beak. Press. Using coordinating thread, secure the head and wing to the body. Switch to Sashiko or embroidery thread and add any desired decorative elements. Proceed to the Construction Steps for the Pillow on page 128.

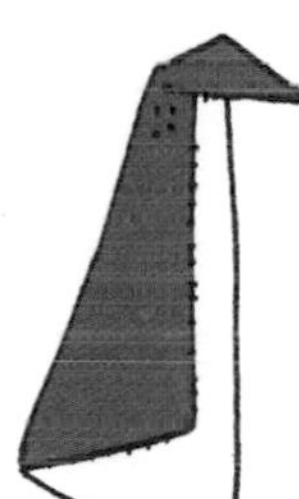

BUTTERFLY

1. Cut two 4-by-3-inch pieces of fabric (either the same or different colors). With the RIGHT sides facing, stitch around the edge with a ¼-inch seam allowance and leave about a 2-inch opening on the bottom.

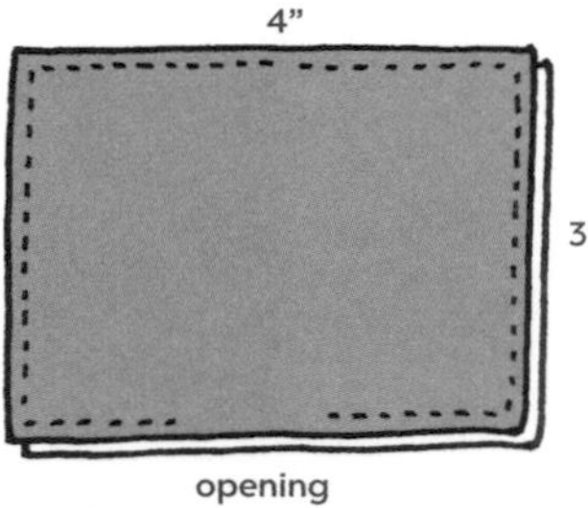

2. Clip the corners and turn RIGHT side out, pushing out the corners with a point turner. Be careful not to poke holes through the seam. Press, making sure to tuck in the seam allowance at the opening so that it is flush with the rest of the seam. You now have a slightly smaller rectangle. (Press and topstitch, if desired.)

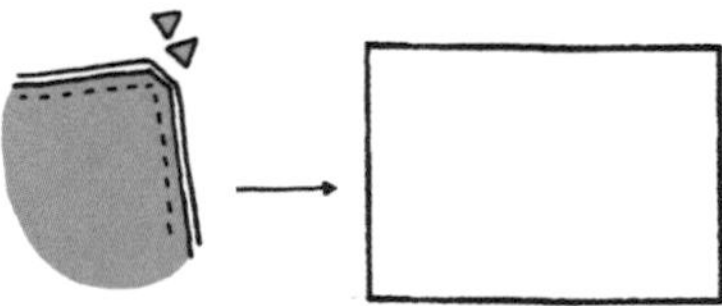

3. Determine the front and back (this is especially helpful if you've used two different colored fabrics). Fold the rectangle in half so that the short halves meet with back sides together. Press.

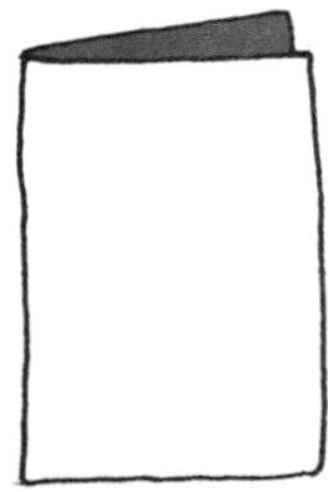

4. Fold in half again, quartering the rectangle. Press.

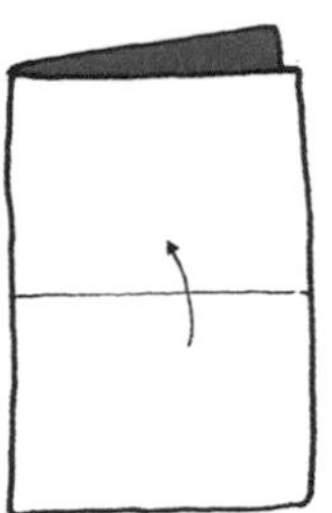

5. Lay the rectangle so that the newest folded edge is closest to you. Then lift the half you just created, open it slightly toward the left direction. It helps to place your index finger inside just where the inner corner of the fold is, guiding the fabric to flatten evenly to create a shape that looks like a house. Press.

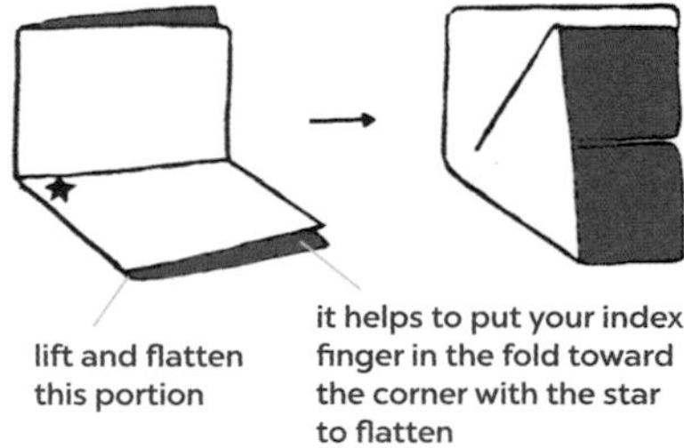

6. Flip it over and it should look like this:

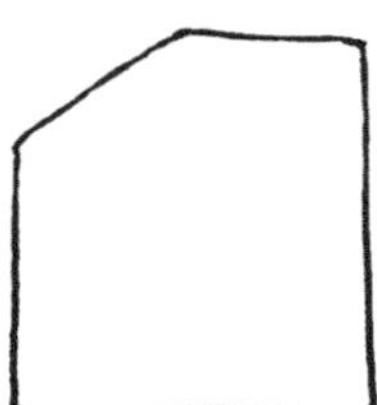

7 Lift the left corner, opening and flattening as you move it toward the right. This should form an identical triangle on top of the one you created previously. Press. It should now look like this:

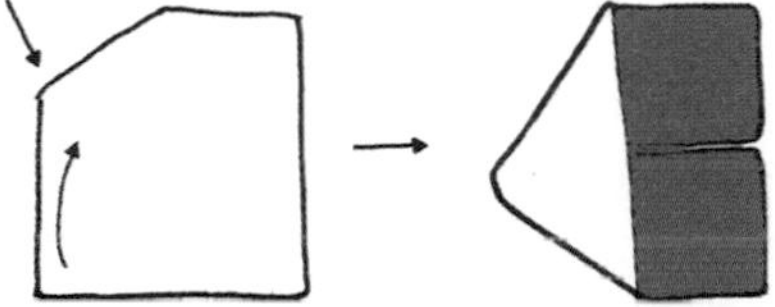

8 Turn the shape so that the triangle is at the top and the two rectangular bases are on the bottom. Beginning with the right rectangle base, push its left corner inward to create a small 45-degree angle. Repeat on the left rectangle with its right corner. Press.

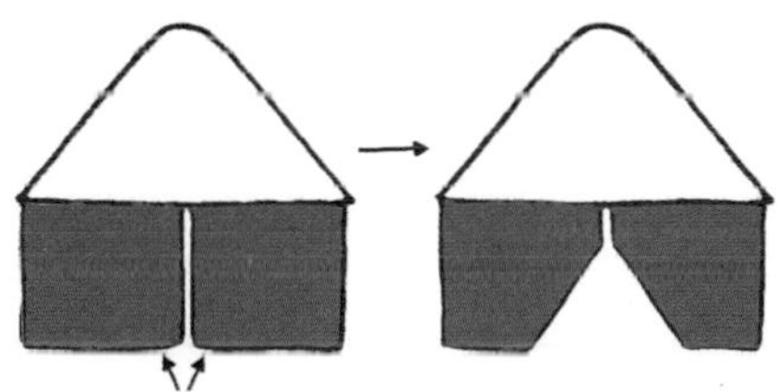

9 With the triangle pointing downward, take the corners indicated by the top arrows in the illustration below and pull them down toward you, meeting in the center. As you pull the corners down, you'll see the top and bottom wings forming. Stitch the lower bottom wings together where they meet in the center.

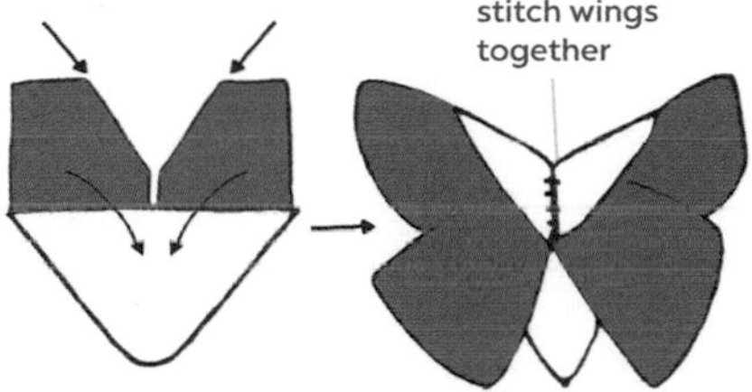

10 Using Sashiko or embroidery thread, add any desired decorative elements to the wings and proceed to the Construction Steps for the Pillow on page 128.

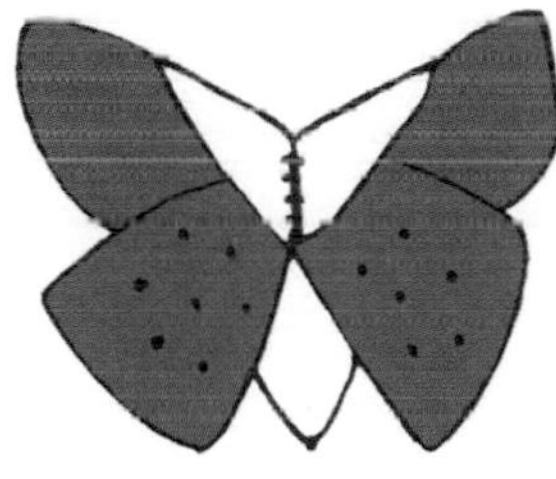

TRIANGLE ECO BAG

I WISH I COULD TAKE credit for this ingeniously designed triangular bag, but it's been around for generations in Japan. The body of the bag is made by folding one piece of rectangular fabric origami-style, and not only is it quite stylish in its simplicity, it's a project that can be sewn up in under an hour. You might be tempted to make multiples in one go!

I've received variations of this design from Japanese friends, but they're typically smaller, to hold bento-style meals. "Bento," if you're not familiar, is the Japanese term for a portable meal of rice, pickled vegetables, and fish or meat. I upped the size to make it a convenient eco tote for farmers' market days, but these would be fantastic lunch box holders too. Photo on pages 20 and 21.

SUPPLIES + MATERIALS

1½ yards woven fabric, for the bag

¼ yard fabric, for the handle

Coordinating thread

FABRIC RECOMMENDATIONS

Linen or cotton feels light and fresh for warmer seasons, but you can also construct these out of a sturdier cotton canvas for year-round use. Try suede or leather for the handle. A handle in a contrasting color made out of linen or cotton looks great too.

Prep the woven fabrics like cotton and linen by washing, drying, and pressing. No need to wash or dry suede or leather, although you might want to press them with a press cloth on a low heat setting.

FINISHED DIMENSIONS

About 25½ inches wide by 18 inches high

FABRIC PIECES: Bag (1), Handle (1)

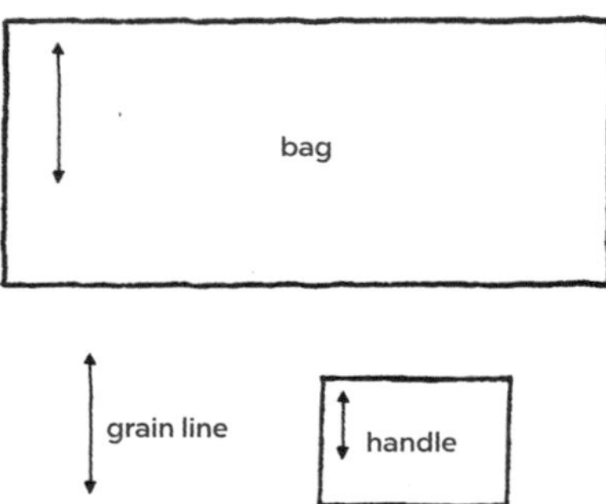

CONSTRUCTION STEPS

1. You can make this bag in any size you desire; all you need to do is start with a 1:3 ratio for the main bag piece before adding in the seam allowance. In my case, for the larger bag, I determined that I wanted to make it about 17 inches high, so that means it's 51 inches wide. Add 1½ inches to the height and width for seam allowance. This means I needed a piece of fabric that was 18½ inches by 52½ inches. Notice how it's not exactly 1:3 with the seam allowance added? This had me scratching my head for a while.

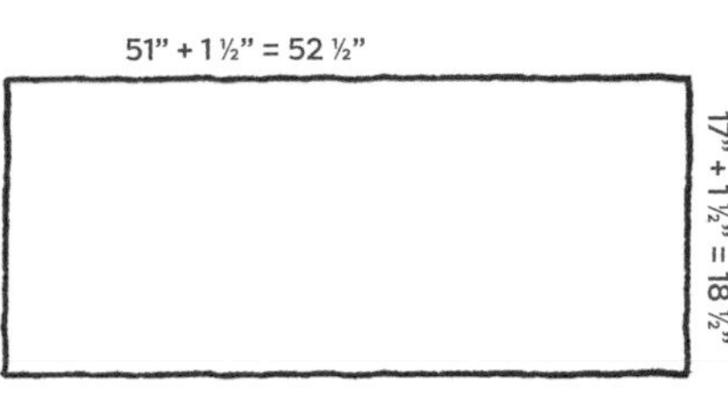

2 Cut out the handle piece from your contrasting fabric. I used leather so I cut a piece that was 6 by 4 inches. If you are using fabric that will fray, add 1 inch to both the height and width for the seam allowance.

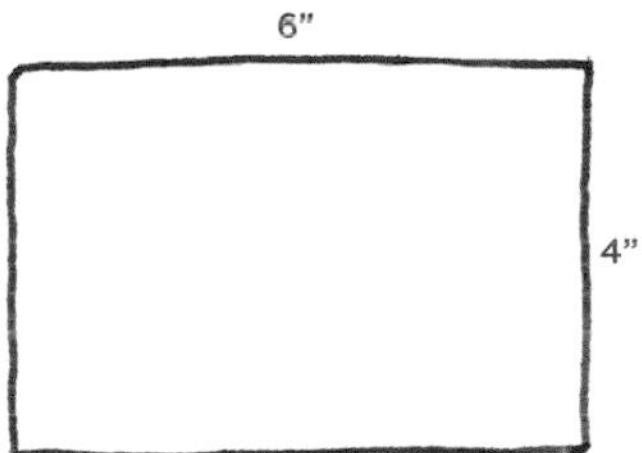

3 To hem all four sides of the main bag fabric, fold over one of the longer sides ⅜ inch and press. Then fold over again ⅜ inch, press, and edgestitch. Repeat on the other long side. Repeat with the shorter sides.

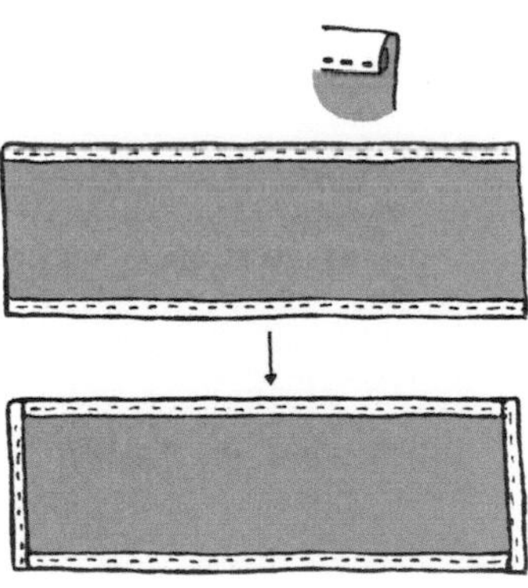

4 Now lay the hemmed fabric with the RIGHT side facing up. Measure out three equal widths using a marking tool (make sure the marks are erasable or will wash out). Taking the right upper corner of the bag, fold the point down toward and along the far right line just to its left. Pin in place.

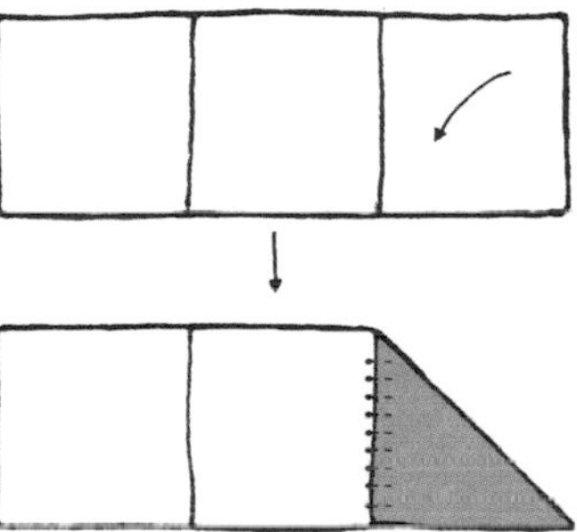

5 Take the lower left corner and fold up toward and along the far left line just to its right. Pin in place.

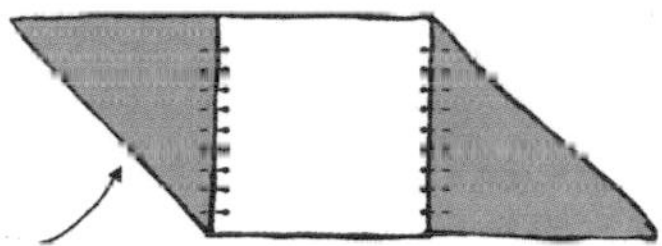

6 This next part is slightly tricky—fold the triangle on the right side up to the far right edge of the left folded triangle. Looking at the top illustration below, the bottom edge between the two triangle folds will be the part you pin to the left triangle (use the two stars as reference). Looking at the bottom illustration with a tipped head to the left, you can see the beginnings of the bag shape. Using the same pins from the first fold (on the left), pin the two edges that meet with the RIGHT sides facing.

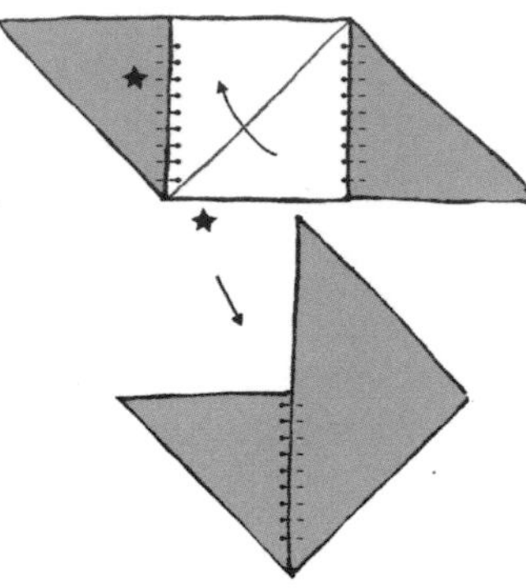

7 Flip the bag over, and repeat the pinning from step 6 on the other side of the bag, using the same pins from the first fold (right side). You might need to futz with the angle a little to make sure the edges line up without distorting the triangular shape. Make sure you are pinning the RIGHT sides facing.

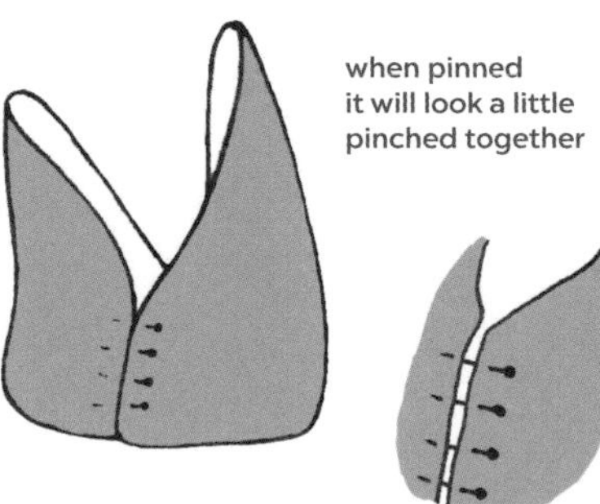

8 Sew along the pinned edges with a ½-inch seam allowance. Make sure to sew to the left of the hemming stitches so they aren't visible on the outer side of the bag. If it's easier, align your presser foot right against the inner fold of the hem, and move your needle so it's just to the left of the hemming stitches. Repeat on the other side of the bag.

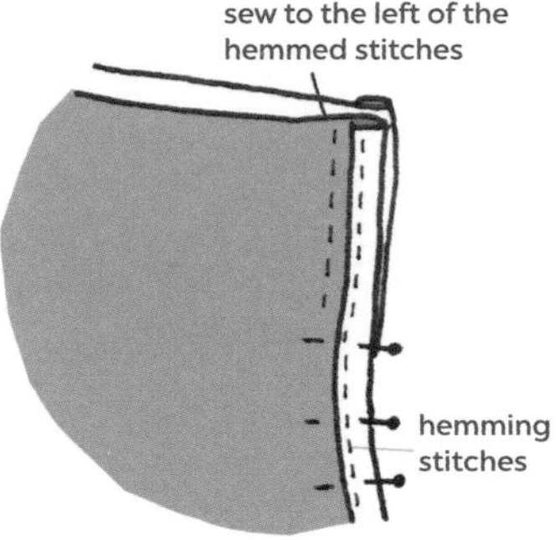

9 Press and sew a few stitches back and forth at the section where the fabric overlaps and the handles start to form, to tidy up and strengthen the area. The hemmed edges meet here and can get bulky, and the stitches also help to flatten the section. Repeat on the other side of the bag.

10 Sew the handle piece. If you're using leather, sew the WRONG side together along the long edge with a ½-inch seam allowance, then trim it down to about ¼ inch, if desired. Slide it onto one of the extended bag handles.

If using fabric that will fray, fold each short end twice by ¼ inch (½ inch total) and edgestitch, then sew the long side with the RIGHT sides facing with a ½-inch seam allowance. Before turning it RIGHT side out, slip the handle piece on one of the extended handles of the bag. It should fit snugly without sliding around. If it is too loose, sew the longer edge with a larger seam allowance to make the opening smaller. Trim the seam allowance. Turn it RIGHT side out and slide onto one of the extended bag handles.

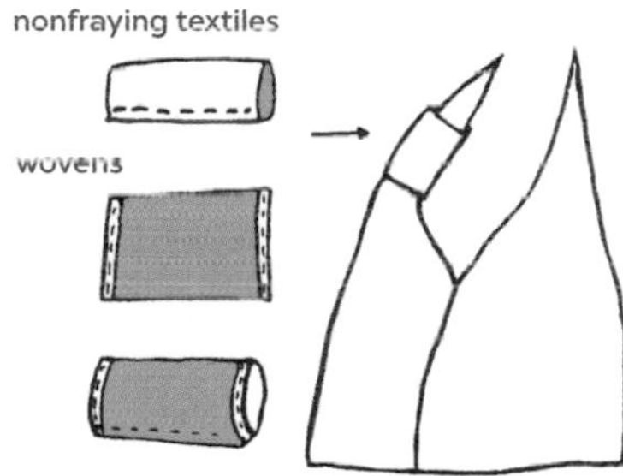

Fun Idea: Try embellishing an indigo linen fabric with a little bit of white Sashiko stitching for the handle piece!

11 Sew the extended bag handles together. This isn't the separate handle piece you created but the top two pointy edges of the bag. Securely stitch them together by overlapping the pointed ends by 2 inches, then stitch a diamond shape. This part may not look as neat and tidy as you'd like, but will be hidden under the handle, so no need to stress about it. Slide the handle over the diamond shape.

Optional: Slip stitch the handle to the bag at each outer edge if you want it to be even more securely attached.

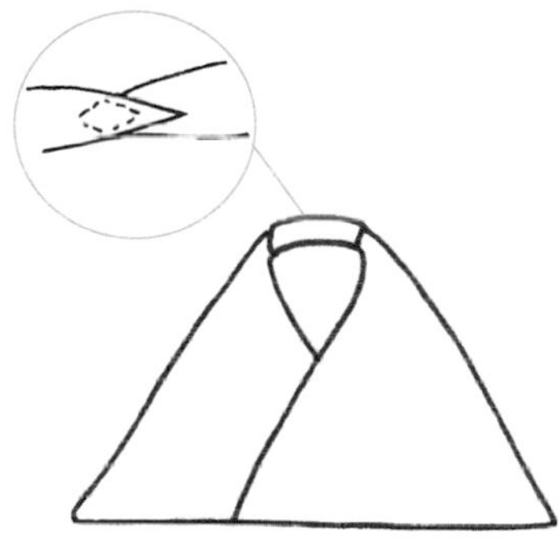

CROSS-BACK APRON

I ADMIT THAT I'M NOT usually an apron person. I'm always sporting a wet spot on my stomach after handwashing dishes, and food splatters during cooking have rarely bothered me. But maybe I'm finally becoming more civilized because I've made a few of these classic Japanese-style aprons, and I adore them. They make me feel efficient and productive, even if all I'm doing is sitting around in my house, trying to motivate myself to start cleaning. To instill some housekeeping mojo in my child, I also created an adjustable kid-size version. Of course, you could follow the steps for the kid-version to make the grown-up version adjustable too.

This is a simple apron with crossover straps in the back made entirely out of rectangles. No closures, no ties, just slip it over your head, easy-peasy. Plus, with some French seam and binding techniques, the underside looks just as clean and streamlined as the front.

As you can see, the pocket sizes vary in the images, but it really doesn't matter—choose a size that looks good to you. That's one of the best parts about sewing, right? You get to make exactly what you want. Photos on pages 22 and 23.

SUPPLIES + MATERIALS

2 yards woven fabric for the adult size or 1½ yards (or less) woven fabric for the kid size

Coordinating thread

FABRIC RECOMMENDATIONS

Cotton or a linen-cotton blend is ideal for this apron, and if you can, try to find fabric that is at least the width of the size you are making; otherwise you'll need significantly more length to cut out two halves that will need to be pieced together. Keep in mind that many fabrics come in 45-inch widths, so most of the sizes listed will not require piecing together. Pure linen is lovely too, but it can be a little finicky and you might find it tricky to get the pocket to look crisp and straight. Then again, the rumpled and askew effect could be wabi-sabi to your eyes. Although you usually want to follow the grain, break the rules and play with multi-directional stripes as I did in some of the examples for a fun effect.

Make sure to prep the fabric by washing, drying, and pressing.

FINISHED DIMENSIONS

Varies (see the charts on pages 141 and 145 for specific dimensions)

FABRIC PIECES: Upper Piece (1), Lower Piece (1), Strap (2), Pocket (1), Binding (1)

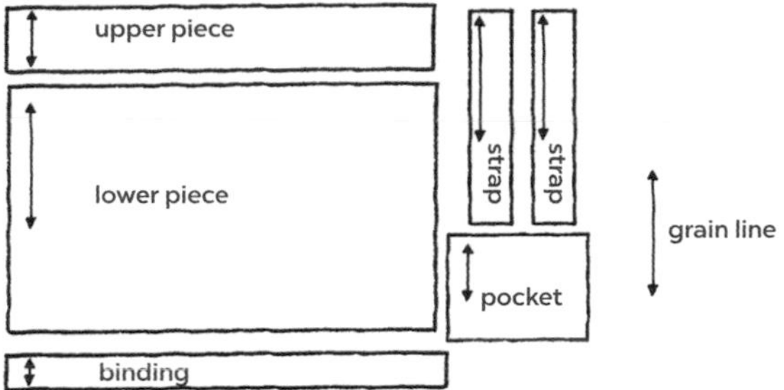

ADULT APRON SIZES (width by height)

	UPPER	LOWER	BINDING	STRAP	POCKET	Approximate finished dimensions width x height (from shoulder to hem)
S	42 x 4	42 x 28	42 x 1½	4 x 18	13 x 7	40 x 39
M	44 x 6	44 x 30	44 x 1½	5 x 20	14 x 8	42 x 41
L	46 x 8	46 x 32	46 x 1½	6 x 22	15 x 9	44 x 43

CONSTRUCTION STEPS

1. Cut out all the necessary fabric pieces based on the measurements in the chart above.

2. Pin together the upper piece and lower piece with the WRONG sides together. Stitch ¼ inch from the top edge. Trim the seam allowance to about ⅛ inch (be careful not to clip into the seam).

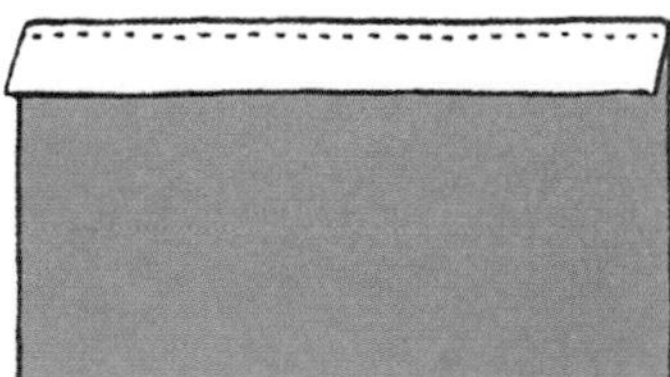

3. From the RIGHT side, press the seam toward the bottom. Then flip the upper piece so that now the RIGHT sides are facing. Press and stitch ⅜ inch from the top edge. This will enclose the raw edge—and that's all there is to a French seam!

4 Press the French seam toward the lower piece, first from the back, and then from the front. Topstitch about ¼ inch from the seam line. Press.

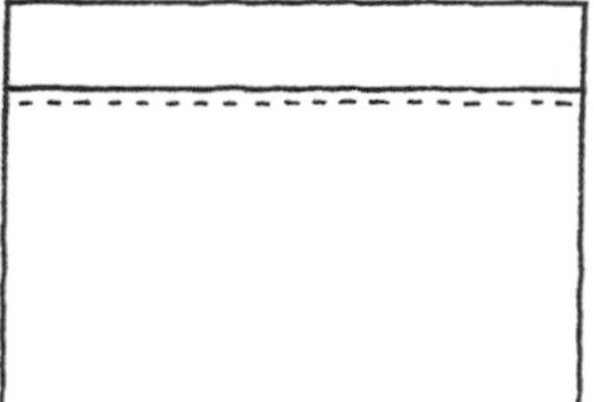

5 Fold one side edge ½ inch to the WRONG side and press. Fold another ½ inch and press. Repeat on the other side. Edge-stitch along the inner fold from the WRONG side. This the main apron piece.

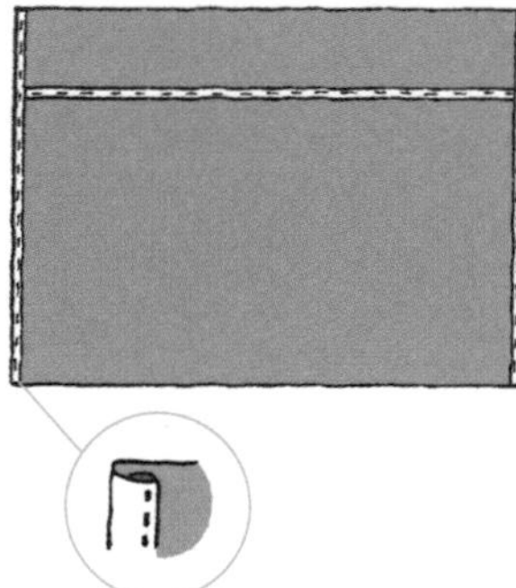

6 Using your preferred marking tool, mark the center of the main apron piece on the RIGHT side. Then make two marks equidistant from the center. The distance of the markings from the center is dependent on the size of the apron you are making: S=3 inches, M=4 inches, L=5 inches.

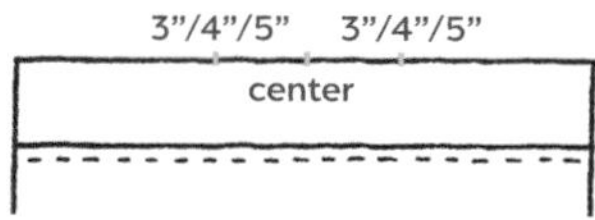

7 To make the straps, fold one of the strap pieces in half lengthwise, with the RIGHT sides facing. Stitch ¼ inch from the edges. Turn RIGHT side out and topstitch both long sides about ¼ inch from each edge. Repeat with the other strap piece.

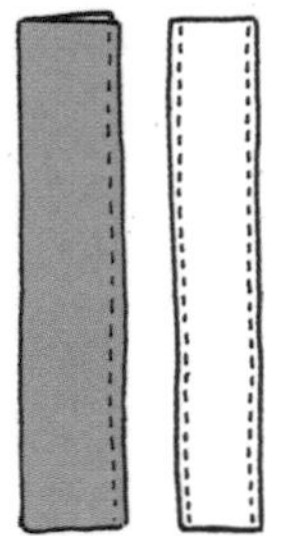

If it's difficult to turn the strap right side out, try using a loop turner (see A Sewing Space, page 87). It's also a good idea to mark the underside with an erasable marking tool. I like to make a quick X on the underside of each piece so I know which side is topstitched (the nicer side) later.

8 Using the markings and the corner edges as a guide, pin the straps to the apron with the RIGHT sides facing (the side you topstitched is the RIGHT side for the straps). It doesn't really matter which strap is on top, but one end of the strap needs to be at the corner edge, and the other end should be on the opposite side of the center marking, making a wide arc.

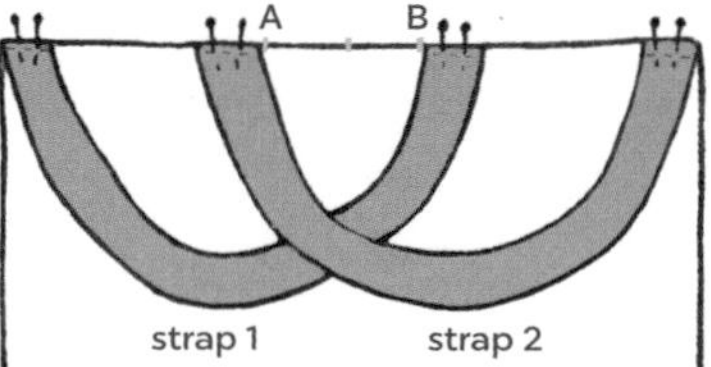

As you can see in the illustration, if you're looking at the apron with the RIGHT side of the apron facing up, you'll need to pin the left end of strap 1 to the left corner of the apron and the right end to mark B and then pin the right end of strap 2 to the right corner of the apron and the left end to mark A. Baste in place about ¼ inch from top. Try on the apron to make sure the straps fit. Your head will go through the biggest gap in the center, and then insert each arm in the smaller gaps on each side of the center gap. Adjust and re-pin the straps as needed.

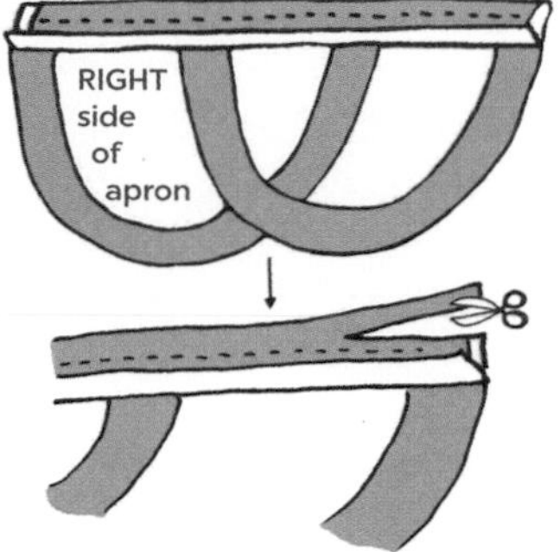

9 To prepare the binding piece, fold each short end toward the WRONG side by ½ inch so that the raw edge will be enclosed, and press. Pin the folded short edges down if you'd like (I usually find that I don't need to). Edgestitch. Next, fold one of the long edges ½ inch toward the WRONG side and press. Although folding and pressing the long edge can be done after you've attached the binding to the apron, prepping it this way makes the process easier.

10 Pin the binding on top of the straps, lining up the raw edges. The binding should be pinned to the apron with the RIGHT sides facing with the folded edge facing up on the bottom. Sew ½ inch from the top edge and trim the seam allowance to about ¼ inch. This helps reduce the bulk.

11 Press the entire binding strip toward the WRONG side of the upper piece to encase the raw edges. Double-check that the straps are securely stitched. Pin and edgestitch along the fold. Keep the straps out of the way as you sew—you don't want to accidentally stitch them in a weird spot!

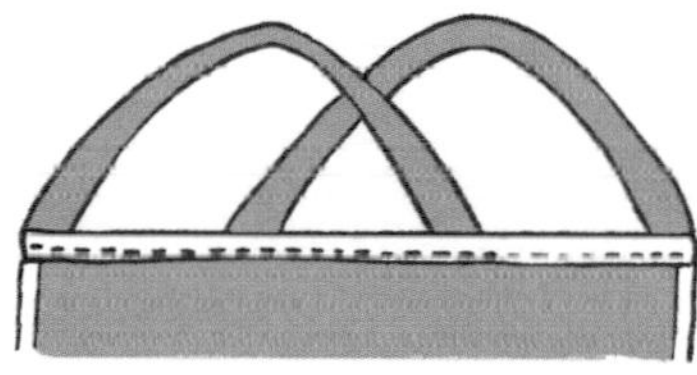

12 To make the pocket, fold the left, right, and bottom edges of the pocket piece ½ inch toward the WRONG side, and press. Optional: Finish the raw edges of these three sides with either pinking sheers, zigzag stitching, or overlock stitching. It won't be visible, so it's not necessary.

Fold the top edge ¼ inch to the WRONG side and press. Fold the new edge down another ½ inch, press, and edgestitch. Leave the other three sides unstitched.

13 Find the center of the main apron piece again, then measure about 7 inches down from the seam line (the one with the French seam), marking with a pin. Place the pocket with its top center at this point. Try on the apron and adjust the pocket placement if it looks too high or low to you.

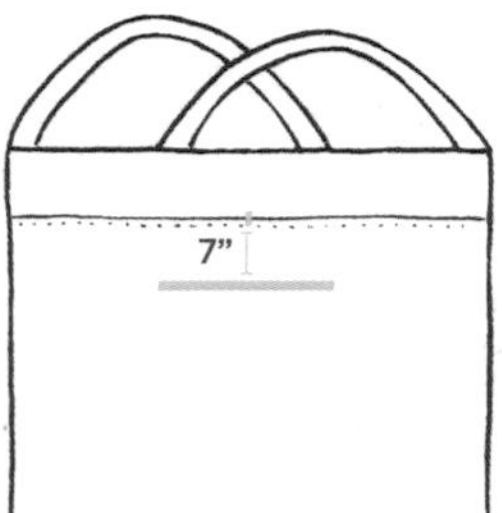

14 Topstitch around the three unstitched sides. I like to get as close to the edge as possible.

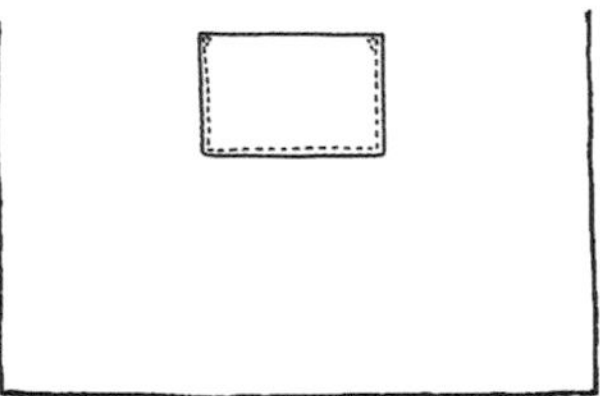

15 If you want to get fancy, sew triangles at the upper left and right corners, which provide additional reinforcement for pockets.

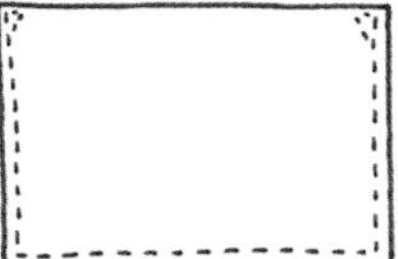

16 For two pockets, simply sew a straight line parallel to the pocket sides as in the example below. Tip: If you would like extra reinforcement, sew a triangle at the top of the dividing seam as well.

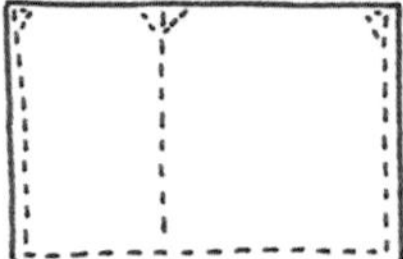

Fold the hem of the apron ½ inch toward the WRONG side and press. Repeat and edgestitch.

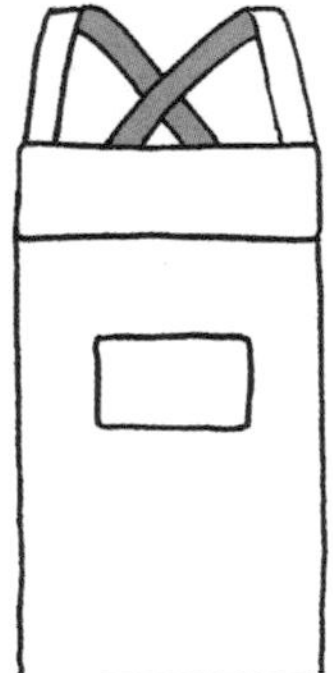

VARIATION: KID'S ADJUSTABLE APRON

I LOVED THE ADULT DESIGN so much that I decided to make mini versions too—and my daughter wholly approves! For the kid version, I extended the length of the straps to make them adjustable—helpful for quickly growing bodies. I experimented with the strap length, and in some cases, I made the straps extra long, which was a quirky design element. Feel free to experiment with the length too. This method can be used for the adult version too—simply add seven inches to the strap measurements, attach straps only at the front, and add buttonholes.

KIDS APRON SIZES (WIDTH BY HEIGHT)

	UPPER	LOWER	BINDING	STRAP	POCKET	Approximate finished dimensions width x height (from shoulder to hem)
XS (2T-3T)	27 x 5	27 x 16	26 x 1½	3 x 19	8 x 5	25 x 19
S (4T-5T)	30 x 6	30 x 18	29 x 1½	3 x 20	9 x 6	28 x 22
M (6-7)	32 x 7	32 x 20	31 x 1½	4 x 21	10 x 7	30 x 25
L (8-10)	34 x 8	34 x 22	33 x 1½	4 x 23	12 x 9	32 x 28

CONSTRUCTION STEPS

1. Follow the directions for the Cross-Back Apron through step 5.

2. Using your preferred marking tool, mark the center of the main apron piece on the RIGHT side. Then make two marks equidistant from the center. The distance of the markings from the center is dependent on the size of the apron you are making: XS=2 inches, S=2½ inches, M=2¾ inches, L=3 inches.

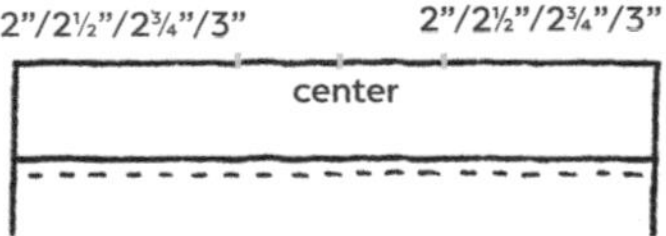

3. To make the straps, fold one of the strap pieces in half lengthwise, with the RIGHT sides facing. Stitch ¼ inch from the edges, pivoting at the end to close up one short end. Clip the corners and turn RIGHT side out, poking out the corners with a point turner. Be careful not to poke holes through the seam. Topstitch the three finished sides about ¼ inch from each edge. Repeat with the other strap piece.

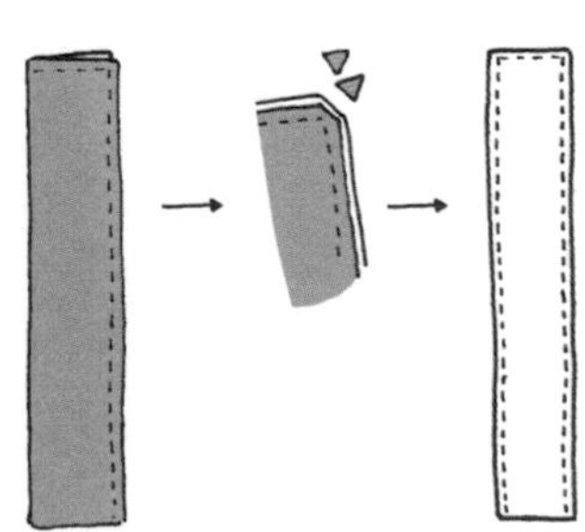

4 Attach one end of each strap to the apron at the marks you made in step 2, leaving the finished end loose and hanging. To prepare the binding piece, fold each short end toward the WRONG side by ½ inch so that the raw edge will be enclosed, and press. Pin the folded short edges down if you'd like (I usually find that I don't need to). Edgestitch. Next, fold one of the long edges ½ inch toward the WRONG side and press. Although folding and pressing the long edge can be done after you've attached the binding to the apron, prepping it this way makes the process easier.

5 Pin the binding on top of the straps, lining up the raw edges. The binding should be pinned to the apron with the RIGHT sides facing with the folded edge facing up on the bottom. Sew ½ inch from top edge and trim seam allowance to about ¼ inch. This helps reduce the bulk.

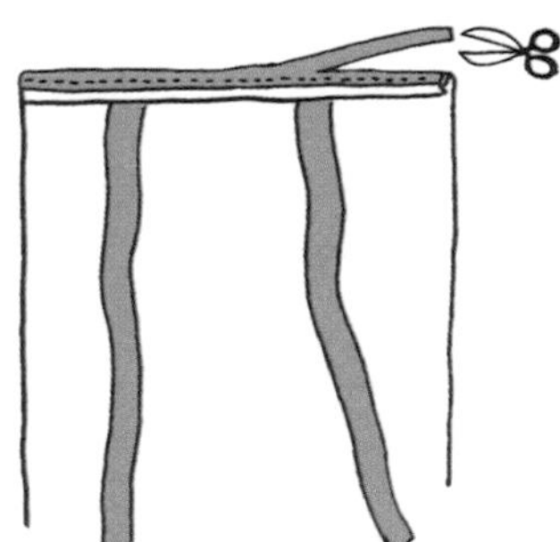

6 Press entire binding strip toward the WRONG side of upper piece to encase the raw edges. Double-check that the straps are securely stitched. Pin and edgestitch along the fold. Keep the straps out of the way as you sew—you don't want to accidentally stitch them in a weird spot!

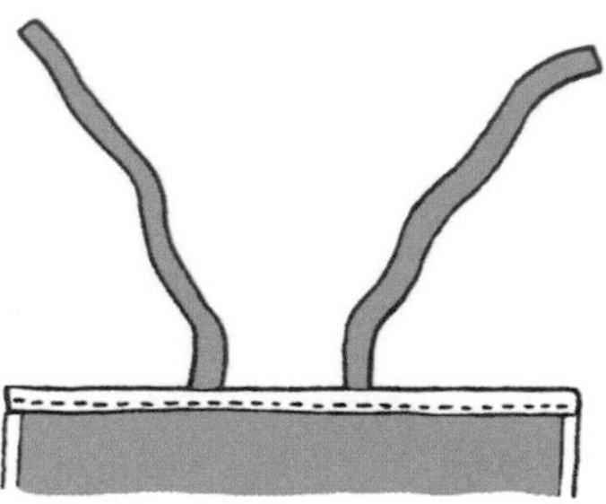

7 Create 1-inch-high buttonholes at the top corners of the apron about 1 inch from each edge.

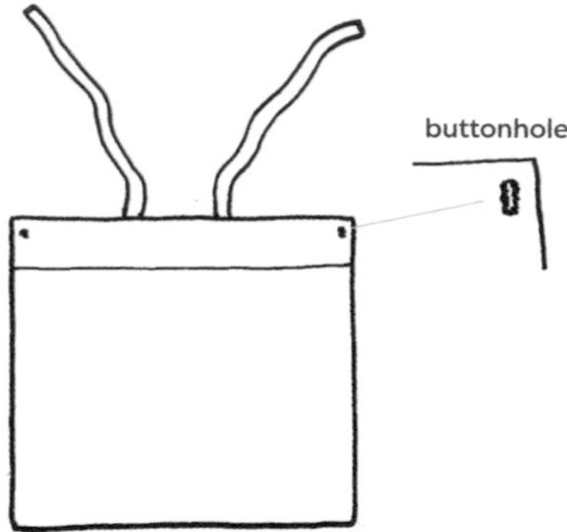

8 Follow steps 12 through 15 for the Cross-Back Apron to construct the pockets and hem the apron.

9 Insert the straps into the buttonholes and tie each into a knot, adjusting for a tighter or looser fit as needed.

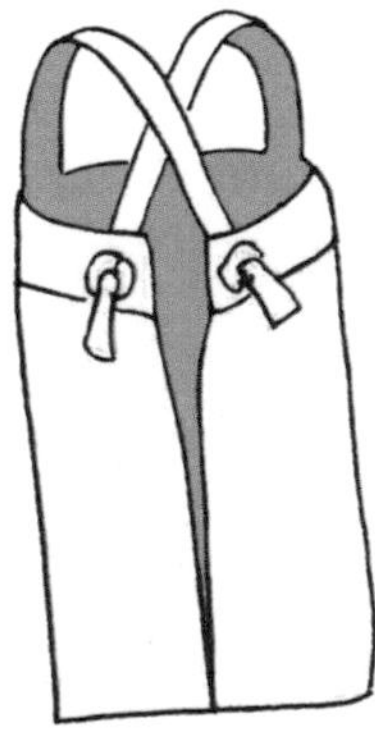

YOGA PANTS

LET'S FACE IT. SOME DAYS are yoga pants days. It doesn't matter if you're actually going to break a sweat or not; it's really a matter of comfort. I balk at the prices of the top-selling brands (though I hear they're engineered to make your abs and derriere appear sculpted and superhuman). Alas, my instructions for a handmade pair may not yield the same results, but you will be able to quickly draft a pair of comfy knit pants using an existing pair, then choose to hit the gym or go sip a latte. The great part about sewing knits is that you don't have to be meticulously precise, and besides, these may never see the outdoors anyway because you'll be too comfortable lounging about at home. Photos on pages 24 and 25.

SUPPLIES + MATERIALS

- 1½ yards knit fabric or 1¾ yards if creating a waistband from the same fabric
- Coordinating thread
- Ballpoint or stretch machine needle
- ¼ yard contrasting knit fabric, for the waistband (optional)
- Drafting kit (see The Drafting Kit, page 96)

FABRIC RECOMMENDATIONS

Look for knit fabric that is about 60 inches wide, if possible. Select a stretchy jersey with great recovery (its capacity to snap back from being stretched without looking lumpy or distended). A knit fabric with a touch (2 to 5 percent) of spandex works really well *and* is easier to sew.

For variety, add a pop of color or print knit fabric for the waistband. Interlock is best for the waistband. It is the least stretchy of the knits, looks extremely smooth (and sometimes slightly shiny), is identical on the front and back, and is firmer and thicker due to its double-knit nature. Performance knit for athletic wear is also a good option.

Make sure to prep the fabric by washing and drying, and if it's particularly rumpled, give it a nice pressing.

FINISHED DIMENSIONS

Modifiable to your size and desired length

FABRIC PIECES: Pant (2), Waistband (1)

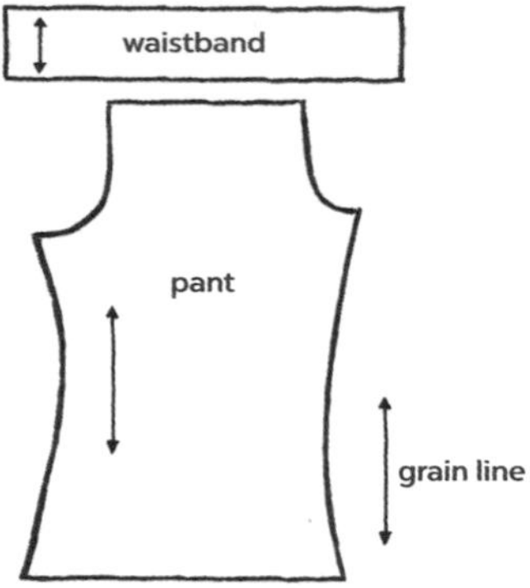

CONSTRUCTION STEPS

1. Take your favorite pair of yoga or stretch pants, and turn them inside out so you can see where the seams meet.

2. To create the back pattern piece, lay out a large piece of paper. Fold pants in half so that the back is facing out. Beginning from just where the waistband ends, trace around the pants onto the paper.

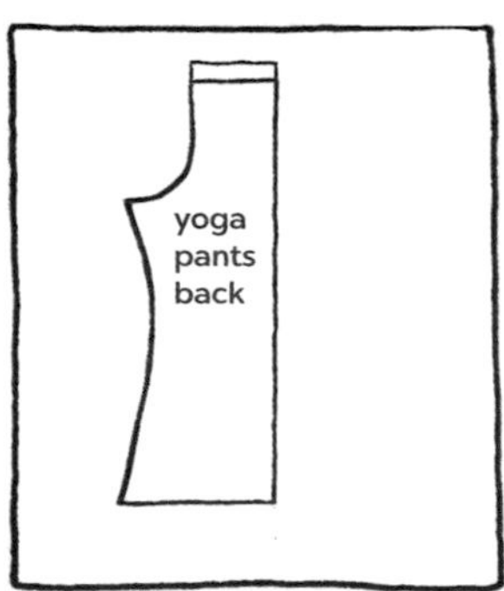

3. Open the yoga pants up and identify where the front rise ends at the bottom. The rise is shorter on the front. Fold the pants in half accordingly with the front facing out. Place with the side seam abutting the side seam of the back pattern piece you just created. Trace so that the front piece is mirroring the back piece, making sure that the bottom of the pant leg lines up. Set the pants aside and sketch a ⅜-inch seam allowance all around the pant leg pattern. Cut out (don't use fabric shears) and label "Yoga Pants—cut 2." Only one more pattern piece to go!

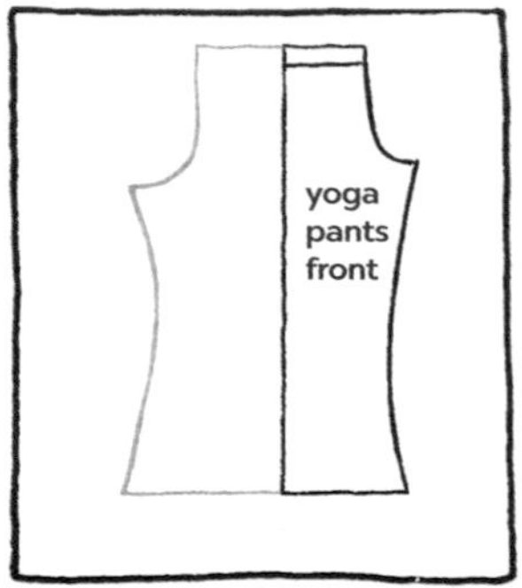

4. Measure the waist length of the pattern. This will be your waistband measurement. Measure the height of your yoga pants' waistband. For example, I used 7 inches for the height. You'll be folding down the waistband after you attach it to the pants, so the height of the waistband will actually be a little less than half of the 7 inches—modify this height to your liking. Cut out and label "Yoga Pants Waistband—cut 1 on fold."

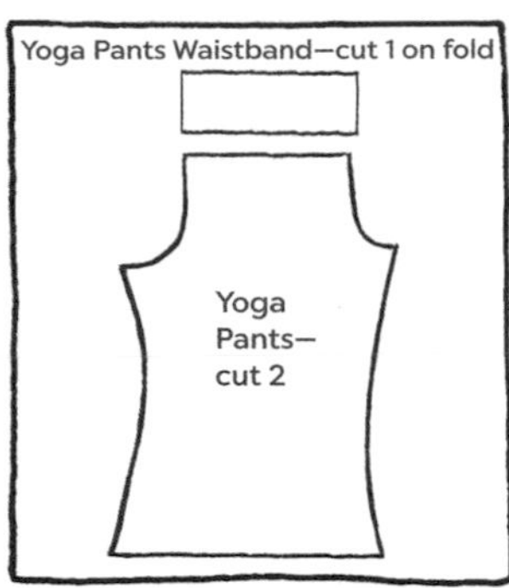

5 Place the pattern pieces on the knit fabric folded in half. The fold line should be parallel to the LESS stretchy side of the fabric. Pin or use weights to hold the pattern pieces in place. Trace with a marking tool and cut out. Let's get ready to sew.

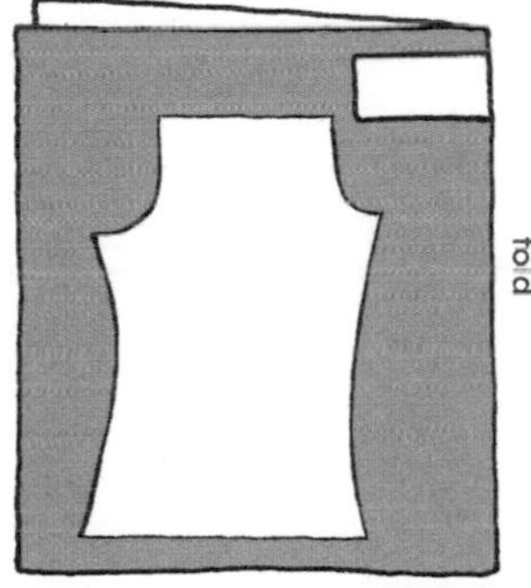

6 Make sure you are sewing with a ballpoint or stretch needle, and adjust your machine stitch to a zigzag or stretch stitch. Pin RIGHT sides together and sew the inseam for each pant leg ⅜ inch from the edge. Finish the edges with zigzag or overlock stitching, if desired. Knit fabrics don't fray, so it's not strictly necessary.

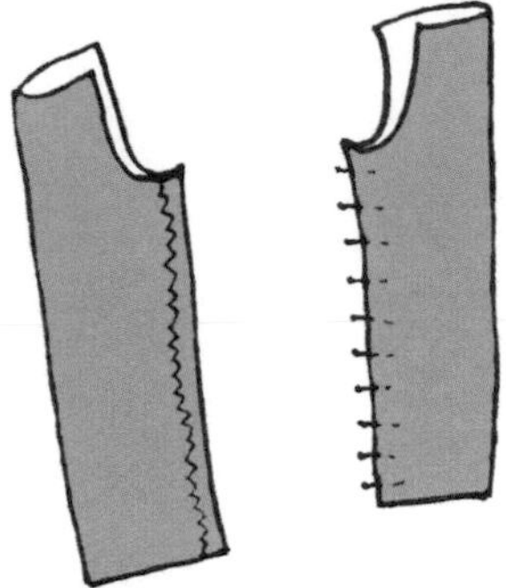

7 Turn one of the legs RIGHT side out. You will slip this leg into the other one so that the inner rise is lined up and RIGHT sides are together. Pin and sew along the curve.

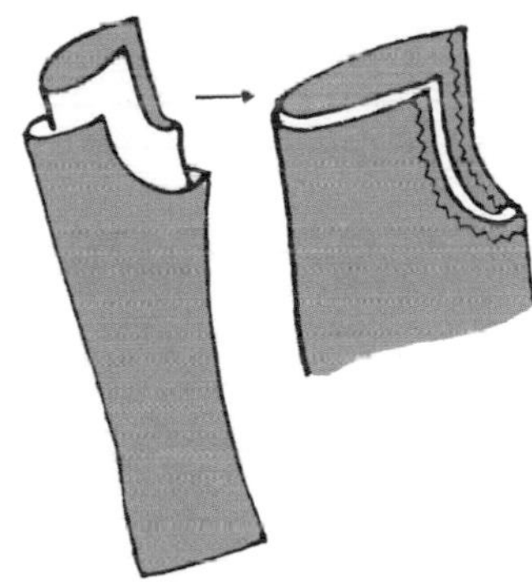

8 Fold the waistband piece in half lengthwise with the RIGHT sides facing. Pin and sew the raw short edges together with a ⅜-inch seam allowance.

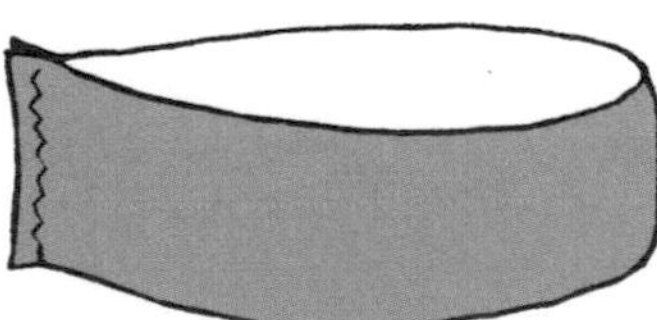

9 Press the seams open and then fold in half with the WRONG sides together. Now try on the waistband. It's important to ensure that it fits snugly before attaching it to the pants—you don't want it slipping down at inopportune moments!

10 With raw edges lined up and the RIGHT sides facing, pin and sew the waistband to the pant legs. I like to place the waistband seam on the center back to indicate which side is the back. Finish raw the edges, if desired.

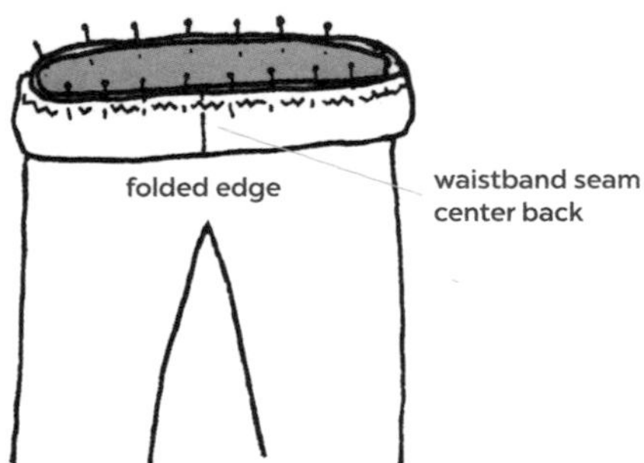

11 Hem the pants. I like to overlock the raw edge with my serger: fold up about ⅜ inch and press. Then edgestitch with a zigzag or stretch stitch along the finished edge. If you don't have an overlocker/serger, simply fold up ⅜ inch, press, and stitch close to the raw edge. Alternatively, you can use a double-needle to finish off the hem (see Sewing Knits, page 105).

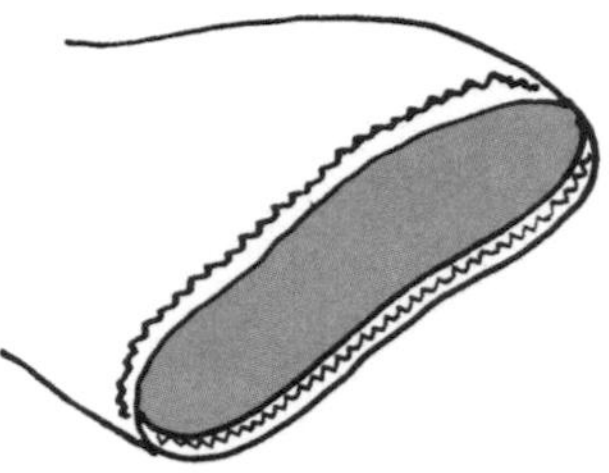

12 Done! Relax in child's pose or engage in any of a plethora of other activities that can be so enjoyable in a pair of well-fitting custom yoga pants.

JOURNAL/BOOK COVER

BACK IN HIGH SCHOOL, A FRIEND of mine gifted me an ancient Greek mythology book. He had created a cover out of brown kraft paper using the precision he inherited from his architect father. He hand-lettered the title on his meticulously folded cover and penned a long, philosophical message on the inner flap, completing his handiwork by reinforcing the entire book cover with clear packing tape. I still treasure the book to this day. I'm sure that he would have made me a fabric version if he had access to a sewing machine, and regardless of the material, the handmade cover is what makes the book extra special to me. This project is a nod to that thoughtful touch as well as a way to fancy up two of my favorite things in the world: journals and books. This is a quick and satisfying project requiring very little in the way of supplies—the hardest part is deciding on the fabric. Photos on pages 34 and 35.

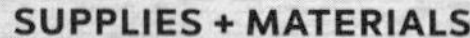

SUPPLIES + MATERIALS

½ yard woven fabric, for the cover*

½ yard woven fabric, for the lining*

½ yard ½-inch elastic

Coordinating thread

Journal or book

½ yard interfacing (optional)

* *Fabric amount depends on the size of book or journal, but ½ yard should be sufficient in general.*

FABRIC RECOMMENDATIONS

MAIN FABRIC: medium-weight cotton, cotton-linen blend, light canvas, twill, quilting cotton

LINING FABRIC: muslin, quilting cotton

Make sure to prep the fabric by washing, drying, and pressing.

FINISHED DIMENSIONS

Modifiable

FABRIC PIECES: Cover (1), Flaps (1 piece that will be cut in half), Lining (1)

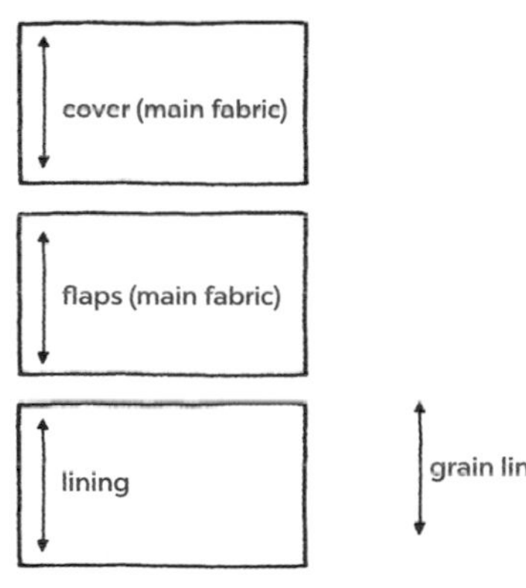

CONSTRUCTION STEPS

1. Determine the cover size by measuring the book, being sure to open the book to do so. Jot down the following:
   - Height
   - Width, including the spine

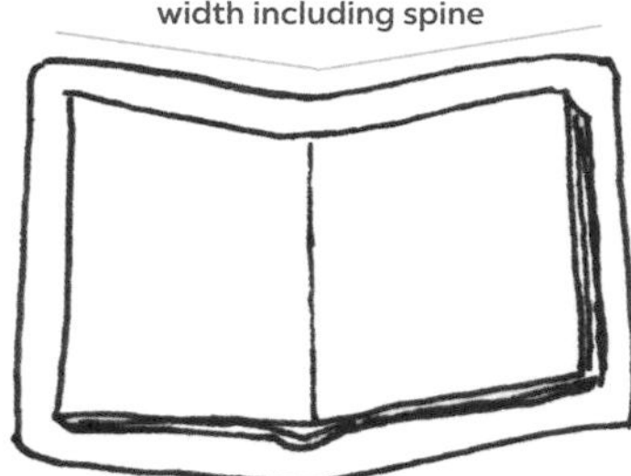

2. Add 1¼ inches to both the height and the width. This is for the ½-inch seam allowance plus a little extra to account for the thickness of the fabric.

3. Let's get ready to cut the fabric! Fold the main fabric so that the selvage edges meet. If you are using a printed fabric and want the print to be placed in a certain way on the cover, lay the fabric with the RIGHT side facing out. Make sure you have enough fabric for the width, then measure out the dimensions and draw the rectangle onto the fabric using chalk and a ruler. Cut through both layers so that you have two pieces.

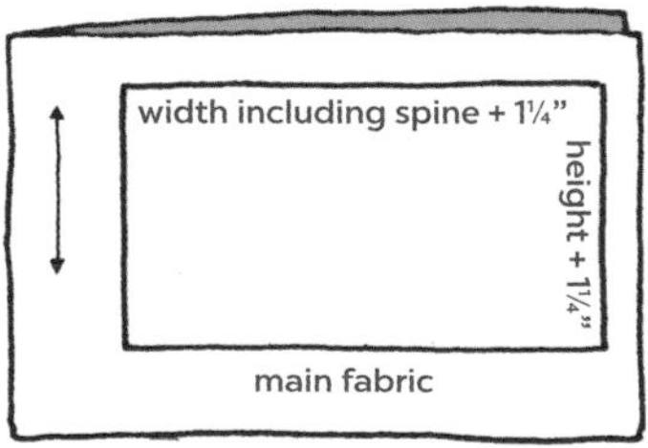

4. On the lining fabric, cut out the same dimensions as the main fabric. You need only one lining piece. If your fabrics feel like they could use a little bit more structure or sturdiness, cut out the interfacing with the same dimensions and iron it onto the WRONG side of the lining.

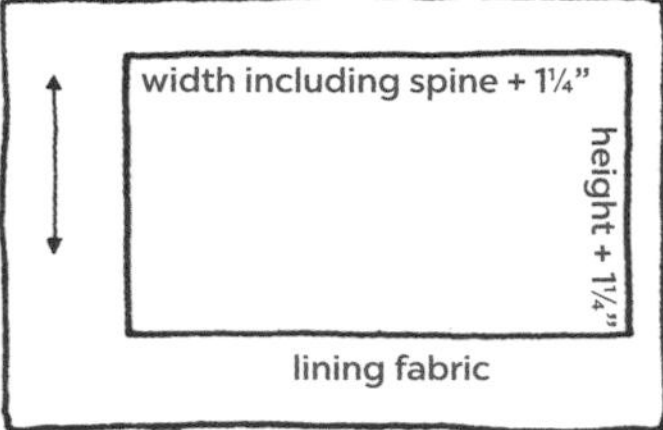

5. Cut a length of elastic equal to the height that you calculated in step 2 (actual height of the book plus 1¼ inches).

6. Cut one of the cover pieces in half to create the two flap pieces (you could measure the halfway point, but I just fold in half, press with my fingers, and cut along the line). Fold one of the flap pieces in half with the WRONG sides facing and press. Stitch about ⅛ inch from the folded edge. Repeat for other flap piece.

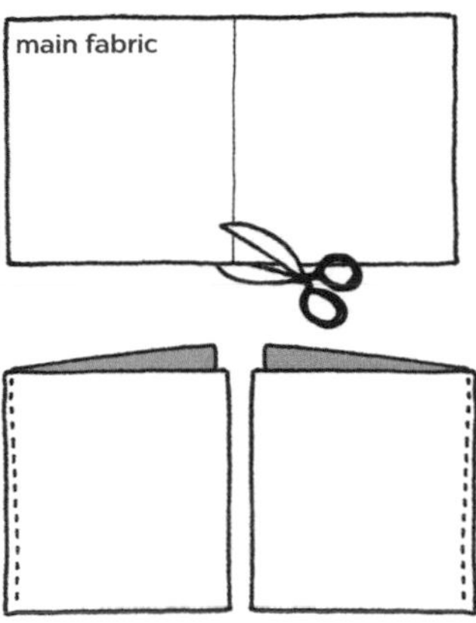

7 Place the uncut cover piece RIGHT side up. The left side of the fabric will be the back cover and the right side the front cover for this project unless you are covering an Asian comic book—then it will be the reverse. Choose whether you want the elastic on the front or the back. If you place the elastic on the front cover, the elastic will snap onto the back side and will not show. I like the contrasting look of the elastic showing on the front, so I sew the elastic onto the back cover area. Depending on which side you would like your elastic to be positioned, measure about 2 inches from the left or right edge of the fabric. Sew ¼ inch from the top and bottom edges so that the elastic is secured but the stitches will not be visible when you assemble the cover.

8 This step is optional, but will help keep the flaps from shifting. Baste the left and right flaps to the main fabric cover piece, the RIGHT sides facing with a ¼-inch seam allowance. If your fabric is directional, make sure that the print is facing the correct way. The raw edges should match up, and the folded parts will be toward the center of the cover.

The elastic will be hidden, sandwiched between a flap and the cover.

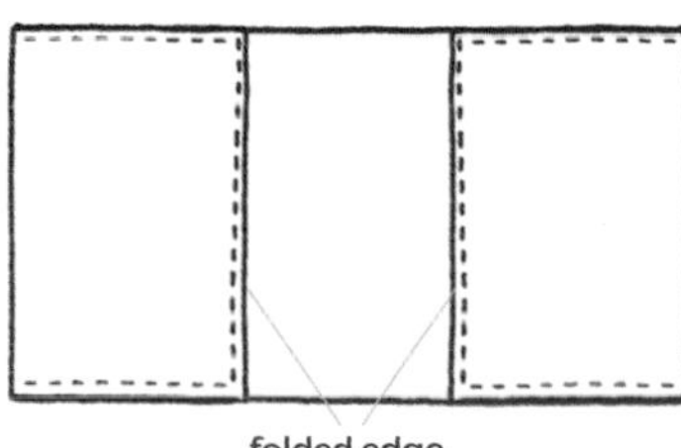

DIRECTIONAL FABRICS have printed patterns pointed a particular direction. For example, you might have a fabric with blue flamingoes all facing left. You'll need to make sure as you cut the fabric that each piece will be sewn with blue flamingoes standing upright, facing left. You don't want part of your cover to have upright, left-facing birds and other parts to have upside down flamingoes. Unless that's the look you're going for, naturally.

9 Place the lining fabric on top of the cover piece with the elastic and flaps, RIGHT sides together. Sew all around with a ½-inch seam allowance, but leave about 4 inches open at the bottom. Keep your needle down at the corners and pivot for a clean, sharp angle.

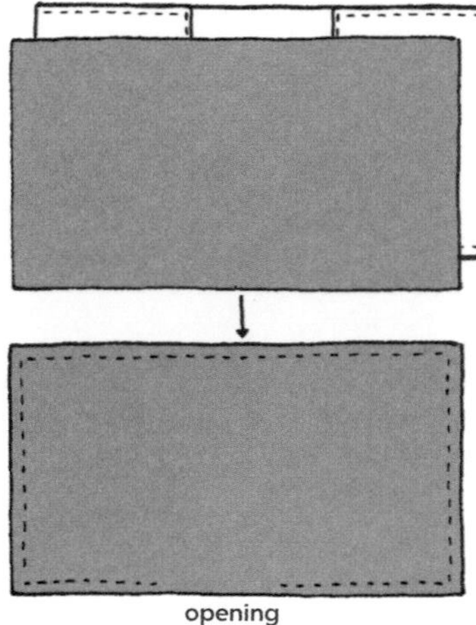

10 Trim the seam allowance to ¼ inch and clip the corners. Be careful not to clip into or too close to the seam. Then, turn the fabric cover RIGHT side out and push out the corners with a point turner. Be careful not to poke holes through the seam. Press, avoiding the elastic, and tuck in the seam allowance at the opening so that it is flush with the rest of the seam.

11 Slip stitch the opening closed, press again, and voila: custom journal or book cover!

QUICK DIY SKETCHBOOK

I'M NOT ONE OF THOSE people who have an onslaught of ideas in the shower. For me, the slow and methodical journaling habit has trained me to record my ideas via words and images in a notebook on a daily basis. As such, I go through a *lot* of journals and sketchbooks. Intrigued by the notion of making my own, I assembled some leather and paper, and voila! In a matter of minutes, I had a lovely idea catcher. This nearly effortless mini–art book can easily slip into a bag for recording inspirations—and makes a terrific gift for kids too. Photo on pages 36 and 37.

SUPPLIES + MATERIALS

10 sheets 8½-by-11-inch (or A4) paper

½ yard nonfraying fabric

1 yard leather cord

Coordinating thread

Leather or denim machine needle (optional)

Utility knife or razor

FABRIC RECOMMENDATIONS

Leather or thicker wool felt are excellent choices for this book. No need to wash these fabrics, although you might want to press them with a press cloth on a low heat setting.

FINISHED DIMENSIONS

13 inches wide by 6 inches high when fully open

FABRIC PIECE: Cover (1)

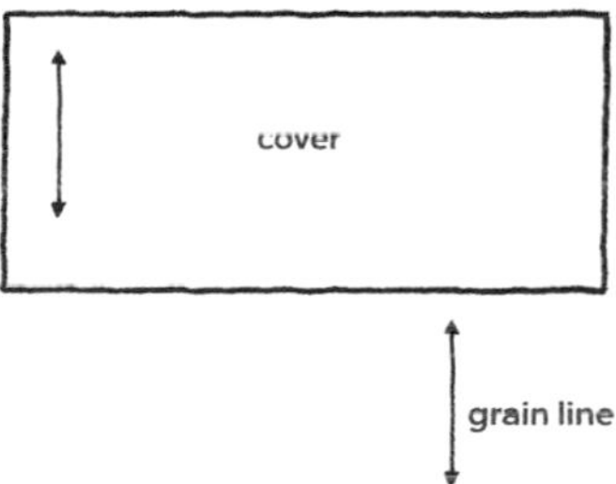

CONSTRUCTION STEPS

1. Cut the paper in half widthwise; the cutting line will be parallel to the shorter, 8½-inch, side. Then score and fold the cut paper at the center lengthwise.

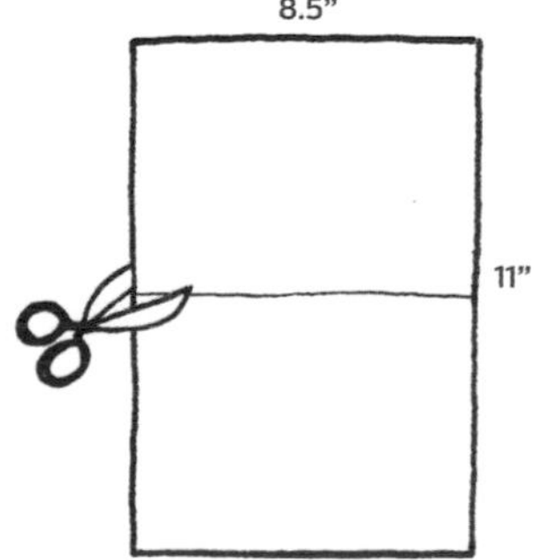

2 You should now have a 4¼-by-5½-inch booklet.

3 Cut a 13-by-6-inch piece of nonfraying fabric for the cover.

Open the booklet at the center and place it on top of the cover piece. Make sure to align the booklet more toward the right of the cover than the left, with ¼ inch of space from the top, right, and bottom. The excess material on the left will become the flap. Sew a straight line down the center of the booklet to attach it to the cover. Wonder clips or binder clips are helpful for keeping the booklet attached to the cover while you sew. If you have to crank the hand wheel and the needle still seems resistant, take out a sheet or two of paper and try again, since some sewing machines are more powerful than others. A leather or denim needle may help as well.

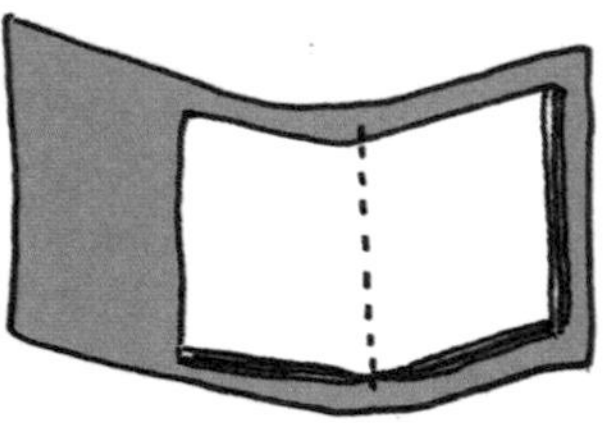

4 Using the utility knife, make two small parallel slits that are each about ½ inch in height on the left flap. Thread the cord through. You now have a DIY journal completed in minutes!

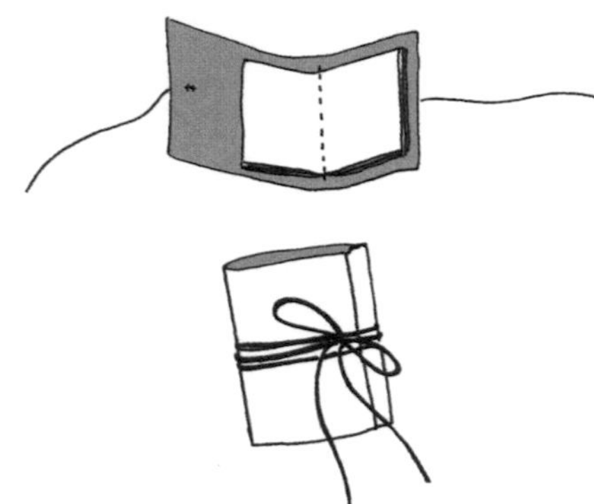

CAMERA STRAP

ON MY DAUGHTER'S FIFTH BIRTHDAY, we rented a section of a local recreation center and had a pool party. When it was time for the cake, I strolled around the perimeter of the pool, calling out to the partygoers to gather round.

"What?" a friend asked. I leaned over to yell a little louder, and then my body started tipping. And tipping. I was quickly submerged underwater, my prized camera in hand.

Now, having a wrist strap would *not* have prevented this occurrence, but at least it could prevent other unfortunate accidents (like the time I dropped my camera mid–photo shoot). I like wrist straps, but if you prefer a neck strap, simply add a few inches to this one and grab yourself another clasp and you're all set!

Bonus idea: By adjusting the length, these would also make lovely key fobs. Photos on pages 38 and 39.

SUPPLIES + MATERIALS

¼ yard woven fabric, for the main strap

Scrap leather or similar, for the connector

Metal clasp with a swivel hook (order these in bulk online)

Coordinating thread

Metal jump ring

¼ yard interfacing (optional)

Leather machine needle (optional)

> If using waxed canvas or leatherlike textiles, wonder clips, binder clips, or even clothespins are helpful.

FABRIC RECOMMENDATIONS

Any type of fabric would work for the camera strap, though if the fabric is on the thin side, I would recommend ironing on some interfacing for some added sturdiness. Linen, cotton, and canvas work *very* well, and I've also tried out a version with perforated lambskin, which was ridiculously easy since I didn't even need to sew the strap. When using wovens like cotton or linen, make sure to prep the fabric by washing, drying, and pressing.

Durable materials like leather and webbing are the recommended options for the connector piece. Keep in mind that you will be sewing through multiple layers of the connector piece and strap ends, so extremely thick textiles are inadvisable. No need to wash these fabrics, although you might want to press them with a press cloth on a low heat setting.

FINISHED DIMENSIONS

1 inch wide by 11½ inches long (clasp and connector) for a wrist strap

FABRIC PIECES: Strap (1), Connector Piece (1)

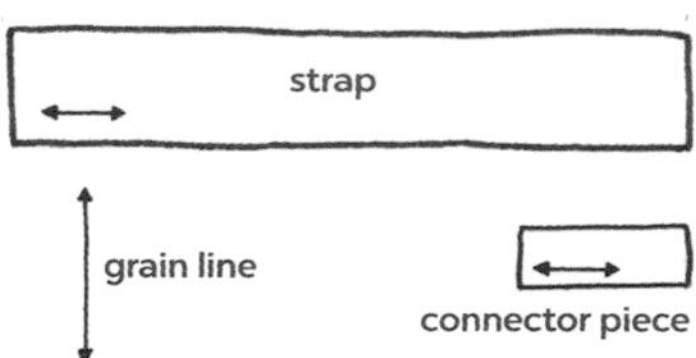

CONSTRUCTION STEPS

1. Measure the desired length for your wrist or neck strap. For my wrist strap, I cut out a 2½-by-21-inch rectangle. The formula:
   - (Desired width x 2) + ½ inch for seam allowance
   - Desired length + 1 inch for seam allowance

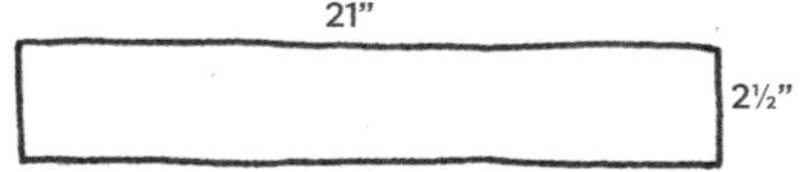

2. Cut the connector piece. Mine is 1 by 3 inches. If you are using webbing, add an extra ½ inch to the length since you will need to fold under the short edges; otherwise the webbing will fray.

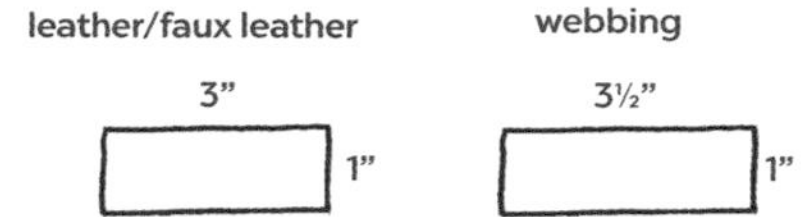

3. Fold the strap in half lengthwise with the RIGHT sides facing and press. Pin and sew the long side with a ¼-inch seam allowance. Turn the RIGHT side out with a loop turner (see A Sewing Space, page 87). Press. Sometimes the fabric stays tucked in at the seam, so you might need to push out the fabric as you press along the seam to make sure it's fully flattened. Fold the end pieces inward to hide the raw edges and press again.

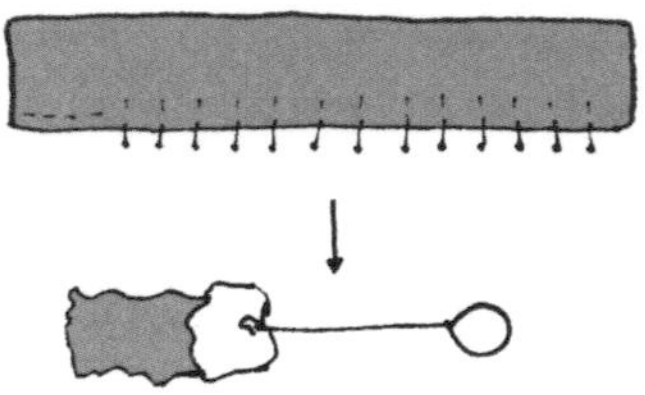

Alternatively, simply fold the strap in half with the WRONG sides together, then fold each long edge toward the wrong side by ¼ inch. Line up the folded edges and edgestitch. Then edgestitch the other side and skip to step 5. This is far easier, but sometimes it's tricky to get the folded edges to line up nicely.

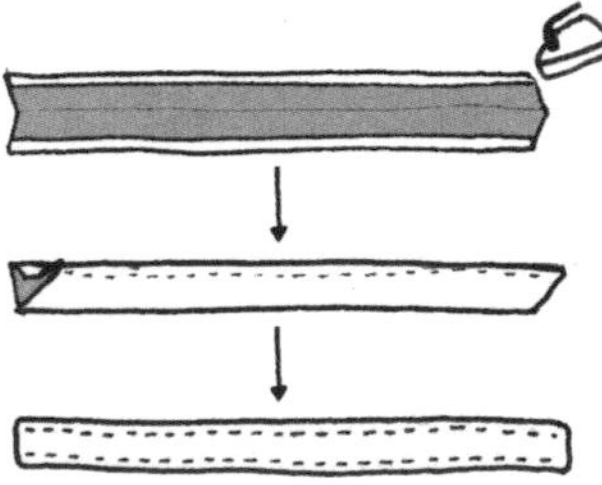

4 Topstitch each long side about ⅛ inch from the folded edge.

5 With the WRONG sides facing, fold the strap over and baste the short sides together about ¼ inch from edge.

6 Insert the connector piece through the hole of the clasp base, and fold over in half, covering the basted side of the wrist strap by about 1 inch on either side. (Use a binder clip or wonder clips to hold the connector piece together, though be careful not to leave unsightly indentations. I often just hold on with my fingers for dear life.)

Increase your stitch length to roughly 3½. Switch to a leather machine needle if your connector piece is especially bulky. Starting from the bottom of the connector piece, slowly and carefully sew a rectangle about ¼ inch from the edge, making sure to catch the main strap. Leave about ½ inch between the base of the clasp and the top of the rectangle so that the presser feet can maneuver across the connector piece at the top without hitting the metal base of the clasp. Finish it off by stitching an *X* within the rectangle.

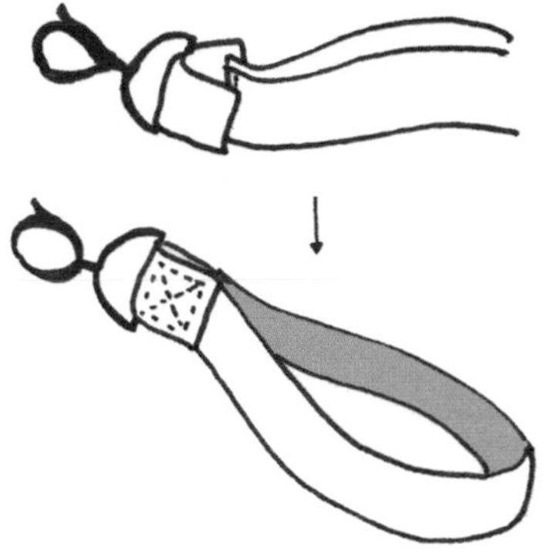

7 If the metal clasp ends up being too big for the strap attach point (the small loops on the side of the camera), add a metal jump ring that is large enough for the metal clasp to the attach point. The strap attach points for both my DSLR and vintage cameras were too small for the metal clasps, so I used jump rings.

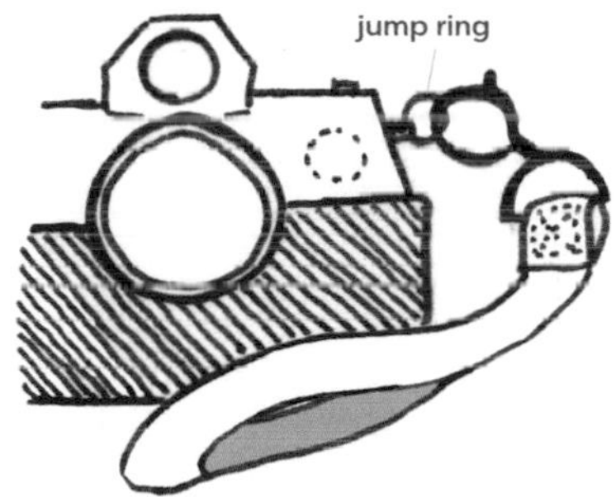

8 Now you can take photos worry-free, but stay away from pools.

FELT FLORAL CROWN

WHO DOESN'T LOVE A GOOD floral crown? I used to make daisy chain crowns for my daughter when she was tiny, and the best part about a felt floral version is that it will never wilt. By limiting the color palette, this type of flora need not look kitschy or as though a preschooler went haywire (though it would be absolutely acceptable and enchanting if your preschooler wants to partake in the making).

Felt is truly the ideal beginner fabric, given the luscious choice of colors, the no-fray edges, and the sturdy yet forgiving surface. Even though the construction of this crown involves mostly hand-stitching and gluing, it is just as satisfying as sewing up a garment—a fun and potentially meditative way (at least the hand-sewing part) to spend an afternoon or evening. The result is sure to be a hit with a pint-sized aspiring princess in your vicinity. It's a fetching addition to a girly Halloween costume—and may end up as a requisite accessory for dress-up. Photos on pages 40 and 41.

SUPPLIES + MATERIALS

Felt in a variety of colors

Coordinating thread

Stamens (found at most craft stores) (optional)

Fabric-covered floral wire (precut into 18-inch pieces or from a roll)

Glue gun

Wire cutter or supersharp scissors (for floral wire)

Tracing paper

Hand-sewing needle

Ribbon or twine (optional)

FABRIC RECOMMENDATIONS

I love working with wool felt, which is more luxurious than the ubiquitous stuff you see at your local craft stores. However, for this project, any type of felt will do! No need to wash these fabrics, although you might want to press them with a press cloth on a low heat setting.

FINISHED DIMENSIONS

Infinitely modifiable, but the sample crown's circumference is 25 inches—and fits both my head and my daughter's head nicely

FABRIC PIECES: Trace the shapes on page 163 or create versions of your own: Petals (6 to 10 per flower), Leaves (2 to 3 per flower), Stamen (1 per flower if using felt, or 4 or 5 per flower if using store-bought double-sided stamens)

CONSTRUCTION STEPS

1. Using tracing paper and pencil, create pattern pieces by drawing the petal, stamen, and leaf shapes provided.

2. For the petals, trace 6 to 10 petals per flower on desired felt colors. Regular old ballpoint pen works wonderfully for tracing onto felt, but chalk pencils are perfectly fine too—and for darker-colored felt, you'll need at least one light-colored chalk.

   For the leaves, trace 2 to 3 leaves per flower on desired felt colors. (I recommend various shades of green for the leaves and the stamens, although aquas would be pretty too.) It's also a good idea to cut out a few extra leaves now to glue here and there as filler later on.

   Tip: As you cut out the shapes, create a pile for each flower so you don't get confused later. (I've made the mistake of just tossing them willy-nilly onto the table and spending way too long sorting through them when it came time to assemble.)

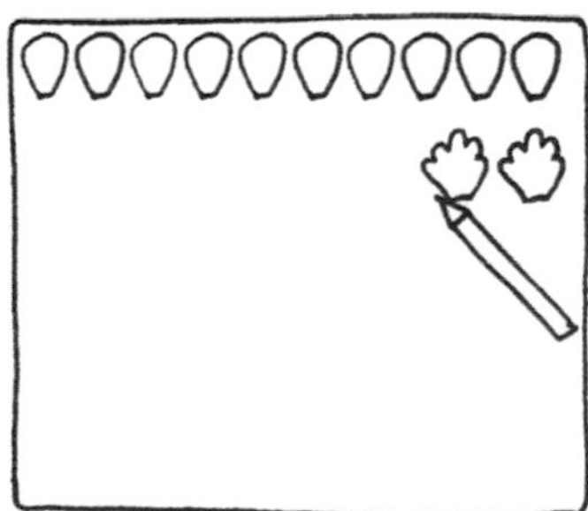

3. To create a fabric stamen, snip parallel lines into each rectangular piece—it will look like a comb—up to about ½ inch from the bottom. Roll it up and stitch the bottom.

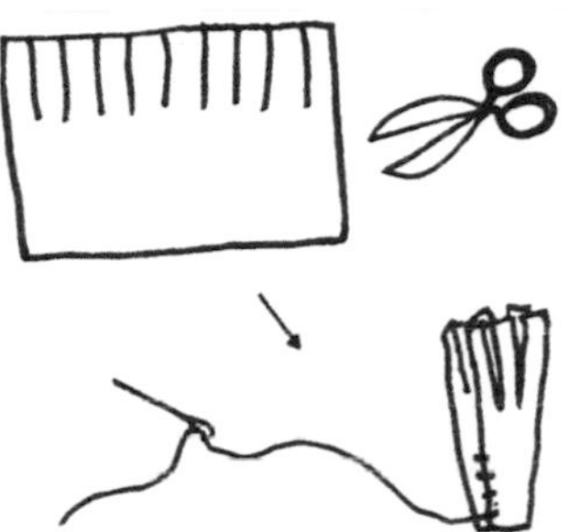

4. Stitch one petal to the stamen, lining up the bottom edges. Don't worry too much about the stitching method, as the base of the flowers will ultimately be covered by glued-on leaves. On the direct opposite side of the stamen, place another petal and stitch. Continue adding petals by overlapping them, until your fingers feel cramped or until it looks sufficiently flower-like. Assemble your desired amount of flowers in different sizes for visual interest.

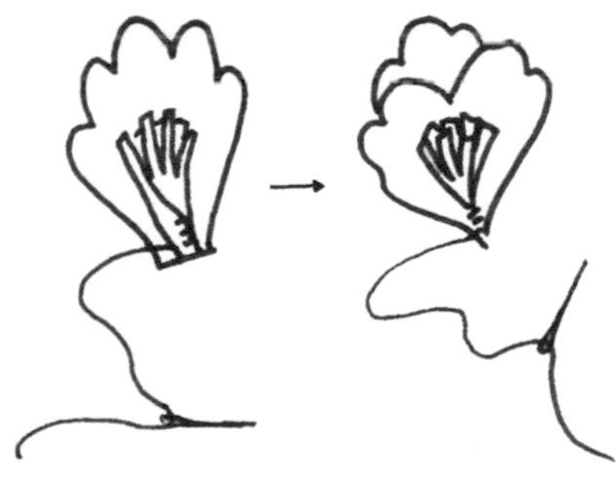

5. To use store-bought stamens instead of felt, fold the stamens in half and wrap the bottom portion of the flower petal around the folded base of the stamen, stitching into place. Repeat with more petals.

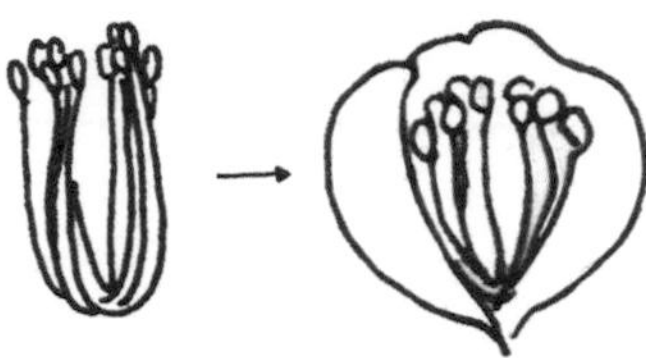

6. Plug in your glue gun. Take one of the larger flowers, place a small bead of glue at its base, and insert one end of 18-inch floral wire. (I used pre-cut wires that come in 18-inch lengths, and this is a good starter length.) Repeat with another larger flower on the other end of the same floral wire. Add a small dollop of glue at the base of a leaf, and attach the leaf to one of the flowers, wrapping the leaf around both the wire and the flower petals at the base. Add a couple more leaves in the same way. Make sure to smooth out where the leaves overlap.

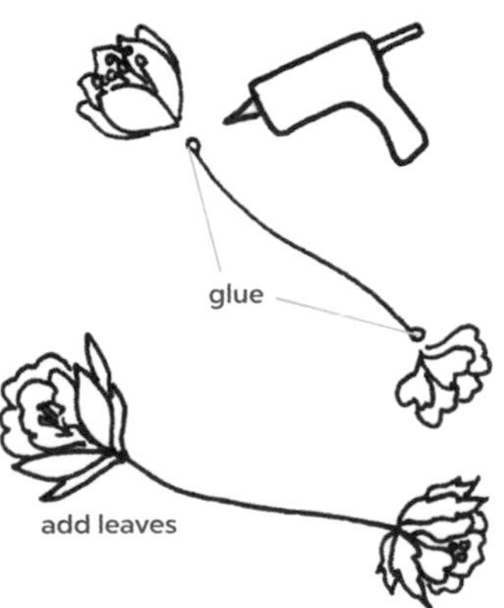

Repeat with another piece of floral wire. You can cut the wire in smaller pieces to cluster the flowers closer together.

7. After you have a few flower-adorned floral wires, twist them together to form a crown. Glue additional flowers and leaves to fill in the blanks as you see fit.

8. If desired, use ribbon or twine to decoratively wrap or hang from the crown. I also found some lovely faux plants at the craft store that look great as accent pieces.

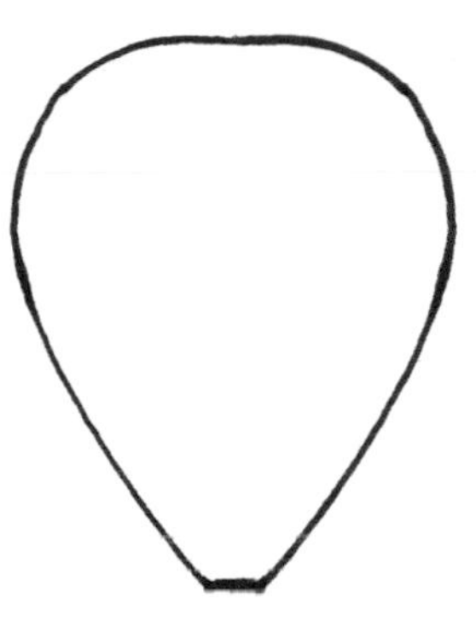

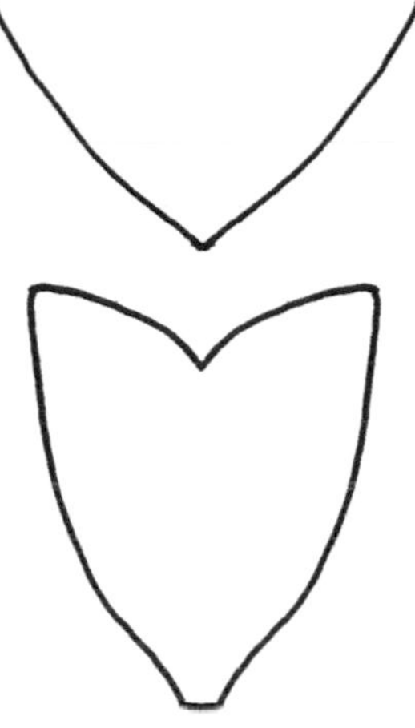

LEAVES

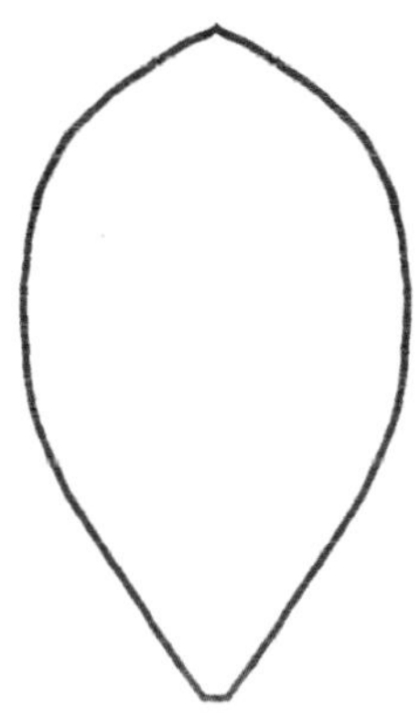

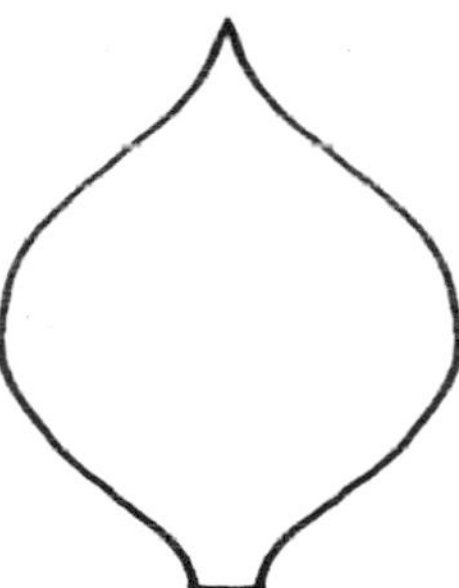

STAMEN

THE STARTER DRESS

WITH THAT FIRST DRESS IN mind—the one I made in late, late summer at the cusp of fall when I relaunched my sewing hobby—I designed a truly simple halter sundress perfect for the special girl in your life, easily adjusted with a slender tie that does double-duty as shoulder straps. Go the minimal and chic route of the A-line style or take a few extra moments to add a couple of gathered tiers to up the girly factor. I've included instructions for inseam pockets too, to allow the recipient of this breezy little number to tuck treasures from the sea, forest, or city as she explores and meanders in the golden light.

The design will accommodate a range of sizes due to the adjustable shoulder straps. As the child grows, the dress will easily become a tunic-length top and as the weather cools, the little fashionista can layer it over a long-sleeved tee.

The main instructions are for the dress with no tiers, but on page 171, I explain how to modify your pattern pieces to create the tiered version. Don't be scared by all the steps! I think you'll find each instruction to be quite simple. Photos on pages 42 and 43.

SUPPLIES + MATERIALS

1½ to 2 yards woven fabric (depends on the size of the child, but this should be sufficient)

Coordinating thread

Drafting kit (see The Drafting Kit, page 96)

FABRIC RECOMMENDATIONS

Drapey fabrics are best for this dress, though quilting cotton would be OK too. Look for lightweight linens, cotton voiles that aren't too sheer, and cotton lawns. Make sure to prep the fabric by washing, drying, and pressing.

FINISHED DIMENSIONS

Modifiable to the child in your life

FABRIC PIECES: Bias Binding, a.k.a. Bias Tape (2), Front (1), Back (2), Pocket (4), Tie (1)

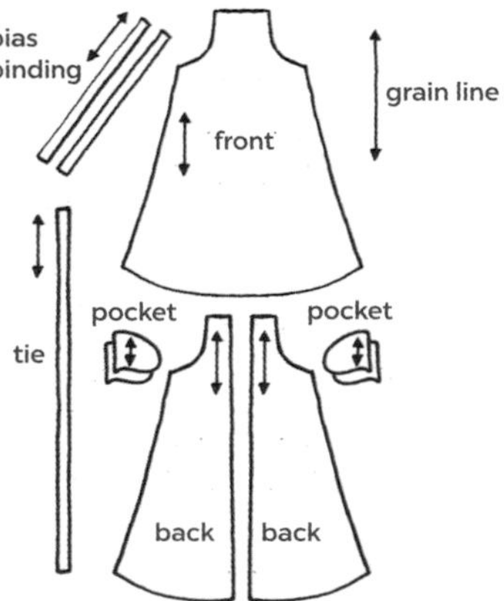

CONSTRUCTION STEPS

1 Let's get a few measurements first. With a tape measure and the lucky young recipient of a custom new dress, determine the following distances—and write it down:

1. From the center of the collarbone (the star in the illustration) over to the outermost edge of shoulder (point A)
2. From the star down to the chest center point that is parallel to just below the armpit (point B)
3. From point B to just below the armpit (point C)
4. From the star down to the finished length—where you want the hem to fall (point D)
5. From point D to how far you want the skirt to extend out—the sweep (point E)

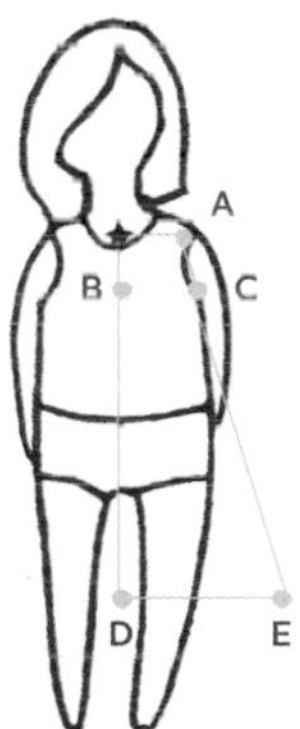

2 On a large, flat surface, place a piece of pattern paper. It should be at least a couple of inches wider than the widest part of the pattern (distance 5 from step 1) and at least three inches longer than the longest part (distance 4 from step 1).

3 We will begin by drafting the front pattern piece. Starting about 3 inches from the top edge of the paper, make a dot or small line with a pencil (mine is indicated with a star).

Measure distance 1 from step 1 and draw a straight horizontal line. This will be the front neckline.

From the star, measure distance 2 downward and make a mark. From point B, measure distance 3, parallel to distance 1 and draw a straight horizontal line. Point C is where the side seam starts.

Again from the star, measure distance 4 downward and make a mark. From point D measure across for distance 5. Draw a straight horizontal line, parallel to distances 1 and 3. This will be the hem.

Connect point A to point C, curving it slightly. (I have a tendency of making the curve too deep, which can result in some embarrassing exposure for the little girl, so you might want to futz with this curve a little to avoid my common mistake.) As a general rule, I shape the curve by keeping the line perpendicular from point A the first inch or two, then I gently arc the line as I connect it to point C. It ends up looking a little like a backward letter *J*.

Using a ruler (so you get a nice straight line), connect point C to point E. You can see how the pattern piece compares to the illustration with the measurement points.

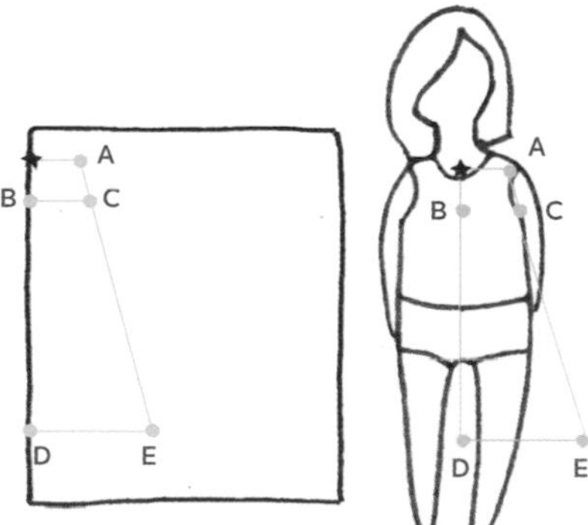

4 At this point, your front pattern piece should be looking pretty good. We need to make just a couple more tweaks. Notice how the corner of the hem is looking quite pointy, like the tip of a pizza slice. We want to make this a right angle so that your front and back pieces will meet up and form a straight hem instead of creating a pointy, asymmetrical appearance.

Now, there are probably more technical methods for doing this, but this is my cheater method and it works for me. Draw a straight line from point C down to the hem. Then take a ruler (a quilting ruler is great for this) and line it up along the angled side line.

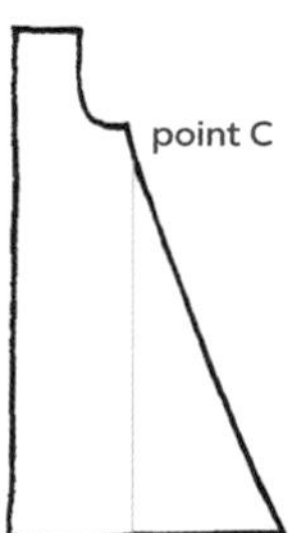

Draw a right angle from the side line, and then gently curve the hemline to the line you drew in step 3. Curved rulers are available for this, but I've never used one and all my hems come out fine.

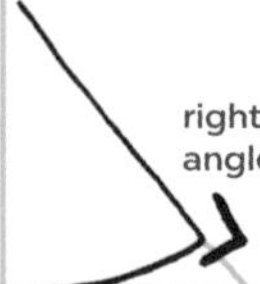

5 Double-check that the underarm section is also at a right angle. If everything looks satisfactory, it's time to add seam allowances. For this dress, I used a ⅜-inch seam allowance for the sides and underarms. For the neckline I added a 1½-inch seam allowance, and for the hem, I added 1 inch. Using a ruler and a pencil, mark the seam allowance amounts along the lines at about two-inch intervals, then connect the dots.

Cut out the pattern piece. Make sure to use your paper scissors and not your fabric shears. You now have your front pattern piece ready to go! Label it "Starter Dress—FRONT—cut 1 on fold" and let's move onto the back pattern piece.

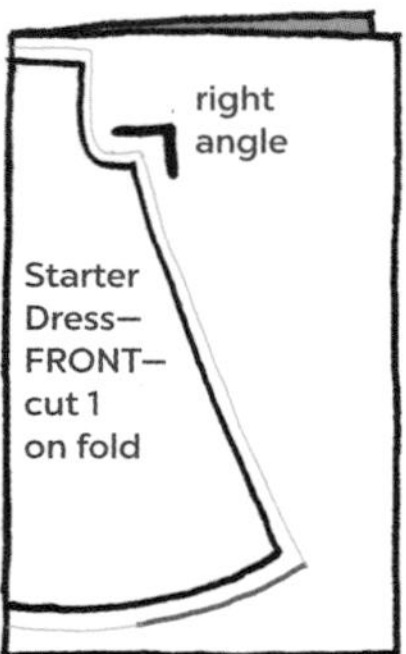

6 Drafting the back piece is a piece of cake. So easy that you might not even need to make a separate pattern piece. If you do, place the front pattern piece onto your pattern paper, making sure that there are a few inches of space to the left. Pin or use weights to hold it in place, if desired. Trace the front pattern piece, and add ⅜ inch to the center line. Cut it out (again, remember to use your paper scissors), label it "Starter Dress—BACK—cut 2," and set it aside. Done.

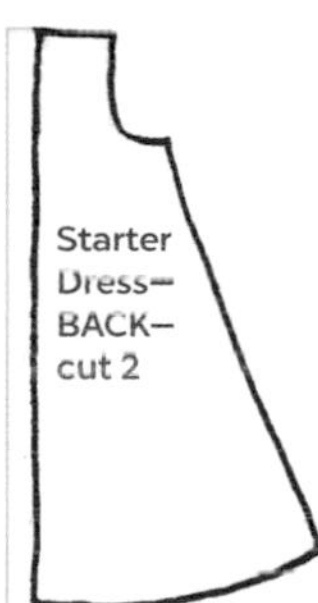

7 For the pockets, you can either find an existing pocket in the child's wardrobe and trace it, or draw one out. You don't need to be too precise. Just make sure one side is straight and extends at least ⅜ inch before you start curving it into a pocket shape. If it's in the general shape of what you would expect a pocket to look like, it will work. One trick I use is to draw a pocket shape directly onto the front pattern piece, and then place a piece of tracing paper on top to create a separate pocket pattern piece.

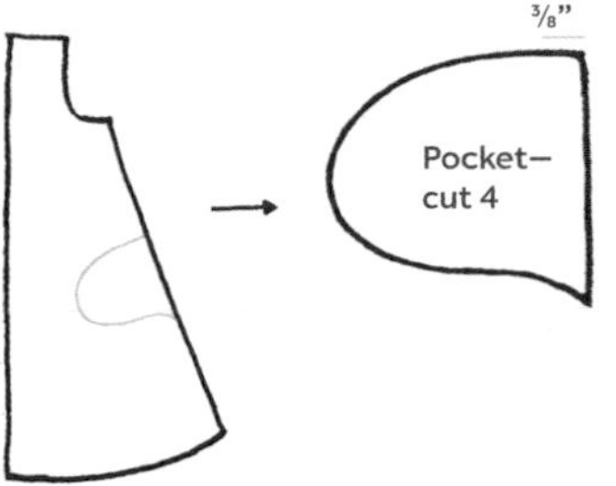

8 You don't need pattern pieces for the bias binding or the tie since you'll measure directly on the fabric.

For the bias binding measurement, line up the front and back pattern pieces side to side so that the side seams match, and measure the armhole curve. Add 1 inch to this measurement and jot it down.

9 It's time to cut out the fabric.

- Fold the fabric in half with the RIGHT sides facing.
- See the illustration that follows for layout suggestions, but whether your pattern pieces will fit this way will depend entirely on the size of the dress and whether the fabric has directional print. Pin or use weights to hold the pattern pieces in place.
- Remember to cut out four pieces for the pockets.
- For the armhole binding, cut out two bias bindings at a 45-degree angle, 1½ inches wide by the length you calculated in step 8.
- For the tie/shoulder straps, start with 50 by 1¾ inches, which will be more than enough for most sizes. Shorten or lengthen as you see fit.

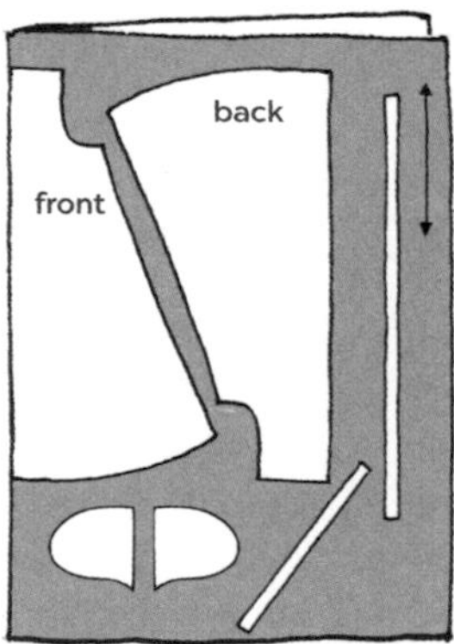

Keep in mind that you might want to create a muslin (also known as a test garment) the first time before cutting into any valuable or expensive fabric—just in case you need to make modifications.

10 Prep the front and back pieces by finishing the raw edges of the sides and center. (If using an overlocker, try not to trim off the edges, if possible.)

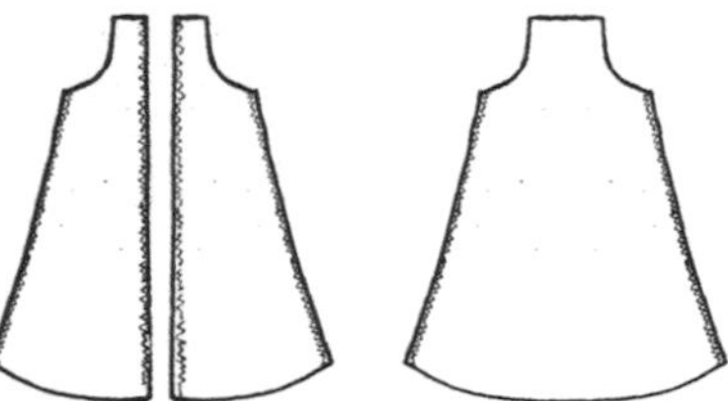

11 With the RIGHT sides facing, pin the back pieces together. Mark 4 inches from the top. Starting from the mark, sew a ⅜-inch seam allowance. Press open. Topstitch along the edge of the opening from the front (in the illustration, the back is shown).

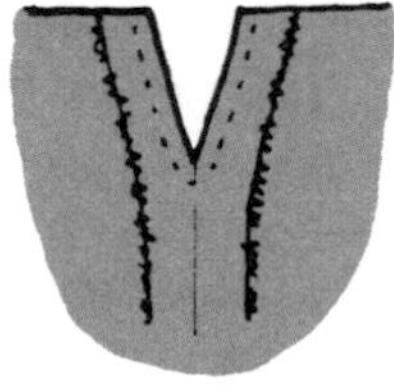

12 Figure out where you would like to place the pockets. You might want to look at existing garments with pockets for reference. Mark where the top of the pocket will start onto one side of the front piece. With the RIGHT sides facing, pin one pocket piece to the front piece. Do this for both sides of the front and the back pieces. Lay the front piece and back piece on top of each other to make sure the pockets line up correctly.

Sew on each pocket piece with a ⅜-inch seam allowance from the edge, and press the seam open.

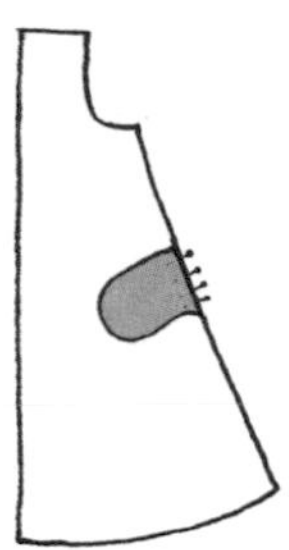

13 With the RIGHT sides facing, pin the front and back pieces together and sew the side seams ⅜ inch from edge. Stop and pivot when you reach about ⅜ inch past the starting point of the pocket. Continue sewing ⅜ inch from the edge following along the outline of the pockets and then pivot again where the side seam resumes. Repeat on other side. Finish the raw edges of the pockets. I like to use the zigzag stitch because I invariably cut into parts I'm not supposed to with the serger.

14 Attach the bias binding. With the RIGHT sides facing, pin the bias binding along the underarm curve. Sew ½ inch from the edge. Trim the seam allowance to about ¼ inch and make little snips along the seam allowance to ensure that the binding will lay flat.

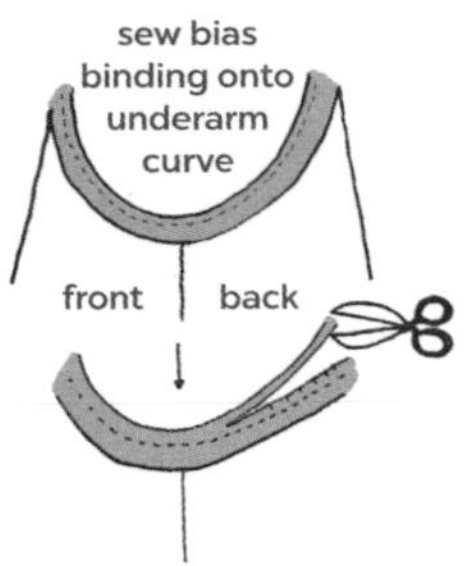

15 Fold the edge of the binding toward the WRONG side so that the edge lines up right against the seam you just stitched. Fold the binding over again along the seam line to completely enclose the raw edge. Edgestitch. Repeat with other side.

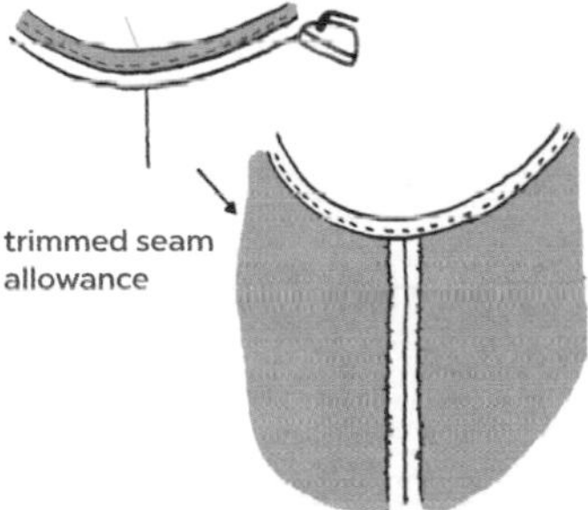

16 To make the neckline casings, fold the top of the neckline toward the WRONG side ¼ inch and press. Fold another ¾ inch and press. Edgestitch. Note that you added 1½ inches of seam allowance, but you're only folding about 1 inch. This is intentional to give a little extra ease for the top of the bodice. Repeat for the back.

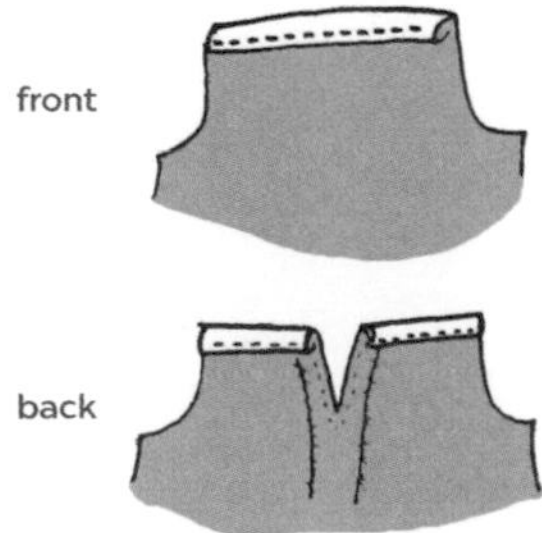

17 Create the tie. Fold the tie fabric in half, lengthwise toward the WRONG sides and press. With the center crease as a guide, fold each side to the center toward the WRONG side and press. Fold each end by about ½ inch toward the WRONG side and press. Then encase the raw edges by folding it in half again along the initial fold lengthwise, and press. Edgestitch.

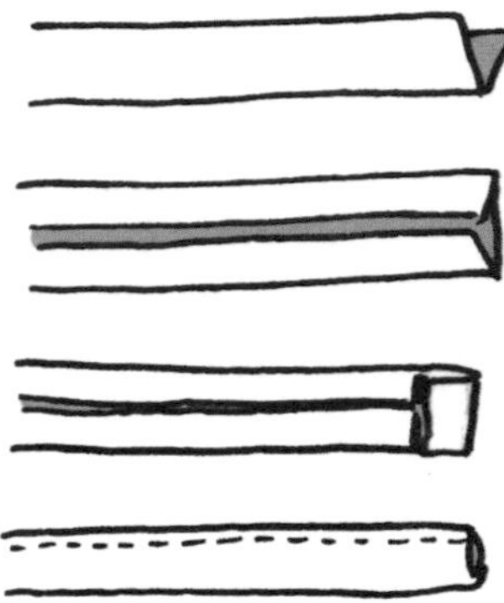

Using a bodkin or safety pin, thread the tie through the neckline casings.

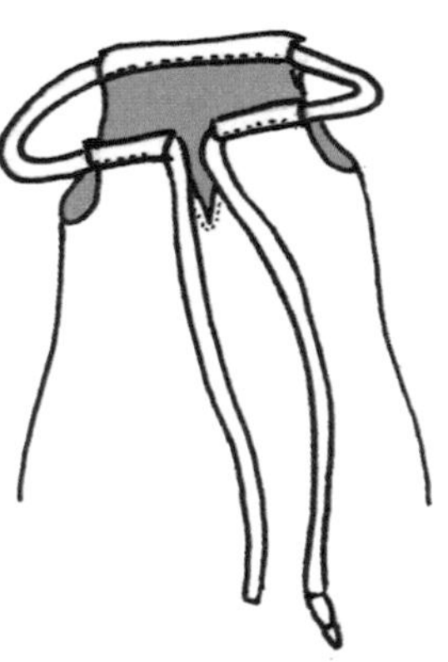

TIP: If you have trouble with sewing the thin tie, first fold up a piece of scrap fabric and stitch the scrap. When the scrap just passes the presser foot, place the beginning of the tie under the foot and pull on the scrap to help ease the tie along.

18 Finally, sew the hem. Fold the bottom of the skirt by ½ inch toward the WRONG side and press. Fold another ½ inch, press, and edgestitch. All done!

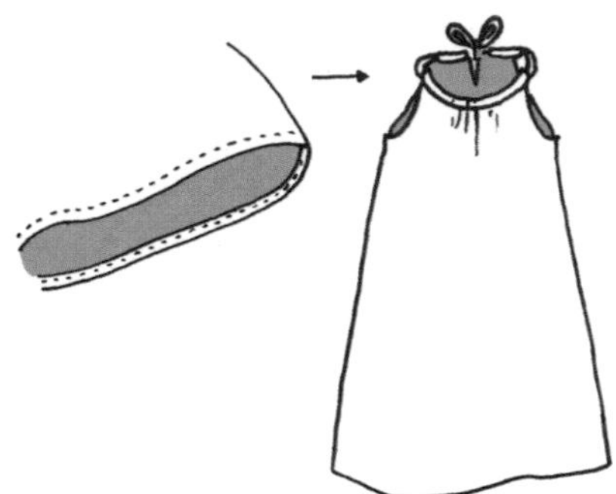

VARIATION: TIERED STARTER DRESS

CONSTRUCTION STEPS

1. To create the tiered dress, you start with the pattern pieces created in steps 1 through 6 for The Starter Dress. Place your front pattern piece on another piece of pattern paper. Trace along the neckline, down the armhole curve and about 5 inches (or whatever measurement looks good to you) down the side seam. Draw a straight, horizontal line from the side seam to the center fold. This is your new front bodice. Trace this new pattern piece to create your back bodice piece, and add ⅜ inch to the center seam. Remember, you will be cutting out two back pieces. Label each pattern piece accordingly: "Front—cut 1 on fold," "Back—cut 2." Cut out the fabric pieces.

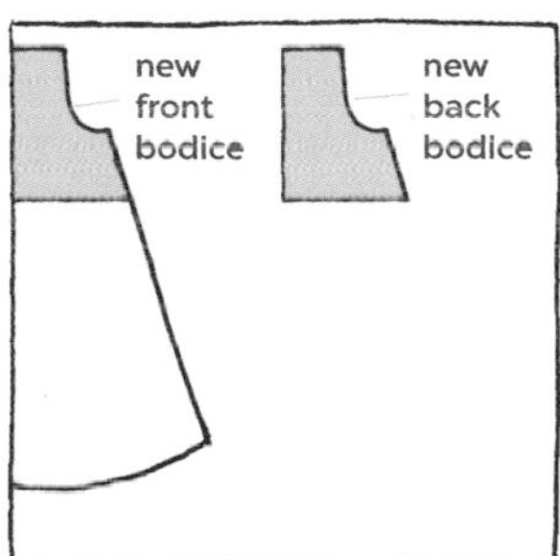

2. To create the tiers of this dress, you need dimensions for two rectangles. It depends on how full you want the gathers to be, but I tend to add about 10 inches to the measurement of the tier above it. So if the bodice base is 10 inches (the pattern piece is 5 inches in width, but remember, this is half of the width since the pattern piece is placed on the fabric fold), the next tier would be 20 inches wide, and the tier after that would be 30 inches.

As for the height, let your inner designer fiddle around with various heights, or you could keep things uniform. It's up to you. Cut two of each rectangle.

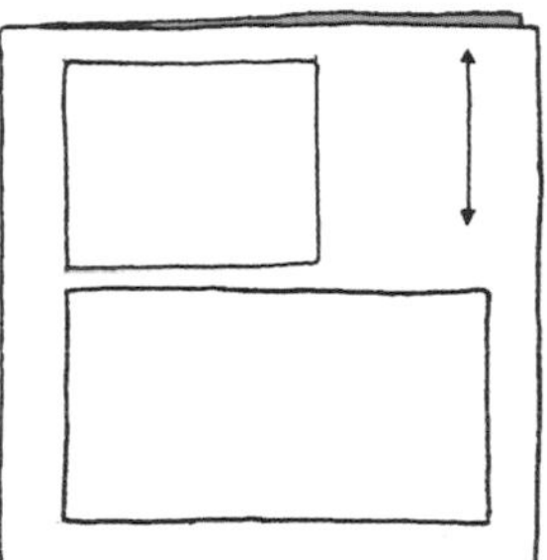

3. To gather the tiers, increase your machine stitch length to the maximum. (My machine goes up to 5.) Without backstitching at the beginning or the end, sew one row about ¼ inch from the edge, leaving a tail of about 3 inches at the beginning and the end of the row. Then sew a second row (again without backstitching) about ⅜ inch from the top row (again leaving 3-inch tails on either end). Now, with the RIGHT side facing up, pull on the two threads that are on the right side. Leave the threads underneath alone. Pull on the threads to gather the fabric, alternating between the left and right sides to get the gathers going.

4 With the RIGHT sides of the new front bodice facing, and the gathered side facing up, pin the ends together and adjust the gathers to fit the length of the bodice. I find it strangely calming to even out the gathers, but this was not always the case. Gathers can be a little frustrating at first, but take heart, they will look adorable.

Change your stitch length back to normal. (I can't tell you how many times I've continued sewing with the basting stitch after gathering a skirt.) With gathered side up, sew ³⁄₈ inch from the edge.

Repeat this process with the bottom tier. Sew the long-stitched (basted) rows, gather, pin, and sew. Finish the raw edges with your preferred method: pinking shears, zigzag stitching, or overlock stitching.

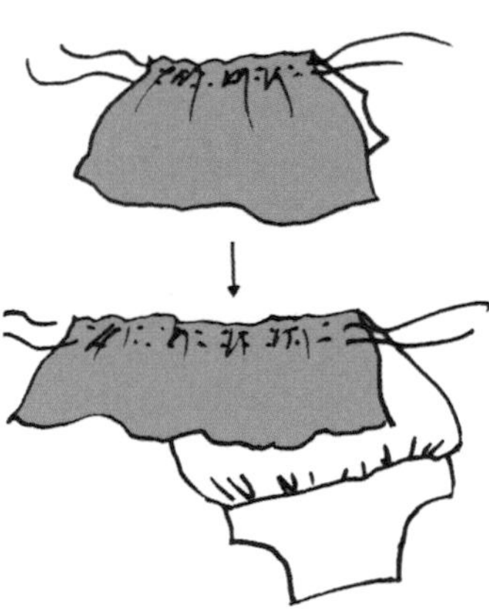

5 For the back bodice pieces, finish the raw edges where the center seam will be. Mark at least 3 inches from the top, and sew the two pieces RIGHT sides together starting at the mark. Press open, and edgestitch around the opening from the front. Repeat steps 3 and 4, and this gives you a front and back piece.

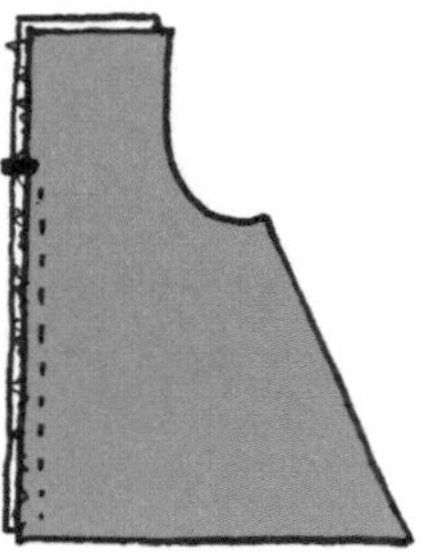

6 Sew the sides together ³⁄₈ inch from the edge and finish the raw edges in your preferred method. Then follow steps 14 to 18 for the non-tiered dress to finish your flouncy wonder! If you decide to add pockets, refer to step 12.

FORTUNE COOKIE ADVENT CALENDAR

IT'S A BRAIN-TEASING EXERCISE FOR me to come up with a different advent calendar design every year. I love it. Each piece needs to look good on its own, but collectively, they must have visual impact as holiday decor. It is very important that they aren't too time-consuming to assemble because I have to make twenty-five of them! I hit the jackpot with the fortune cookie idea with numbered "fortunes" coming out of them. They are ludicrously easy to make, although the step that requires flipping the ends might be a bit perplexing at first.

The scavenger hunt element I added in prior years was so well-received that I am thinking of incorporating it into these fortune cookies too. Alternatively, funny or pithy "fortunes" can be written on them. If coming up with scavenger hunt or fortune ideas seem like too much to take on, you can double the circle size and simply tuck in a small treat. Just use a touch of craft glue to seal a portion of the "cookie" shut to prevent the treat from falling out. Photos on pages 52 and 53.

SUPPLIES + MATERIALS

½ yard fabric

Coordinating thread

Paper, for the fortunes

Craft glue (optional)

FABRIC RECOMMENDATIONS

Leather and wool felt are ideal for these clever little fabric cookies. No need to wash these fabrics, although you might want to press them with a press cloth on a low heat setting.

FINISHED DIMENSIONS

Approximately 2¼-inch-wide cookies

FABRIC PIECES: Circle (25)

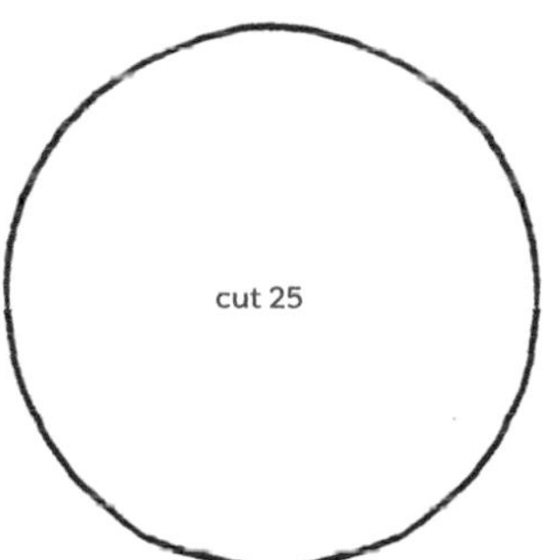

CONSTRUCTION STEPS

1. Onto a piece of pattern paper, trace the bottom of a cup or a small bowl that measures about 3 inches in diameter, and cut out. Or measure out a circle manually by folding a paper into quarters and plotting the radius (see illustration on the following page), and cut out that circle.

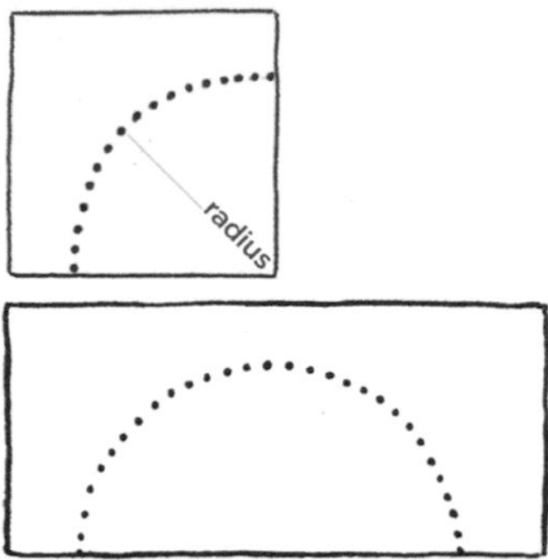

2. On the WRONG side of your fabric, place the pattern piece and trace 25 circles close together. Cut them out.

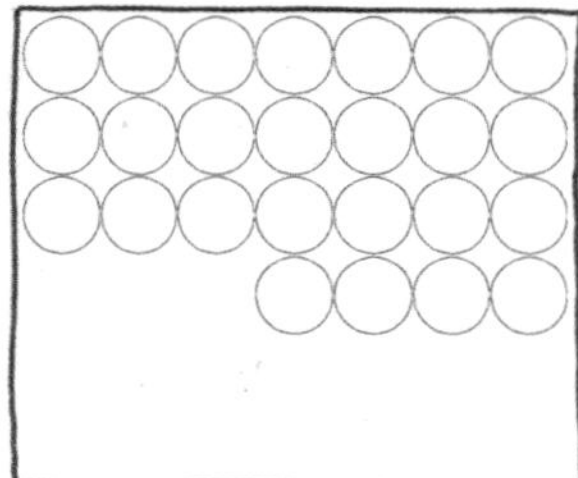

3. Fold a circle in half with the RIGHT sides together, and sew about 5 or 6 stitches down the center from the flat edge.

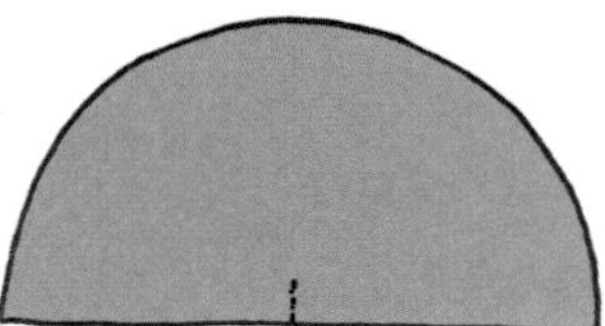

4. Flip each end so that the RIGHT side of the fabric is on the outside. The way you flip it is at first counterintuitive. If you're holding the half circle as shown in the following illustration with the flat side pointing upward, turn the "cookie" 90 degrees so you're looking at the side view and into the "cookie." Then you will turn the side you're looking at inside out in a upward direction. Do the same thing on the other side. You might have to fiddle with it a little bit to make it look like a fortune cookie, but that's basically it.

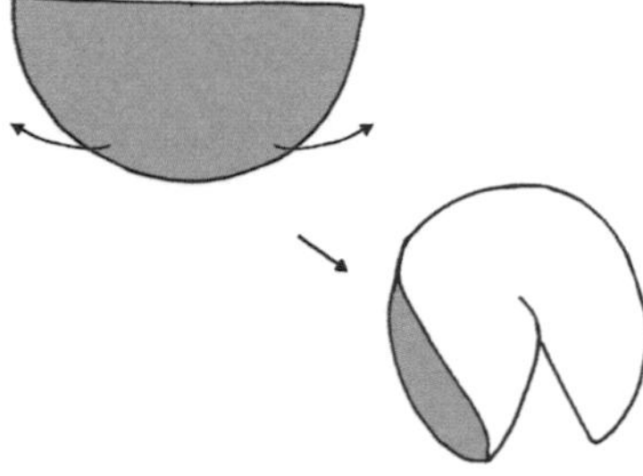

5. For the fortunes, cut out strips of paper about 3 by ¾ inches. Write or stamp numbers 1 through 25 close to the short edge of the strip. Add a message to the back side if you like, and slip the piece of paper into each cookie with the numbers visible to the outside.

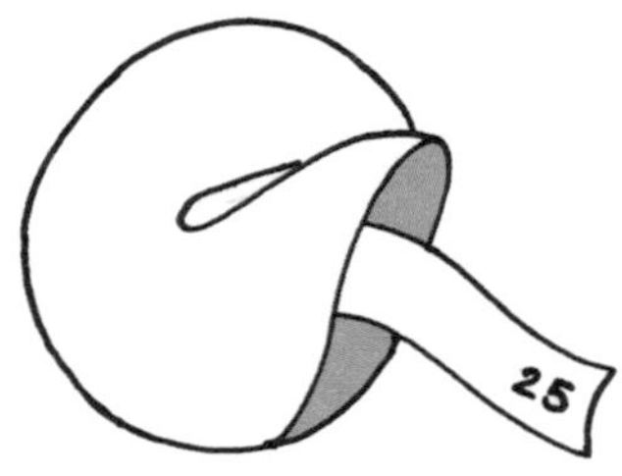

6. Aesthetically arrange all 25 fortune cookies in a bowl—and let the countdown begin!

DOPP KIT

I'VE RESEARCHED QUITE A FEW versions of DIY Dopp Kits, and the stickler is the raw edges for these decidedly effortless bags. I chose to forego the whole issue by sewing with waxed canvas, outdoor fabric, and wool felt. Using pinking shears to trim the raw edges is sufficient (it is, in fact, unnecessary for the wool felt, which won't fray at all)—think of it as the industrial look.

All projects in this book require backstitching (see Handy Terms + Techniques, page 100), but for this hardy bag, I recommend creating reinforcement with extra backstitching throughout.

Note: Although they will be rugged and durable, these bags will not be stiff. Regardless, they are an excellent way to corral a panoply of small travel items. Photos on pages 54 and 55.

SUPPLIES + MATERIALS

½ yard durable fabric, for the bag

3-by-1-inch (at least) coordinating fabric, for the tab

14-inch zipper (or any zipper longer than 14 inches trim since you can extra length)

Coordinating thread

> If using waxed canvas or leatherlike textiles, wonder clips, binder clips, or even clothespins are helpful

FABRIC RECOMMENDATIONS

Try waxed canvas, leather, coated fabric (often found in the outdoors section of fabric stores), or wool felt for the main fabric. Coordinating webbing or leather works well for the tab. No need to wash these fabrics, although you might want to press them with a press cloth on a low heat setting.

FINISHED DIMENSIONS

8 inches long by 6 inches high by 4 inches deep

FABRIC PIECES: Dopp Kit (2), Tab (1)

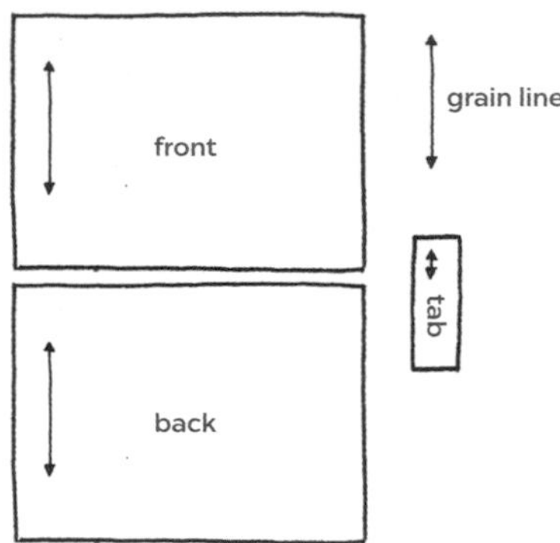

CONSTRUCTION STEPS

1. Cut two 14-by-10-inch pieces of fabric.

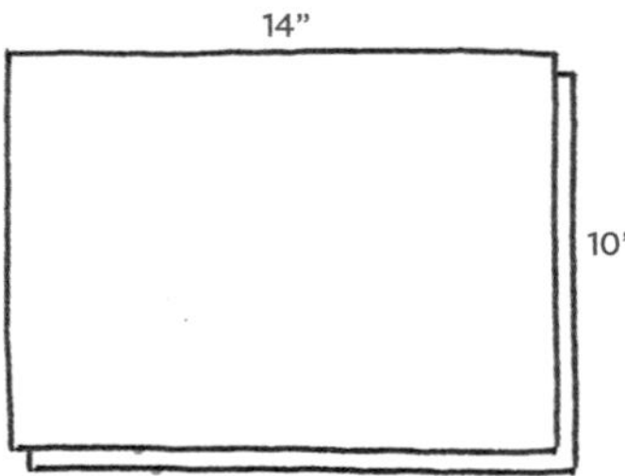

2. With the RIGHT side of the zipper facing toward the RIGHT side of one fabric piece, clip or pin the zipper to the fabric. Using your zipper foot, sew ¼ inch from the outer edge of the zipper tape.

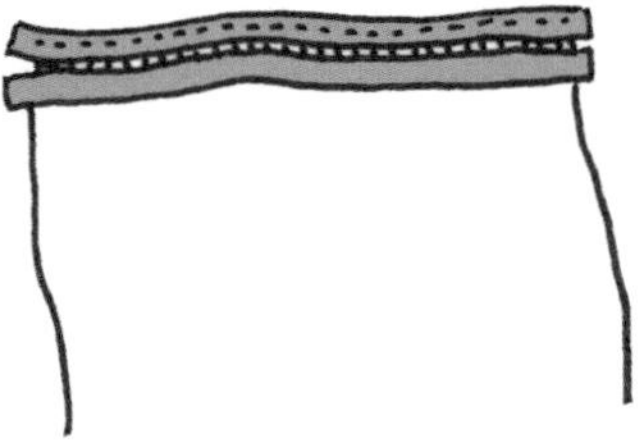

3. Repeat on the other side, attaching the zipper to the other piece of fabric.

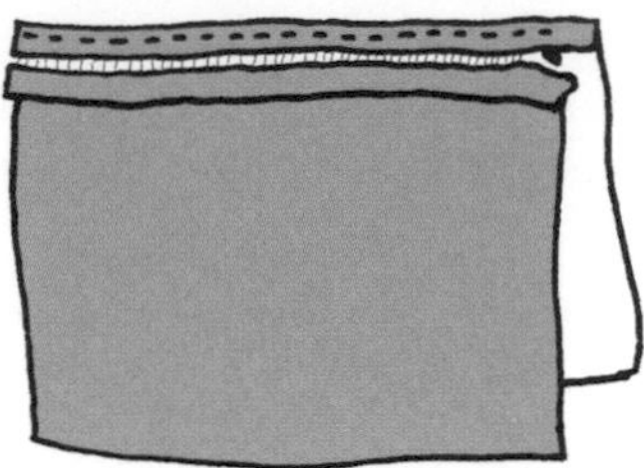

4. First test your fabric before ironing to prevent scorching. Press the fabric away from the zipper—and be careful not to melt the zipper if you're using a plastic one. Topstitch about ⅛ inch from the zipper teeth on both sides. It might be helpful to first partially unzip the zipper, sew a few inches, then with the needle down, pivot the fabric in a way that allows you to close the zipper back up. The zipper pull will remain out of the way and enable you to sew an even, straight seam along the zipper teeth with this method. If you used a zipper that's longer than the width of the bag, snip off the excess at this stage.

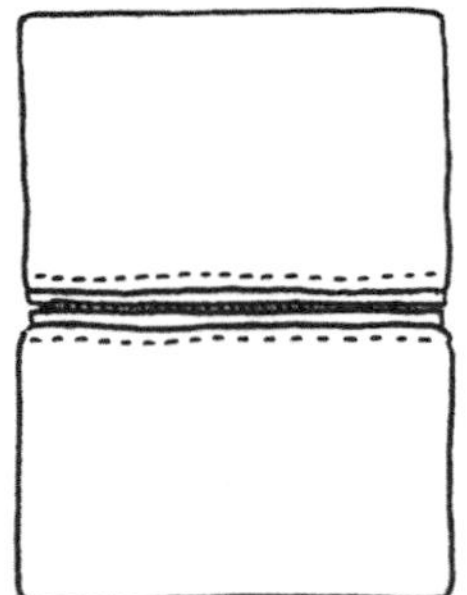

5 To create a French seam for the bottom, start with the WRONG sides facing and sew the bottom edges together with a ¼-inch seam allowance. Trim the seam allowance to ⅛ inch and press to one side. Then turn the bag inside out (the WRONG sides will be facing outward), press the folded bottom edge. With the RIGHT sides together, sew the bottom of the bag with a ½-inch seam allowance to enclose the raw edge. Press the French seam to one side.

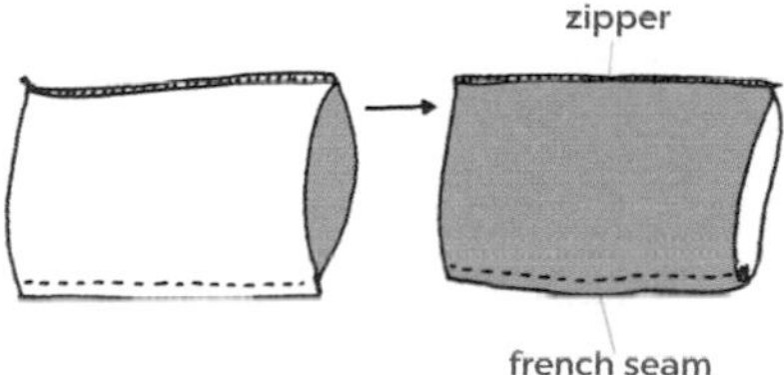

6 Arrange the fabric so the zipper is lined up above the bottom seam. On the side where the zipper ends (the pull side), place the tab folded in half, centering it on the bottom seam with the raw edges lined up. Pin or clip in place. Baste the tab about ¼ inch from the edge.

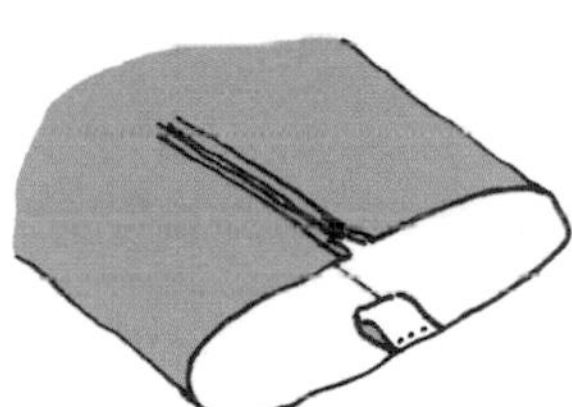

7 VERY IMPORTANT: Open the zipper halfway; otherwise, it will be very challenging to turn the bag RIGHT side out later! Clip the unzipped ends to the bottom of the bag so that the zipper is touching as though it's still zipped. Check to ensure that the bottom seam is lined up with the center of the zipper teeth. Clip the other side to the bottom of the bag too. Measure in ½ inch and draw a line with a marking tool on each side.

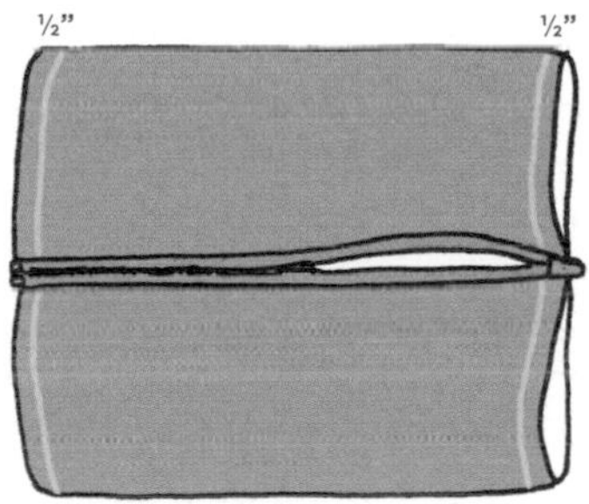

Then mark 2-inch squares on all four corners, starting from the ½-inch line, so each marked box will actually be 2½ by 2 inches. (You can measure the boxes with these dimensions on each corner from the get-go, but I've found that my method of adding a line for the seam allowance to the sides first prevents me from getting confused. Cut out the corners.

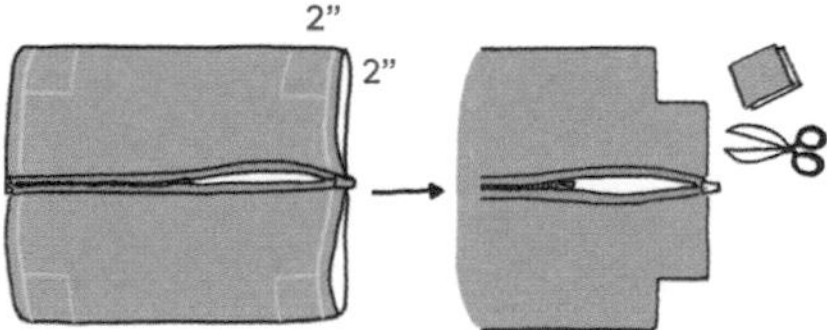

8 If it makes it easier for you, attach clips to the sides to prevent shifting (you don't want to poke holes with pins for waxed canvas, and wool felt might be a little too thick for pins) though I can usually hold the fabric in place with my hands. With the zipper side facing up, stitch on top of the marked lines you made on each side, making sure to backstitch securely at the beginning and end. Finish the edges with pinking shears. When you get to the section with the tab, it will be pretty thick, so it may require a little extra strength to use the pinking shears.

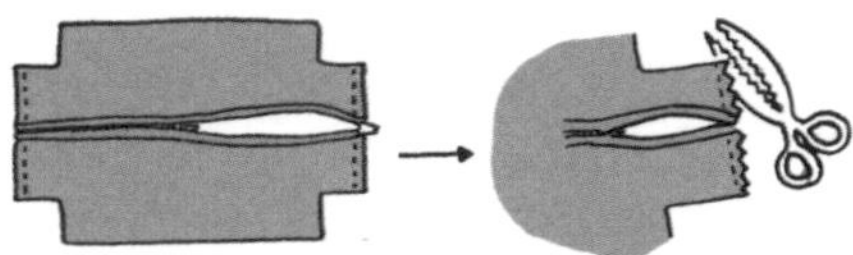

9 Open up one of the corners, sort of how you might pull open a ziplock bag. This should flatten the corner to create an angled line. You'll notice that if you try to pull it the other way, it won't flatten, so there's only one direction to go. Sew along the angled edge with a ⅜-inch seam allowance. Sew with the side seam pointing away from the zipper, toward the bottom of the bag. Repeat on the remaining three corners, and trim all with pinking shears.

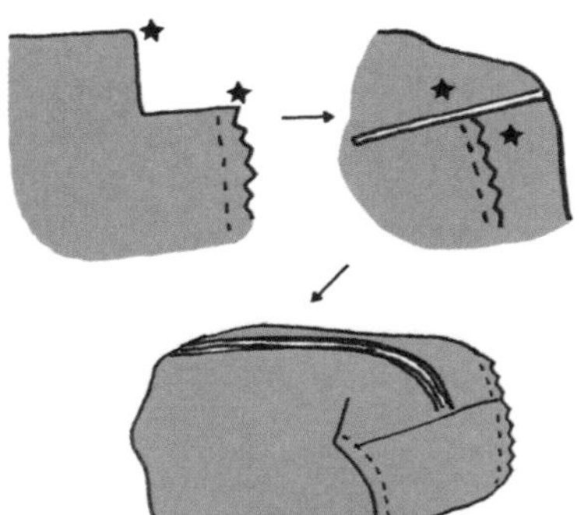

10 Turn the bag RIGHT side out and poke the out corners with a point turner. Be careful not to poke holes through the seam. You could press the final bag if you'd like, though I just use pressure from my hands to mold it into the shape I want. Fill it with manly toiletries and gift to your would-be well-groomed man (or woman, as this also makes an excellent travel cosmetic bag).

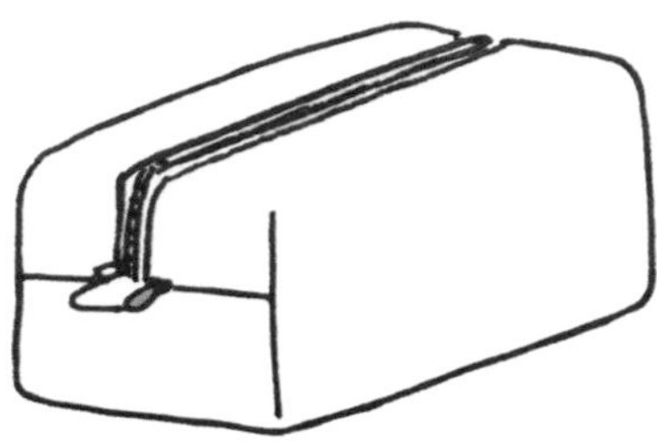

FUN TO TRY: Instead of a tab, try creating a handle with leather. In step 9, after you've flattened the corners, you would insert each end of the handle on one side of the bag before sewing the flattened corners shut. I recommend a handle size that is approximately 8 inches long and 1 inch wide.

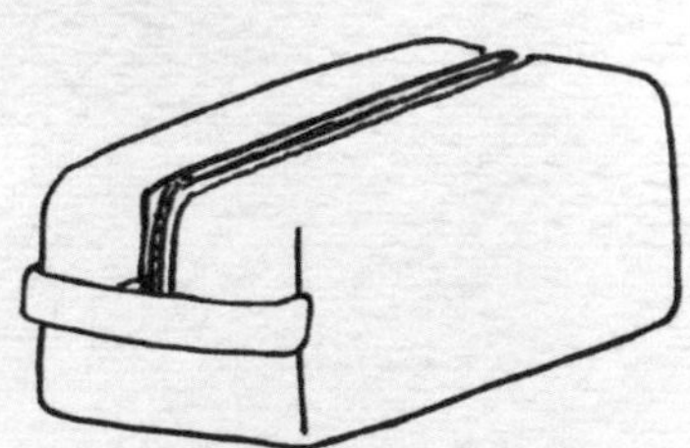

HEATING PAD

EVERY HOLIDAY GIFT-GIVING SEASON, I'M AFFLICTED with a condition called Crafter's Delusion. Symptoms include a total disregard for realistic time management, an overblown sense of crafting skills, and a rather worrisome need to hoard supplies and materials *just in case*. This condition manifests itself when strolling through retail stores where a deluge of thoughts invade the mind. Thoughts like, "Pshaw, I can make that in five minutes for 50 cents," or "That's pretty cool, but wouldn't it be cooler with a giant hand-embroidered monogram?" or "So what if I've never knit socks before? I'll just go buy twenty skeins of yarn. That looks totally easy." *Never* the case.

To combat this tendency, I've come up with a super simple project in the form of a heating pad. When making these, you can experiment with fun shapes and play with the sizing: the possibilities are limitless! You can also reimagine these as festive beanbags for the little ones.

Stay on your toes when microwaving these—overheating will result in an unpleasant charred odor or worse, a fire hazard. Start with a minute and add thirty-second bursts until it's nice and toasty. Since you'll be using grains and/or food products to fill them, consider replacing these each season. Though these can't be washed, you could create a cover using the envelope method from the Origami Pillow instructions. Do make sure to provide recipients with heating instructions. Photos on pages 56 and 57.

SUPPLIES + MATERIALS

¼ yard woven fabric

Coordinating thread

2 to 3 cups filling

Essential oil (optional)

FABRIC + FILLING RECOMMENDATIONS

Look for natural fibers such as cotton (quilting, ticking, or flannel are all good choices) or wool. Please avoid any fabrics with metallic threads since these will combust in a microwave. For the filling, I've used rice, groats, and whole flax seed with much success. Make sure to prep the fabric by washing, drying, and pressing.

FINISHED DIMENSIONS

You can create these heating pads in any size you desire, but for reference, here's what I made.

CLOUD: 7½ by 12 inches

MOON: 8 by 3½ inches at the center

SQUARE: 5 by 5 inches

FABRIC PIECES: You simply need 2 pieces of the same shape. An Internet search will yield plenty of options for shapes to trace, or you can use household items to create pattern pieces too (I've been eyeing one of the Valentine's Day heart-shaped cards that my daughter gave me).

CONSTRUCTION STEPS

1. Fold the fabric with the RIGHT sides together and trace the desired shape onto the WRONG side. Cut two mirror pieces. With the RIGHT sides together, pin and sew along the shape with a ⅜-inch seam allowance. Make sure to leave a 2- to 3-inch opening on one of the sides.

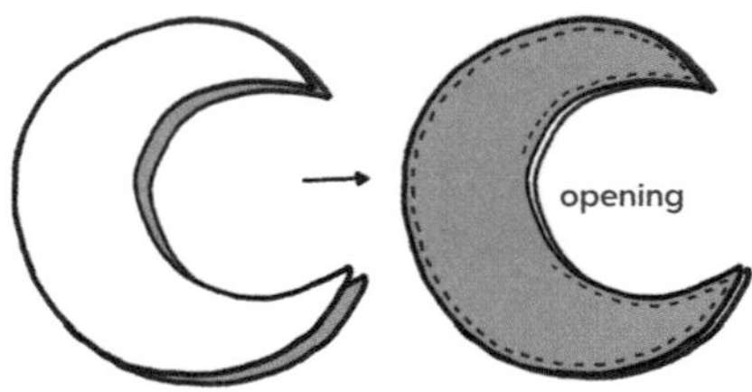

2. Clip any pointy edges and corners.

3. Turn the shape RIGHT side out and poke out any corners with a point turner. Be careful not to poke holes through the seam. Manipulate curves to smooth them out. Tuck in the raw edges at the opening so that it is flush with the seam. Press.

4. Pour the filling into a measuring cup. Start with 1 cup and work your way up if more is needed. At this point, add a drop or two of essential oil to the filling, if desired. Alternatively, you could give a bottle of essential oil as part of the gift, which is always a thoughtful touch.

   Create a funnel out of paper, insert it into the fabric opening, and fill the shape with your choice of rice, groats, or whole flax seeds. Don't overfill it; when it's flat on a surface and the filling is evenly distributed, the thickness should be about ½ inch.

5. Slip stitch the opening closed with the stitches very close together to prevent any filling leakage.

6. Done! Now it's all ready to become toasty and fragrant.

BABY KIMONO TOP + BLOOMERS

IS ANYTHING CUTER THAN BABY OUTFITS? Although you don't need to make these as a matching set, there's something about the traditional kimono shape combined with the rounded bloomers that amp up the adorableness. These are sized for newborns (up to three months), and to make it extra easy for sleep-deprived caretakers, the top has a hidden snap closure and is front-tie style. No fiddling with tugging and pulling the garment over delicate noggins! The bloomers are straightforward and once you get the hang of them, you'll be able to whip up a pair in under thirty minutes. Sure to be a hit with new parents, these make lovely baby gifts all year round. Photos on pages 58 and 59.

SUPPLIES + MATERIALS

1¼ yards of 44-inch-wide fabric, if using the same fabric for both the top and bloomers

Coordinating thread

16 inches ⅜-inch elastic

16 inches ⅛-inch elastic

1 set size 2/0 (approximately ⅜ inch) snaps

Drafting kit (see The Drafting Kit, page 96)

Ribbon or tag (optional)

¾ yard fabric, for contrasting bias tape or store-bought bias tape (optional)

> You may be able to squeeze out the bias tapes if the fabric is wider than 44 inches, but if not, you can definitely get the bias tape from 1¼ yards of total fabric. Note: If you want to make either the kimono top or the bloomers but not both, ½ yard is sufficient for each.

FABRIC RECOMMENDATIONS

Since these are sized for newborns, seek out soft, breathable fabric like cotton, double-gauze, and linen. Make sure to prep the fabric by washing, drying, and pressing.

FINISHED DIMENSIONS

KIMONO TOP
Sleeve to sleeve: 14½ inches
Chest: 16 inches
Length: 10½ inches

BLOOMERS
Waist: 15 inches
Hips: 20 inches
Height: 7 inches
Leg openings: 7½ inches

FABRIC PIECES: Kimono Top: Front (2), Back (1), Tie (3); Bloomers: Pant (2)

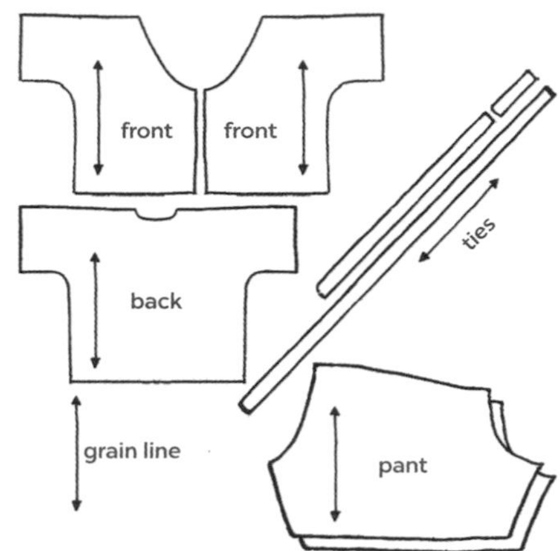

CONSTRUCTION STEPS FOR THE KIMONO TOP

1. Let's start with the Kimono Top. (If you want to make the bloomers out of the same fabric, draft the Bloomers pattern piece before cutting out and constructing the kimono top.) For the kimono top back, measure out a 12-by-8-inch rectangle. On the right vertical line, measure 4½ inches from the top. Draw a perpendicular 3-inch line extending to the left. This is the underarm portion of the sleeve.

   Measure 3 inches from the bottom right corner of the rectangle toward the left on the horizontal line. Draw a perpendicular line up that connects this point to where the underarm ends above. Now round out the underarm corner just a touch and create the neckline opening.

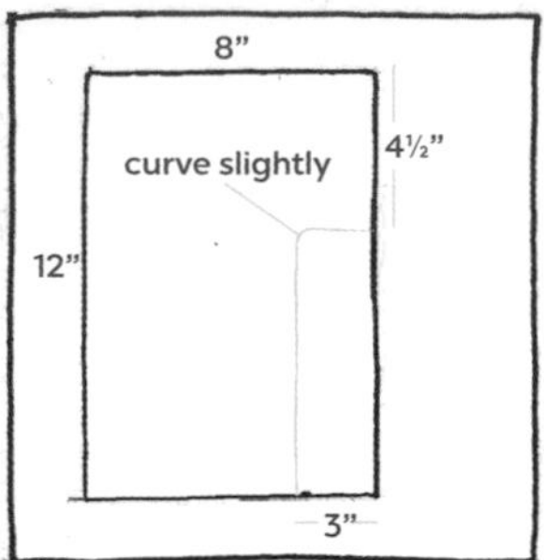

For the back neckline, from the upper left corner, measure 1½ inches to the right and make a mark. From the same corner, measure ¾ inch down and make a mark. Draw a 1½-by-¾-inch rectangle within the upper left corner. Create the back neckline by sketching a curve between the two marks. IMPORTANT: Make sure the line at the base of the neck is initially perpendicular to avoid weird pointy edges or a funky curve. Cut it out and label it "Kimono Top—BACK—cut 1 on fold."

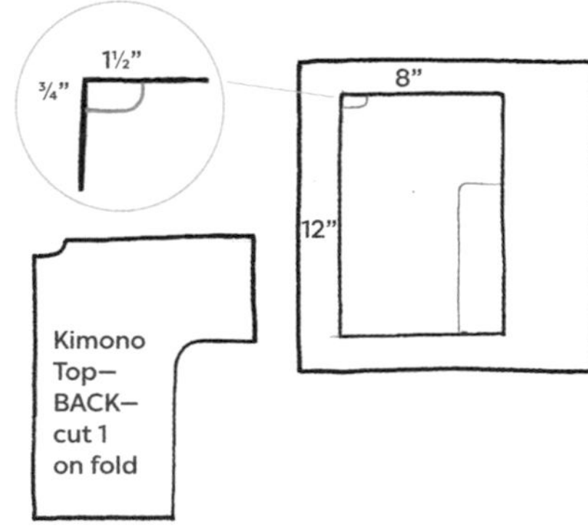

2 For the kimono top front, place your freshly created kimono top back pattern onto another piece of pattern paper. This pattern piece will be a bit bigger, so give yourself a few extra inches to the left of the top back pattern piece. Trace the pattern piece. Extend the bottom of the pattern piece to the left by 3 inches. Draw a 7-inch perpendicular, vertical line from the bottom of this line. From the neckline point to the top of the 7-inch line, draw a smooth curve, making sure to form a right angle where the curve meets at the top of the 7-inch line (a.k.a. the front flap corner). To indicate where the ties and elastic will be attached, mark ¾ inch down from the armpit. Cut out the pattern piece and label it "Kimono Top—FRONT—cut 2." Congrats! You've finished the hard part.

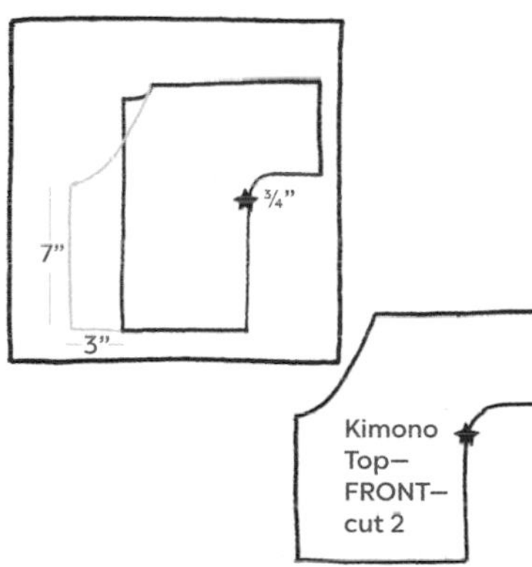

3 If making the bloomers, draft the bloomers pattern piece at this point, especially if you want to cut it out of the same fabric as the top. Directions are on page 187. If you are just making the kimono, proceed to the next step.

4 Fold your fabric in half selvage to selvage with the WRONG side facing out, and trace your beautifully drafted pattern pieces. (If you are using a print and are particular about print placement, fold the fabric with RIGHT side facing out.) Arrange the pieces to fit, keeping in mind that you will need some diagonal space if you choose to use the same fabric for the bias tape. (You will need two bias tapes, but this will be measured directly onto the fabric, so we'll worry about that a little later.)

If you are cutting out the bloomers from the same fabric, place the pattern piece on the fabric at this time too. Otherwise, cut out the bias tape from contrasting fabric or use store-bought tape.

Below is my suggested layout. Pin or use weights to hold the pattern pieces in place. With a marking tool, trace the pattern pieces, making sure to mark the tie placement on the front. Cut out pieces.

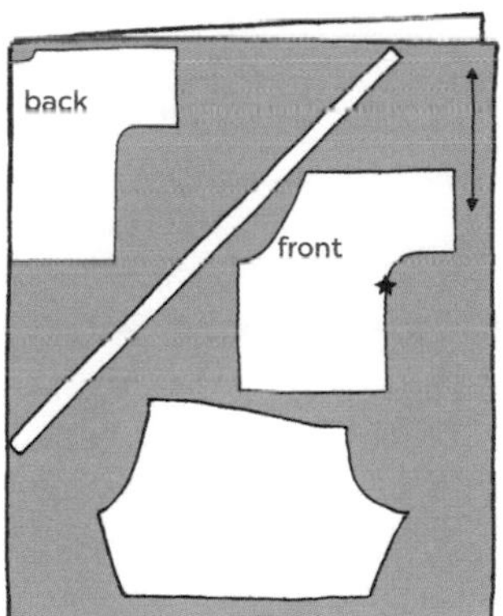

5 I'm prone to forgetting which side is which, so I like to make an *L* with my marking tool on the WRONG side of the left piece. Also, if it's hard to tell which side of the fabric is the WRONG side, I quickly mark *X*s on the WRONG side of all of the other pattern pieces.

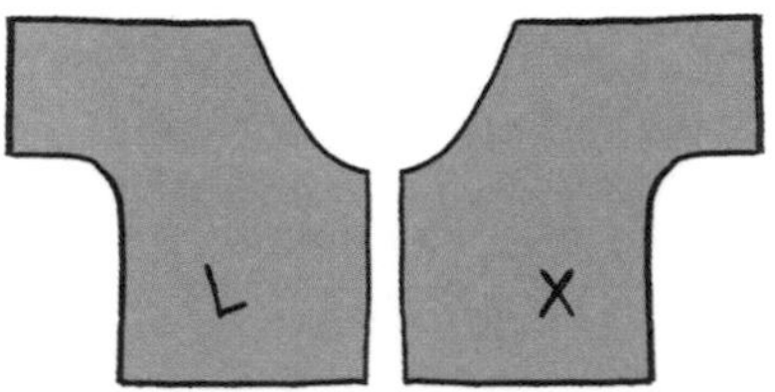

Cut your 1½-inch wide bias tape into two strips: (long) 33 inches and (short) 16½ inches.

The shorter strip will be cut into two strips in the next step, so if you are using store-bought 1½-inch wide bias tape, cut it into three strips:

- 33 inches
- 13 inches
- 3½ inches

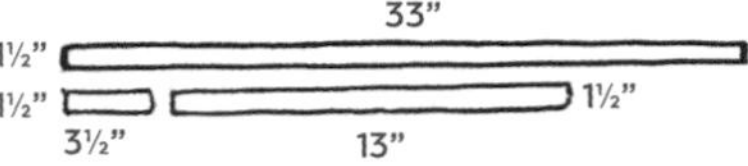

6 When making the bias tapes, a bias tape maker is useful, but you can simply press the tape in half, toward the WRONG side, then press the upper and lower edges toward the center crease (also toward the WRONG side). Your bias tape should measure 1½ inches wide.

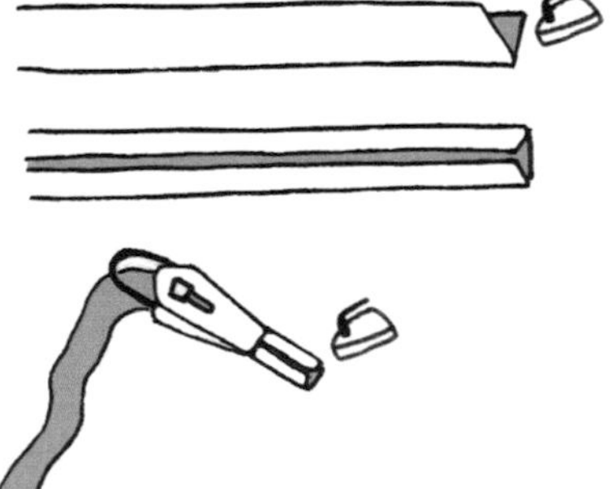

7 Sew the 16½-inch long tie. Open the bias tape, fold one end toward the WRONG side by ¼ inch, fold back up and edgestitch the tie. Once you've sewn the entire tie, measure 3½ inches from the raw end of the tie and cut. This will be the piece to which you'll be attaching the snap later.

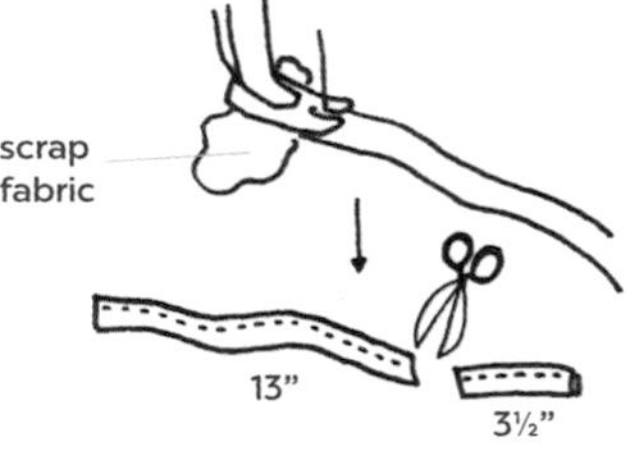

TIP: If you have trouble sewing the thin tie, first fold up a piece of scrap fabric and stitch the scrap. When the scrap just passes the foot, place the beginning of the folded end of the tie under the foot and pull on the scrap to help ease the tie along.

8 Traditionally, a kimono top with the left flap on top is for boys and the reverse is for girls, but it doesn't change its functionality either way. The following instructions are for the left flap to be on top. Zigzag stitch one end of the shortest tie (3½-inch length). Pin the non-zigzag-stitched, raw end to the WRONG side of the left front piece at the tie mark. Baste about ¼ inch from the edge.

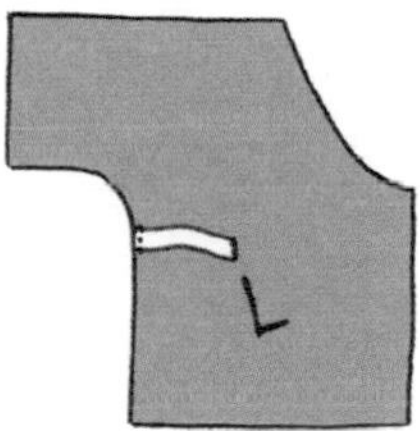

9 Pin the 13½-inch-length tie at the tie mark on the RIGHT side of the right front piece with the raw edges lined up. Baste about ¼ inch from the edge.

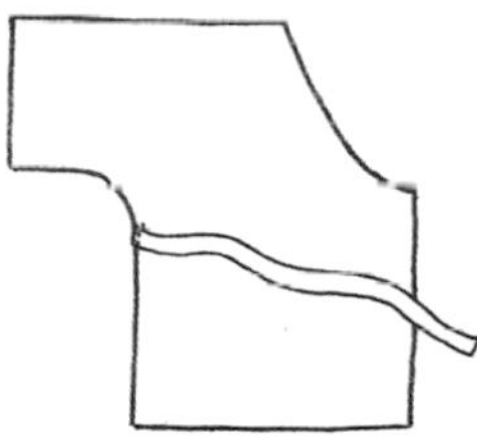

10 With the RIGHT sides facing, pin the front pieces to the back piece at the shoulders, and sew a ⅜-inch seam from the edge. Finish the raw edges with a zigzag or overlock stitch. Press the seam allowance toward the back piece.

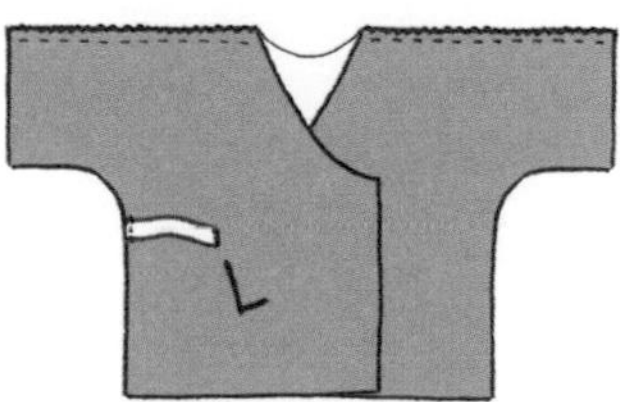

11 With the RIGHT sides still facing, pin and sew the sides ⅜ inch from the edge, sandwiching the longer tie that is basted onto the RIGHT side of right front piece—make sure the tie doesn't get tangled and accidentally sewn into other parts of the side seam. I advise back-stitching several times to secure the ties really well. Clip the underarm curves, then finish the raw edges with a zigzag or overlock stitch. Press the seam allowances toward the back piece.

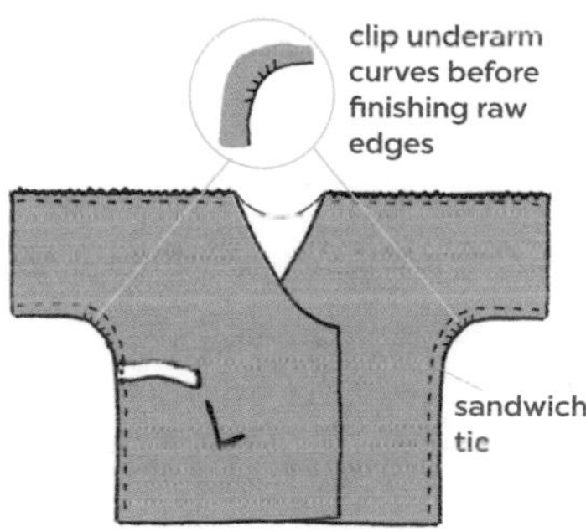

12 Fold the edge of one sleeve toward the WRONG side by ⅜ inch and press. Repeat, and edgestitch. Repeat for the other sleeve.

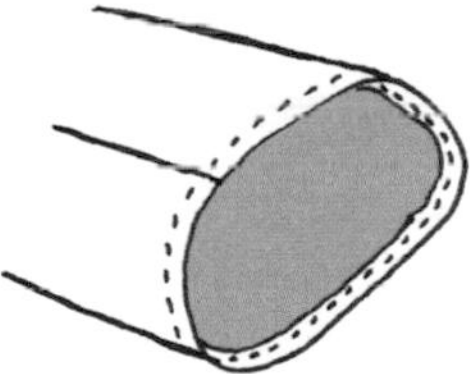

13 Fold the flap edge of the front piece toward the WRONG side by ¼ inch and press. Repeat and edgestitch. Repeat for the other flap.

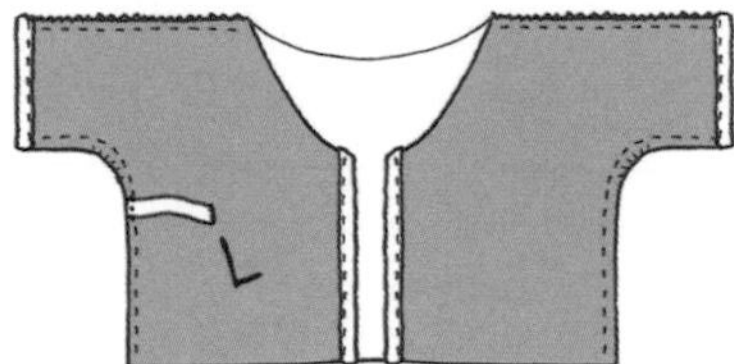

14 Fold the hem toward the WRONG side by ⅜ inch and press. Repeat and edgestitch.

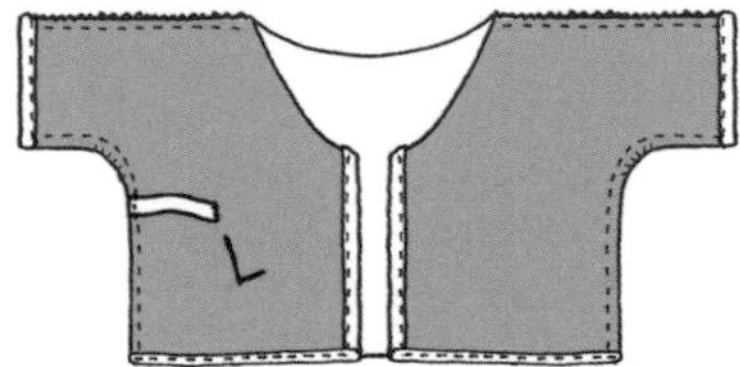

15 Open up your long bias tape and fold one short end toward the WRONG side by ⅜ inch and press. Starting at the corner of the right flap of the front piece, pin the bias tape to the WRONG side of the kimono top all along the top, leaving a tail of the tie hanging off the corner of the left flap.

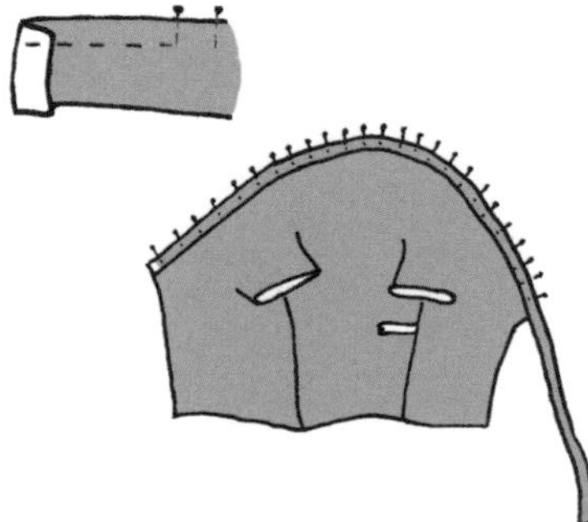

Turn the garment RIGHT side out and check the lengths of the ties by tying them into a bow. (For some reason, depending on the fabric I used, the length of the ties can be dramatically different.) If needed, cut off any excess from the pinned tie to even it out with the shorter tie when formed into a bow. Fold the hanging raw edge of the tie toward the WRONG side by ¼ inch and press. Sew bias tape onto the top about ¼ inch from edge. (I follow the crease line formed when I first created the bias tape.)

16 Trim the seam allowance to about ⅛ inch up to the corner of the left flap. Fold over the bias tape toward the RIGHT side of the kimono top so that the raw edges are neatly enclosed (remember to press the short edge of the hanging tie to the WRONG side to hide the raw edge). Edgestitch.

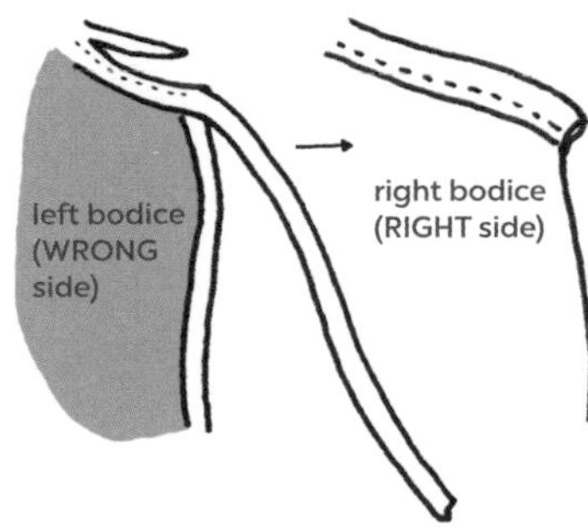

17 Sew on the snaps. Make sure that the short tie reaches the corner of the right flap. Fold the zigzag edge of the short tie about ½ inch (or the appropriate amount to just overlap with that corner) and hand-stitch. Add snaps by attaching the male (stud) snap on the bodice and the female (socket) snap on the tie so the baby is never being prodded by the pointy part of the snap. Now you're all set!

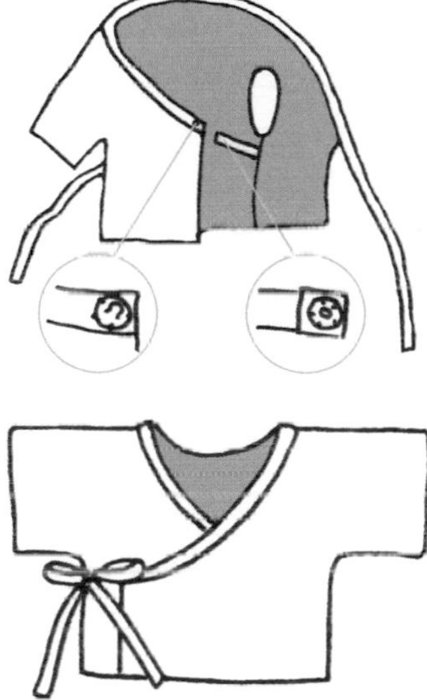

18 Next, make the bloomers. If you cut out the bloomers from the same fabric as the top, skip to step 5.

CONSTRUCTION STEPS FOR THE BLOOMERS

1 Trace a 10-by-16-inch rectangle onto the tracing paper. Then draw three vertical lines from the left: 3 inches, 8 inches, and 13 inches. On both of the two short sides, mark 4 inches from the bottom. On the bottom base of the rectangle, from the left side, mark 2 inches and 14 inches.

Now you'll make a few marks on the vertical lines. On the 3-inch vertical line, mark the top edge. On the 8-inch vertical line, measure 1 inch from the top and make a mark. On the 13-inch vertical line, measure 2 inches and make a mark.

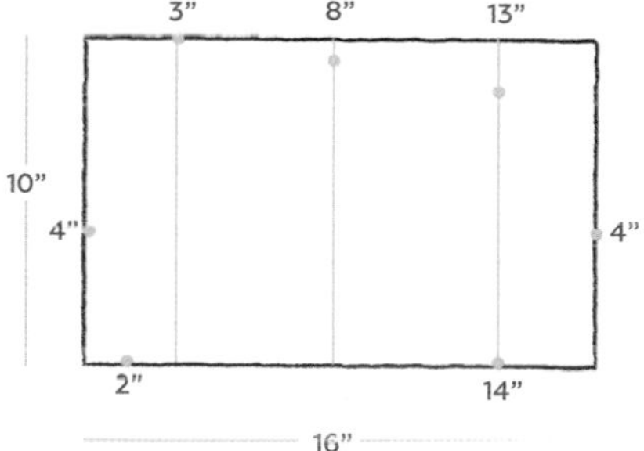

2 Connect the dots, as pictured. Don't worry too much about the curves—you just want to make sure that the pointed ends (the 4-inch marks on the sides) are at right angles so they match up nicely.

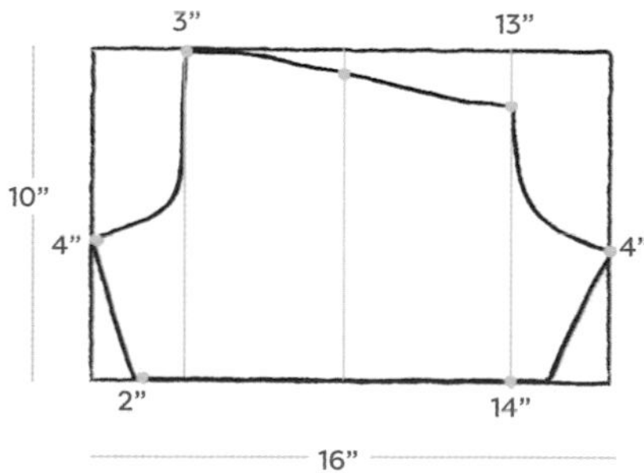

3. Cut out the shape and there you have it: a bloomers pattern piece! Label it "Bloomers—cut 2."

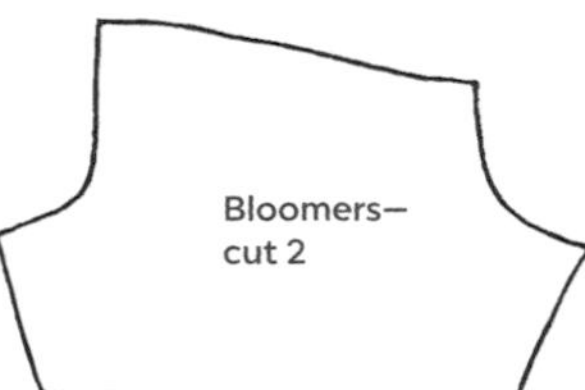

4. With the RIGHT sides facing, fold your fabric in half and place the pattern piece on top. Cut two pieces.

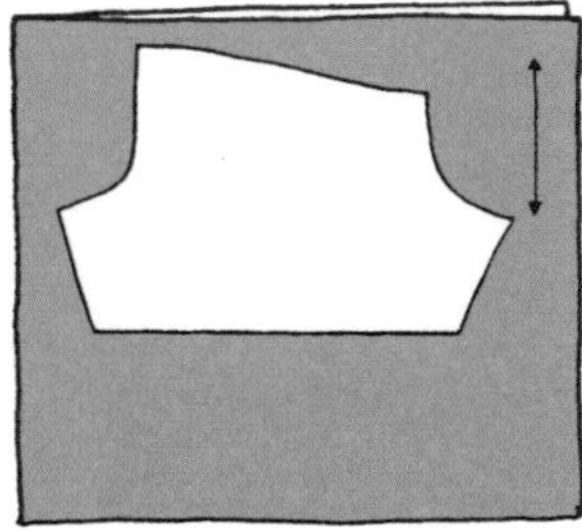

5. With the RIGHT sides facing, pin one leg piece and sew the inseam with a ⅜-inch seam allowance. Finish the raw edges with a zigzag or overlock stitch. Repeat for other leg piece. Press the seam allowance toward the same side for both legs.

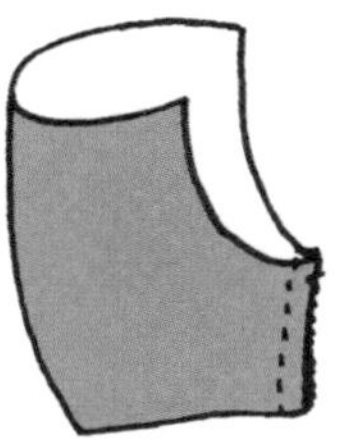

6. Turn one leg RIGHT side out and insert into other leg that has the WRONG side facing out, matching up the curve of the rise. The legs should be facing RIGHT sides together. Sew along the curve with a ⅜-inch seam allowance. To reduce bulk, the inseam seam allowance for each leg should be pointing in opposite directions. Finish the raw edges with a zigzag or overlock stitch. Press.

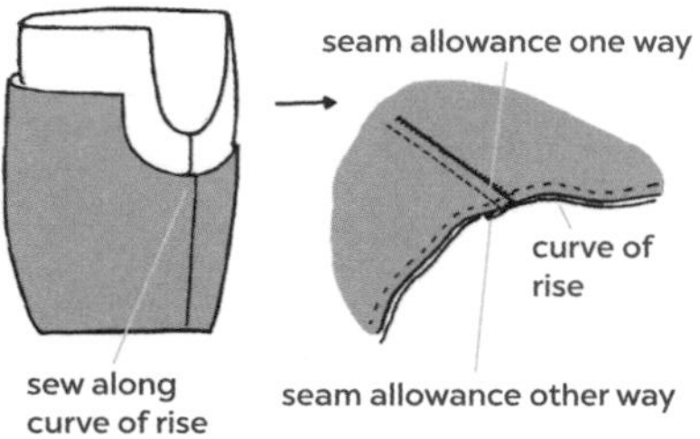

7. To create the waistband, fold the top edge toward the WRONG side by ¼ inch, and press. Then another fold ½ inch toward the WRONG side, and press. Edgestitch, leaving an opening of about 1½ inches at the back center seam.

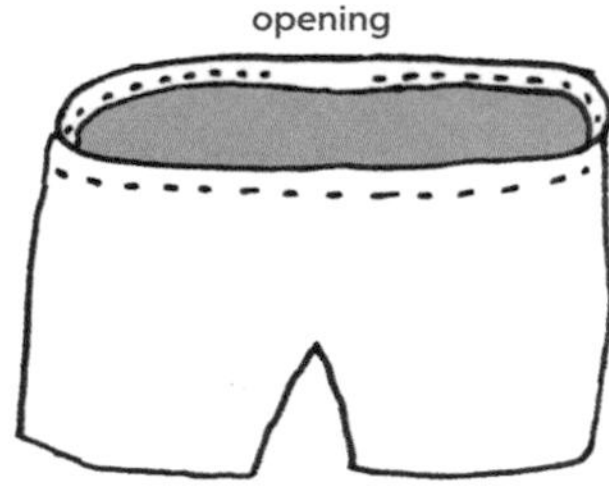

When folding and pressing to create the waistband casing, you may find that some parts are curved in such a way that makes it trickier to keep the seam allowance the same width throughout and might require a slight stretching of the fabric as you press.

8 To create the elastic casings for the legs, fold the bottom edge of one leg opening toward the WRONG side by ¼ inch, and press. Fold another ⅜ inch toward the WRONG side, and press. Edgestitch, leaving an opening of about 1½ inches on the inseam side. Repeat for the other leg opening.

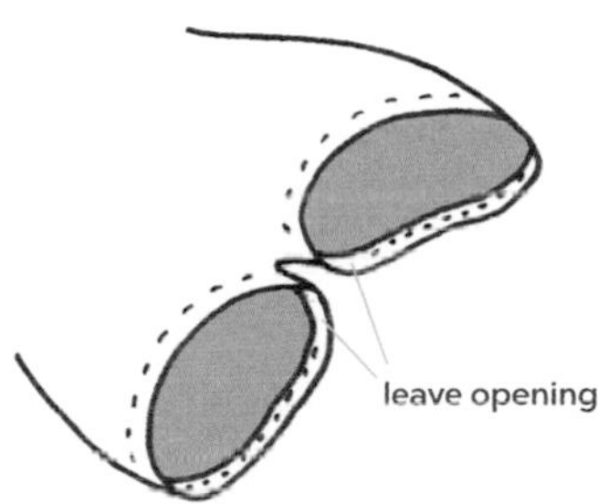

9 Thread the 16-inch length of ⅜-inch elastic through the waistband casing. Use a small bodkin for one end and attach a safety pin at the other end to avoid losing the elastic inside the casing. Check that the elastic isn't twisted or stretched, then overlap the elastic ends about ½ inch and sew together with a zigzag stitch. Then stitch the opening closed OR fold a piece of ribbon with WRONG sides together, insert it into the opening so that it looks like a tag, and stitch closed. It's a good idea to stretch the casing as you sew since the elastic will cause the casing to gather and bunch up.

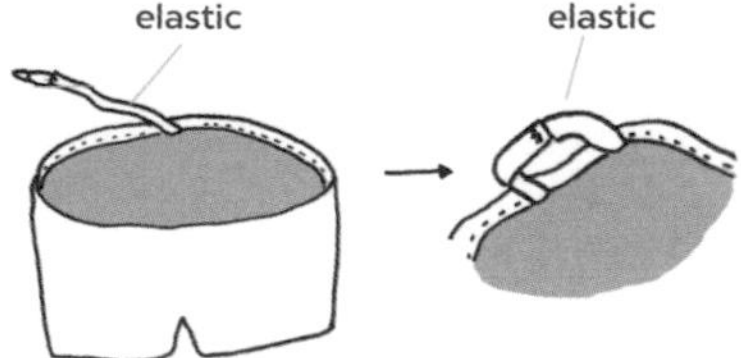

10 Cut the 16-inch length of ⅛-inch elastic in half, yielding two 8-inch pieces. Thread one length of elastic through each leg casing, following the same guidelines as the waistband: check for smoothness within the casing and stitch the ends together. For the thinner ⅛-inch elastic, it may be difficult to overlap, so simply line them up side-by-side or on top of each other if possible and sew with a zigzag stitch a few times. Stitch the inseam openings closed, stretching the casing as you sew.

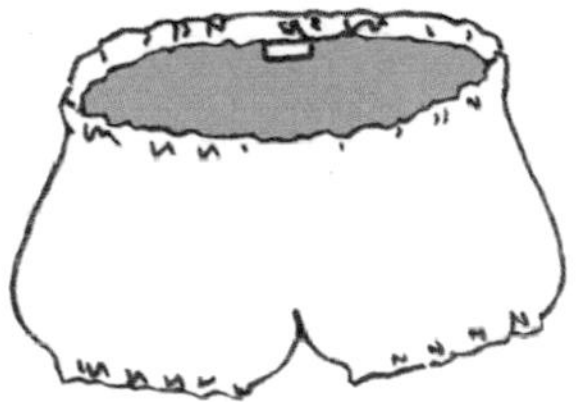

11 Coo with delight as a diapered darling kicks up his/her legs in these fashionable bloomers!

COLOR-BLOCK ZIP POUCH

THE OTHER DAY I WANDERED into a fancy boutique and my jaw hung open at the price tag of a simple handmade zip pouch—and it wasn't even lined! I wanted to rush home and become a zip pouch mogul, but these are much more rewarding to give as gifts. I end up using them all the time myself to hold pens and pencils and the assorted odds and ends that accumulate in my purse. I believe few things are as utilitarian as a zip pouch, making it a quick and almost fail-safe holiday gift option. As with all sewing projects, changing up the fabric completely transforms the look, and I highly encourage experimentation, not only with fabric choice but with sizing as well. I've made tall ones, wide ones, and even teeny tiny ones (which my daughter loved). For this zip pouch, I added a small color-block feature for kicks. You could dress up the pouch by adding a suede or embroidered element perhaps. Fully-lined, functional, and attractive, this is my go-to present time and time again! Photo on pages 60 and 61.

SUPPLIES + MATERIALS

½ yard woven fabric, for the pouch

½ yard woven fabric, for the lining

¼ yard contrasting woven fabric, for the color-block triangle

10-inch zipper (longer is OK)

Coordinating thread

Double-sided tape or Wonder clips (optional)

FABRIC RECOMMENDATIONS

The usual suspects: cotton, linen, canvas. Test out a variety of different materials for the color-block to give it some glam or spunk or some unique factor. Make sure to prep woven fabrics such as cotton and linen by washing, drying, and pressing.

Use suede, leather, or leatherlike fabric for the color-block contrasting fabric. No need to wash suede or leather, although you might want to press them with a press cloth on a low heat setting.

FINISHED DIMENSIONS

9 inches wide by 6¼ inches high

FABRIC PIECES: Pouch (2), Lining (2), Color-Block Triangle (1)

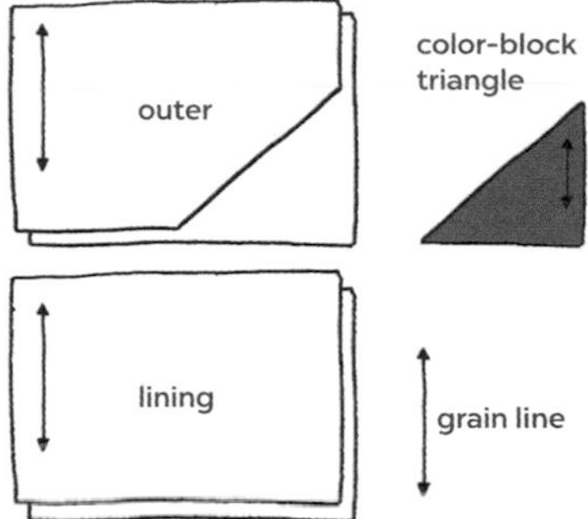

CONSTRUCTION STEPS

1. Cut two 10-by-7-inch pieces from the main fabric and two from the lining fabric.

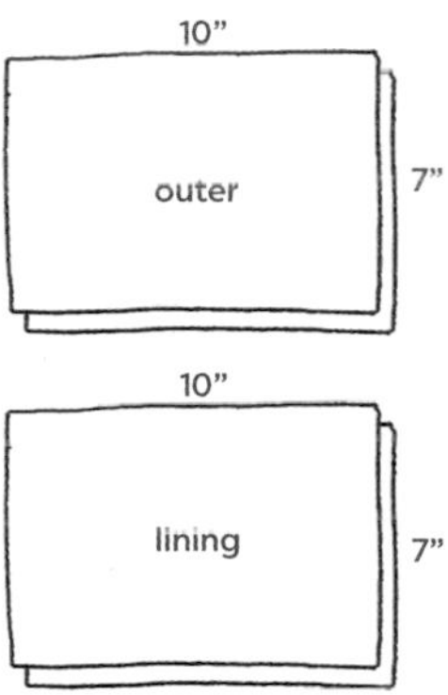

2. Determine the size of your triangular color-block piece. Cut it from one of the main pieces. You will use this triangle to create the triangle on the contrasting fabric.

3. Place the WRONG side of the triangle on the RIGHT side of the contrasting fabric. Measure a $\frac{3}{8}$-inch seam allowance all around, mark it on the fabric, and cut out the color-block piece from the contrasting fabric. Tip: Mark the side of the triangle that will be attached to the corresponding outer piece (see star below).

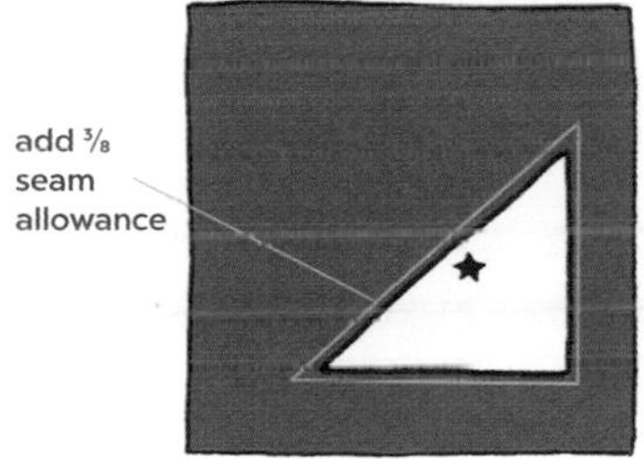

4 With the RIGHT sides facing, sew the color-block piece to the main fabric from which you cut the triangle with a ⅜-inch seam allowance. Press the seam allowance open and topstitch along the diagonal line, if desired. You may need to trim a bit of the color-block piece to make the edges flush.

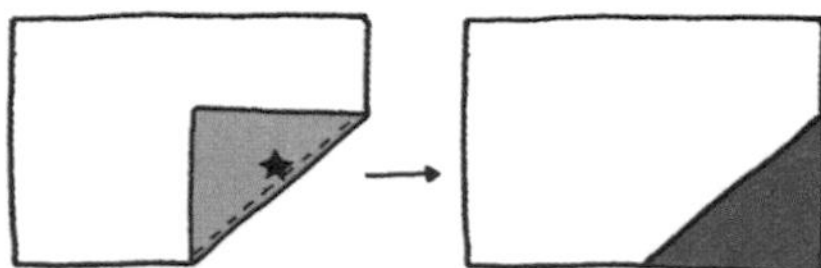

5 Place the RIGHT side of the zipper facing the RIGHT side of one of the outer pieces; then place one of the lining pieces WRONG side facing up, sandwiching the body of the zipper. I like to hand-baste the zipper in place first since, for me, this absolutely prevents the shifting of the fabric and zipper. But you can use pins, wonder clips, or double-sided tape to hold it in place as well. Switch to your zipper foot and sew about ¼ inch from outer edge of the zipper tape. It helps to start with the zipper unzipped halfway, and after a few inches, with the needle still in the fabric, I close the zipper and continue sewing the rest of the length of the pouch. Repeat with the other main and lining fabrics with the other side of the zipper.

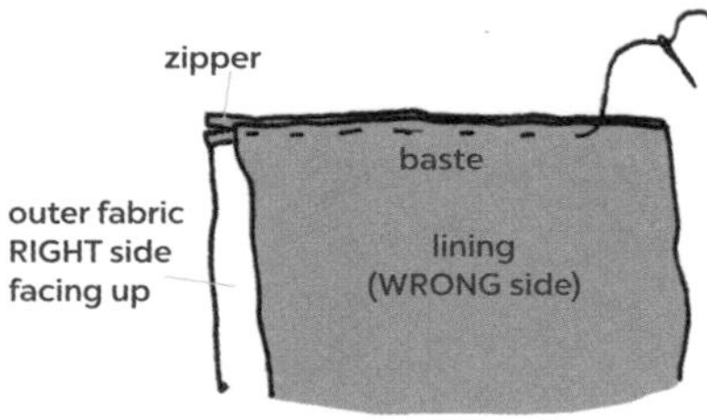

6 With the zipper in the middle and open half way (VERY IMPORTANT), position the pouch so that the RIGHT sides of the main fabric are facing together on one side and the RIGHT sides of the lining pieces are facing together on the other side. The zipper teeth should be folded up and away from outer fabric. Think of it like a taco: the right side of the zipper teeth are inside the taco, and the zipper tape helps form the taco shell.

Starting a couple of inches to the side of the center on the bottom of the lining, sew all the way around with a ½-inch seam allowance, slowing down as you get close to the zipper teeth and stitching as close as you can to the teeth without going over them. I've broken many a needle during this step, so be very careful! End your stitching a couple inches away from the other side of the center on the bottom of the lining, leaving an opening.

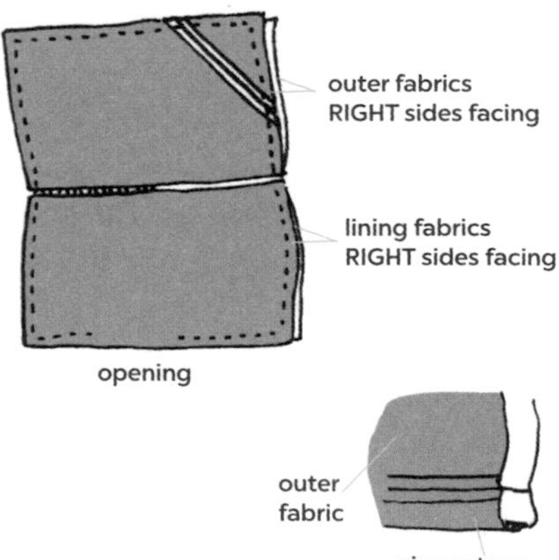

7 Clip the corners and trim the seams down to ¼ inch.

8 Pull the outer fabric through the half-open zipper and the opening in the lining, and turn the pouch RIGHT side out. Poke out the corners with a point turner. Be careful not to poke holes through the seam. Press.

9 Slip stitch the lining opening closed. Alternatively, you could machine stitch all the way across the bottom of the lining, push it back into the pouch, and no one will be the wiser!

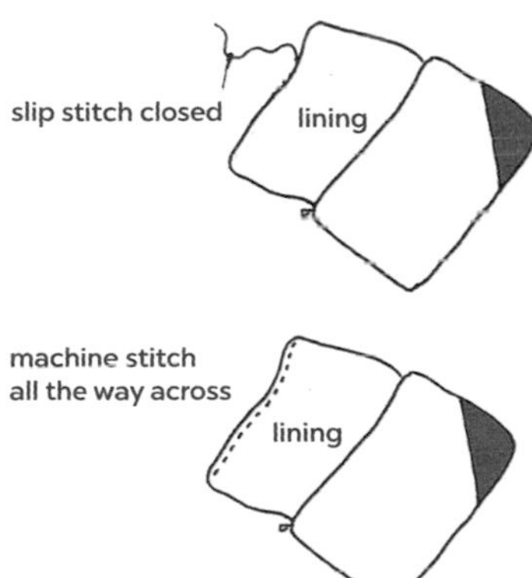

10 Give the pouch one final press, then pat yourself on the back because you just saved some pretty pennies and will make someone's day with this über-useful and dashing present!

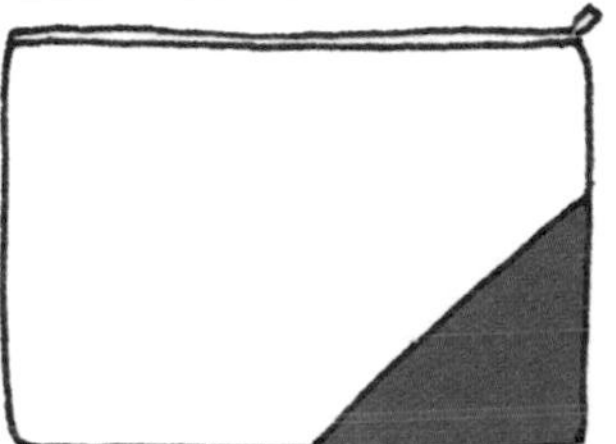

INFINITY SCARF

I LOVE A GOOD SCARF—AND whoever invented the infinity design deserves a medal for its pure genius. Here in the Pacific Northwest, the weather stays fairly chilly up until June. I'm a native Californian and had no idea just how frigid it could be. Way back in March 2002, I drove from San Francisco to Seattle in a yellow Penske moving truck with my then-boyfriend (now husband). He'd convinced me to uproot my whole life although I had wanted desperately to stay in San Fran. Two days after our arrival, I started my new job, woefully underdressed. As I waited for the bus to take me to the Eastside, I felt the icy kisses of big, fluffy snowflakes. They flurried and piled on my shoulders and around my neck and my predominant thought was, *I've made a huge mistake. HUGE.* Perhaps a pretty handmade scarf would have alleviated the situation. Fortunately, I now savor living here, and I've discovered that the calm grayness of Seattle suits my temperament. Even though the scarf instructions are included in the Spring section, switching up the fabric to a knit jersey or a light wool will make it fall and winter worthy too. These are phenomenally easy to make, and once you get in the groove, you could easily pump out one in roughly twenty minutes. To add a bit of challenge and embellishment, try some Sashiko stitching here and there. Photos on pages 72 and 73.

SUPPLIES + MATERIALS

1½ yards 45-inch-wide fabric or 1 yard 60-inch or wider fabric

Coordinating thread

Sashiko or extra long needles (optional)

Sashiko thread or embroidery thread (the kind that isn't shiny) (optional)

FABRIC RECOMMENDATIONS

Lightweight fabrics such as cotton voile, cotton lawn, polyester, rayon, and linen work best for a spring scarf. Knit jersey is a good option too. If you plan on adding embroidery, choose a fabric that isn't too sheer. Also, the tighter the weave, the better; cotton is usually the best option for embroidery. Make sure to prep the fabric by washing, drying, and pressing.

FINISHED DIMENSIONS

24 inches wide by 59 inches around

FABRIC PIECES: Scarf (1) or, if your fabric doesn't have enough width (2)

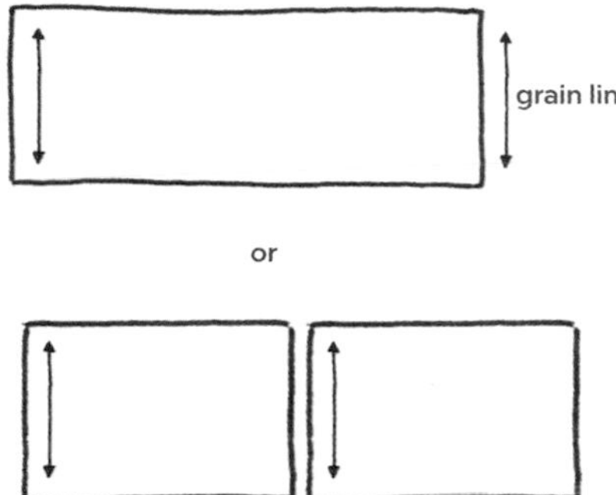

In general, a 60-inch scarf will loop around the neck twice, and an 80-inch loops around three times. However, fabric comes in various widths, and depending on the size of the fabric you'll be using, you can maximize the width and just cut from selvage to selvage. I've made 40-inch (great for children—I kept the same height of 25 inches) to 90-inch ones, and they've all been fantastic. Varying the height will also give the scarf different looks. Try a few different sizes and see what feels right for you, keeping in mind that you will lose two inches to the seam allowances. If all these choices feel overwhelming, just stick to 25 inches high and 60 inches long as a starting point.

CONSTRUCTION STEPS

1. If using a 60-inch fabric, cut all the way across the width of the fabric (perpendicular to the selvage) at 25 inches high.

If your fabric isn't wide enough for a single scarf pattern piece, cut two 25-by-31½-inch rectangles. Sew the short ends together ½ inch from the edge.

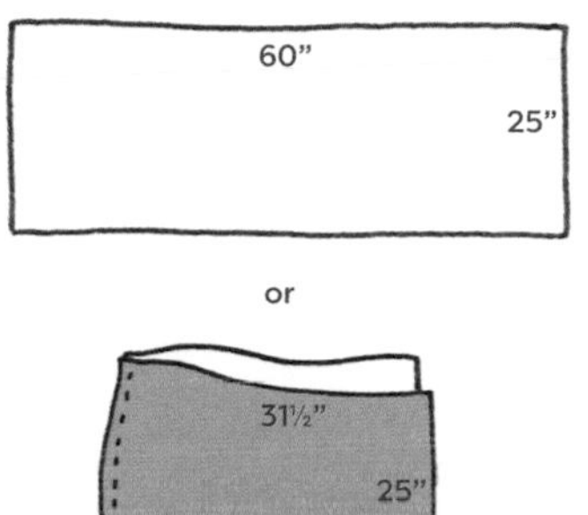

2. Skip this step if you are not embroidering your scarf. However, if you would like to add Sashiko stitches, mark the design on the RIGHT side of the fabric with your preferred marking tool—first testing it to make sure it comes out easily.

Using either a Sashiko or extra long needle with cotton thread, follow the marked design using running stitches. See The Mini Sashiko Primer (page 109) for design inspirations and a quick how-to. Personally, I enjoy adding a few subtle straight running stitches in random places on a solid-colored fabric to give it a little texture and a design element.

In this example, I placed the designs in a way that would overlap each other, assuming a 60-inch fabric so that the rows of stitching would cross in the front. Try looping the fabric around your neck to figure out where you want the designs to be.

3. With the RIGHT sides facing, sew a ⅜-inch seam allowance along the long edge. If you're using silk or a sheer fabric and you want to encase the raw edge so the fraying won't show through as much, create a French seam (see Handy Terms + Techniques, page 100). Press the seam to one side.

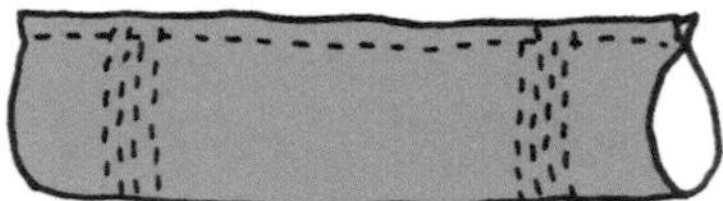

4. With the WRONG side still facing out, start to turn the scarf right side out, but stop when the two end openings line up with RIGHT sides together. Make sure that the scarf doesn't get twisted during this step (although you could also deliberately twist it if you like that look). Pin and sew a ½-inch seam allowance from the raw edges, making sure to leave about a 4-inch opening.

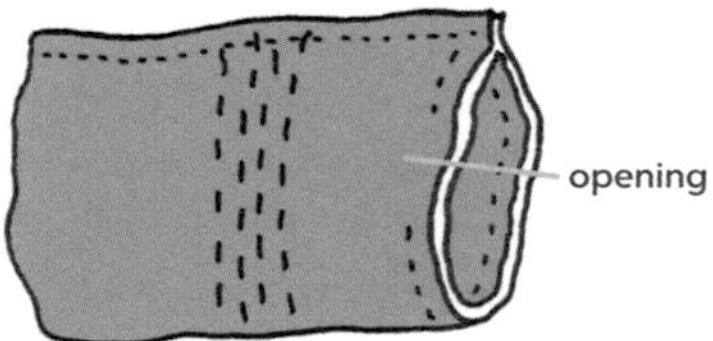

5. Turn the scarf RIGHT side out by pulling out the fabric through the opening.

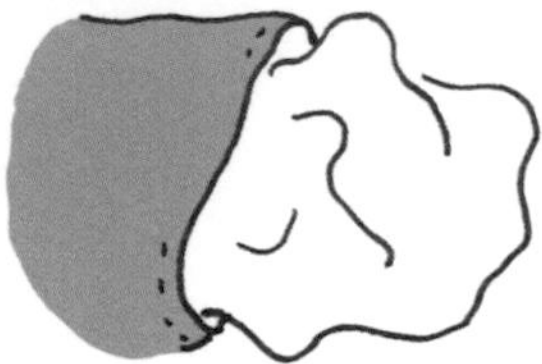

6. Slip stitch the opening closed, press, and wear!

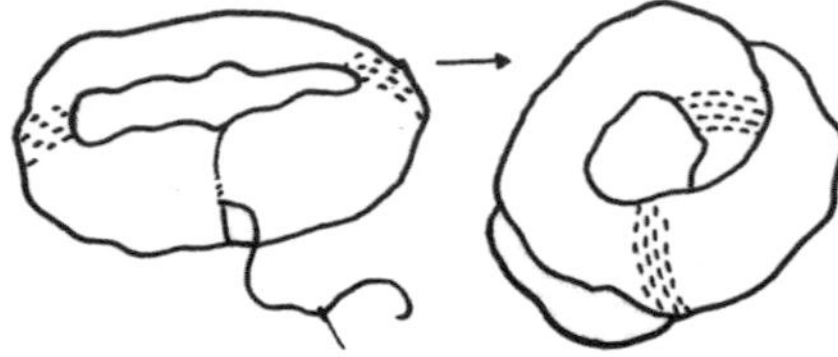

EVERYTHING BUCKET

THERE'S SOMETHING ABOUT CONTAINERS THAT makes my heart flutter. My husband has complained about my tendency to accumulate a massive number of baskets and fabric boxes and miscellaneous holders of things. I'm of the opinion that one can never have too many containers, and I have yet to be proven wrong. After I finished making these buckets, and placed them in the entryway, my husband spotted them and asked (in a horrified tone), "Did you buy more baskets? These look expensive!" Shhhh . . . they cost far, far less than the fancy ones I love. They also require minimal effort to stitch up, especially if you opt to omit the handles and the color-blocking.

What makes this project extremely adaptable is that you can create all manner of fabric buckets in any size imaginable, with or without handles, and all you need is a simple formula to figure out the dimensions. Photos on pages 74 and 75.

SUPPLIES + MATERIALS

1 yard woven fabric, for the bucket

1 yard woven fabric, for the base

1 yard woven fabric, for the lining

Decor-weight interfacing (optional)

Coordinating thread

Screw-on metal hardware (I used ¼ inch screws) (optional)

FABRIC RECOMMENDATIONS

Sturdy fabrics like duck canvas, burlap, jute, and faux leather work best for these buckets. Duck canvas is fantastic as a lining too, although the one I used had an overpowering smell. A word of caution if you decide to use burlap or jute: the fibers get everywhere. I wanted a softer feel for the burlap/jute baskets so I didn't use interfacing. Make sure to prep woven fabrics by washing, drying, and pressing.

FINISHED DIMENSIONS

14-inch-high two-fabric bucket with a 10-inch-diamenter base

FABRIC PIECES: Bucket Upper (1), Bucket Lower (1), Base (1), Bucket Lining (1), Base Lining (1), Strap (2) (optional)

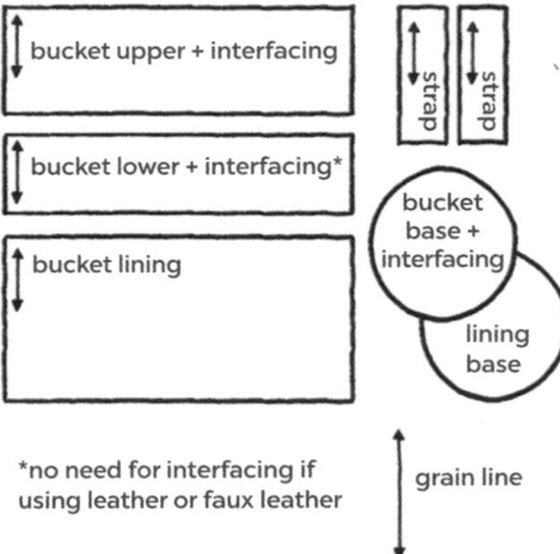

INTERFACING + LINING INFO

I highly recommend using heavier, decor-weight interfacing for this bucket. It will help keep the sides upright and look more professional. The iron-on interfacing I used didn't actually stick that well to the fabric, but you end up stitching it in, so it shouldn't be an issue. But feel free to baste it on if it's a concern. If you want to make the bucket extra sturdy, consider fusing interfacing on both the outer and lining fabrics. If you do, you'll probably need to use a thicker needle, such as a leather or denim needle, to sew it all together.

CONSTRUCTION STEPS

1. We'll start with a little math that's not too daunting. Let's use a ½-inch seam allowance throughout and tackle these first two measurements: circular base and bucket width (a.k.a. circumference). Be sure to jot them down once you've figured them out:

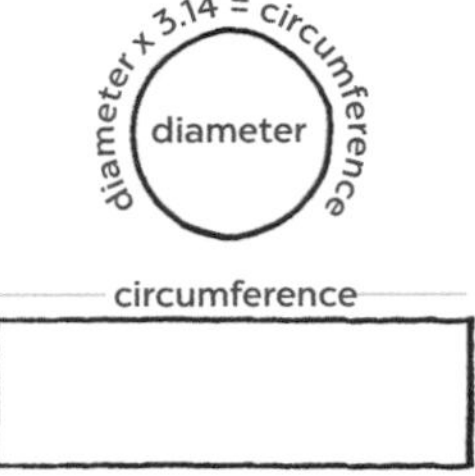

Circular Base
It can be as small or as big as you want! I made mine 10 inches because it was a nice even number. It will be 1 inch smaller after it's sewn because of the seam allowance. So if you want to end up with a 10-inch base, you'll cut out an 11-inch-wide circle.

Bucket Width (Circumference)
We're going back to grade school math here: diameter x π = circumference. Pi (π) is approximately 3.14. With a 10-inch base, it's easy to calculate: 31⅖ inches. But 31⅖ inches is sort of awkward to me, so I rounded it up to 31½ inches. Add the 1-inch seam allowance and the width is 32½ inches. It turned out to be just fine, but a word of caution not to round up too much since attaching the circular base may become more fiddly.

2 Next, calculate the bucket height: For this example, I chose 14 inches for the height. If you just want a plain and simple bucket without color-blocking, simply add 1 inch to the height. Because I wanted to color-block with canvas and faux leather, I split up my 14 inches this way:

- Canvas = 8 inches high
- Faux leather = 6 inches high

The fabric will need a ½-inch seam allowance, so 1 inch should be added to the height for each piece. This means 9 inches for the canvas piece and 7 inches for the faux leather piece. Jot down your measurements.

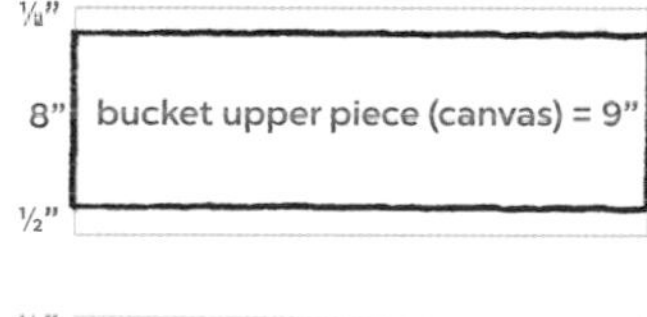

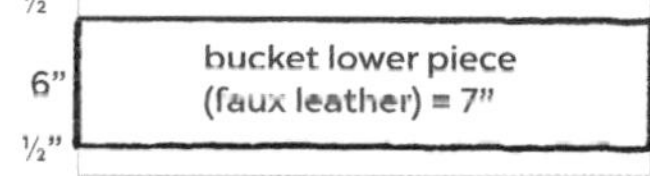

For the lining, just add a 1-inch seam allowance to the 14-inch height, making the lining piece 15 inches high.

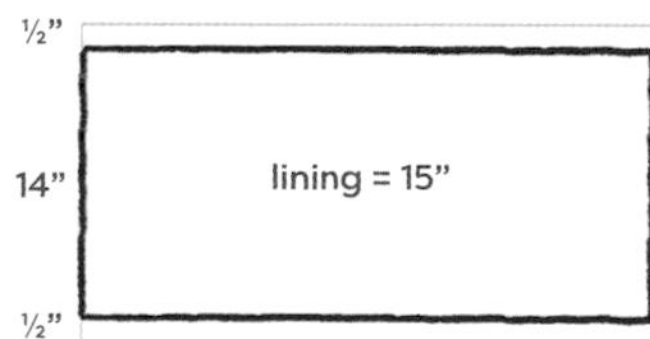

Jot down these height numbers for future reference.

> **TIP:** A good rule of thumb is, the taller the height, the bigger the base should be. This is to avoid the bucket from toppling over.

3 To reduce bulk it's a good idea to make the interfacing ever so slightly smaller than the fabric on which you are fusing—¼ inch smaller should do the trick. In this sample bucket version, the interfacing will be fused onto the upper bucket piece only since the faux leather is thick enough on its own.

A note on the lining: I used the same dimensions as the main fabric, but for a more snugly fitting lining, reduce the lining dimensions by a scant ⅛ inch on all sides for both the rectangular and circular pieces.

4 Finally, calculate the handle strap width and height, if desired. I would recommend two 5-by-10-inch pieces for the handles, but you may want your handles to be shorter, longer, thinner, wider, etc. If you are using leather or similar, there is no need to calculate for a seam allowance, but for woven fabrics like cotton, keep in mind that the handle pieces will be folded in half lengthwise and that you will need a ½-inch seam allowance. As with all the other measurements, jot down the dimensions you choose.

You should now have the measurements for all the pieces you need; I've noted mine here:

- Bucket Upper Piece: 32.5 by 9 inches
- Interfacing for Bucket Upper Piece: 32.25 by 8.75 inches
- Bucket Lower Piece (faux leather so no interfacing): 32.5 by 7 inches
- Circular Base for Bucket and lining: 11 inches
- Bucket Lining: 32.5 by 15 inches
- Handle Strap (if using them): 5 by 10 inches

If you are not using faux leather, you may want to just attach interfacing to the lining piece to make it easier. The only pattern piece you need is for the circular base, since all the other rectangular dimensions can be directly marked on the fabric. A plate is extremely handy for creating the pattern piece. Or, to measure out a pattern for your circular base, you can fold a square piece of paper into quarters and plot out a 5.5-inch radius for your 11-inch circle. Or create a half circle pattern and just flip it over to trace the other side.

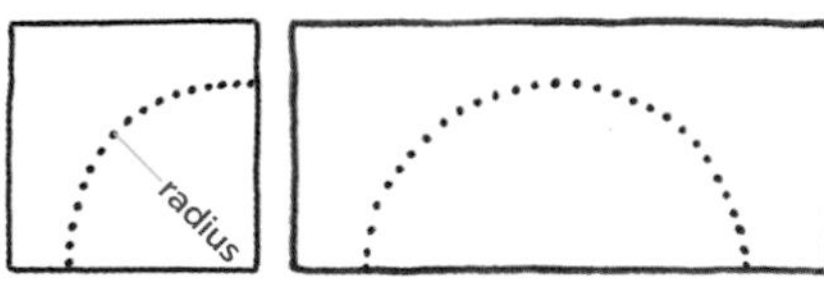

5. Cut out all the pieces from your fabrics. Remember, these are all the pieces you need if you are using color-blocking with a faux leather base and are including handles:

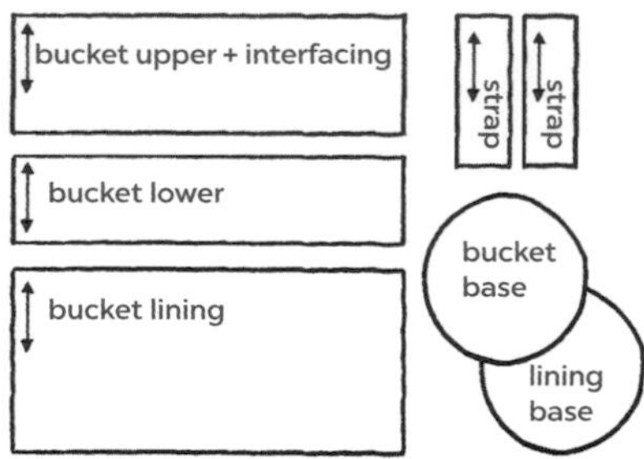

6. To prep, iron-on and/or baste the interfacing to the WRONG side of the main upper piece.

If you are not using faux leather for the base, iron-on and/or baste interfacing to the outer circular base as well.

7. Time to sew! Note: If you don't want to color-block your bucket, skip this step and go to step 8. Sew the bucket upper and lower pieces together RIGHT sides facing, ½ inch from the edge. Press the seam open. (With leather, remember to use clips rather than pins since pins may leave holes.) This is now the main bucket piece.

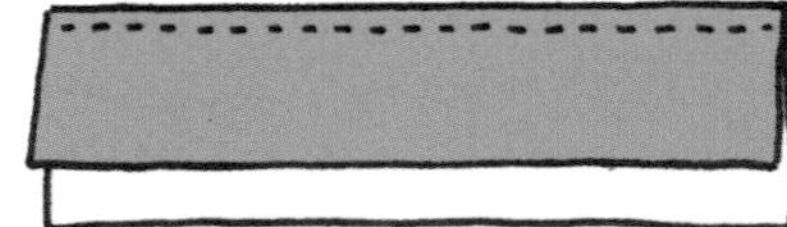

8 With the RIGHT sides facing lengthwise, sew ½ inch along the side edges of the main bucket piece. Press the seam open, again being careful with any leather or leatherlike material.

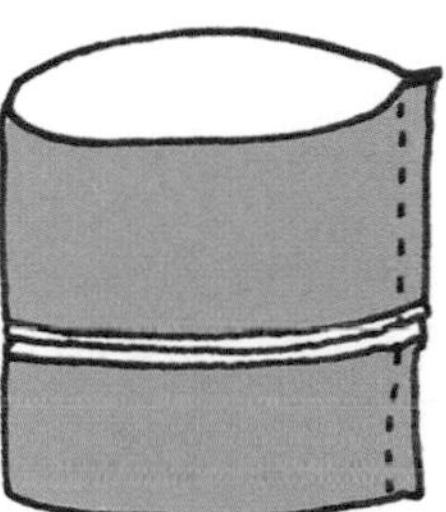

9 Find four equidistant points on both the bucket lower piece and the bucket base, as shown. With the RIGHT sides facing, clip or pin the two pieces together.

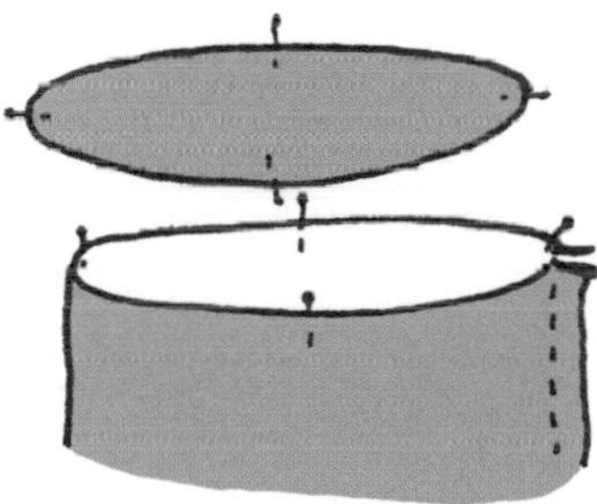

10 Stitch together, ½ inch from the edge, working with the bucket lower piece on the top so you can gently pull and adjust the fabric to keep it lying flat as you sew around the circle. To do this, place the bucket edge under the presser foot with the WRONG side of the bucket piece facing up and the base on the underside.

Leather and faux leather tend to stretch a little, causing the fabrics to shift, so ease up on the foot pedal and stitch slowly.

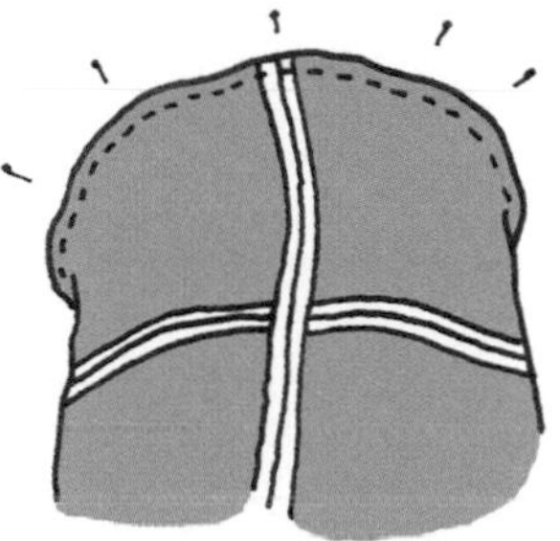

11 Cut notches into the seam allowance, taking care not to snip the seam. This will help prevent puckering and smooth out the curve.

12 Make the handles, if desired. If you are using a leatherlike material, skip to step 13 since there is no need to sew anything. If you are using fabric, such as canvas, fold the handle piece in half lengthwise with the RIGHT sides facing, and stitch ½ inch from the edge. Trim the seam allowance to ¼ inch, turn RIGHT side out, and press. Topstitch three parallel rows. Repeat to make the second handle piece.

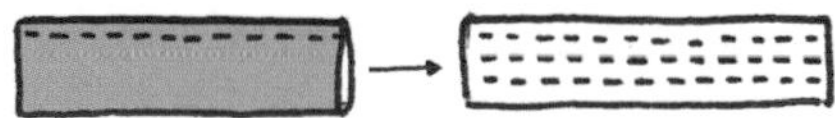

13 Positioning the main bucket piece with the seam in the back, mark the desired handle positions. Pin or clip the straps to the main bucket piece with raw edges matching, RIGHT sides together. Baste the straps ¼ inch from edge.

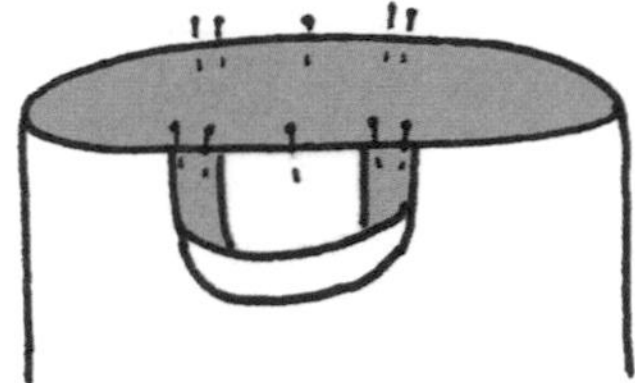

14 Repeat steps 9 to 11 for the through lining and the lining base.

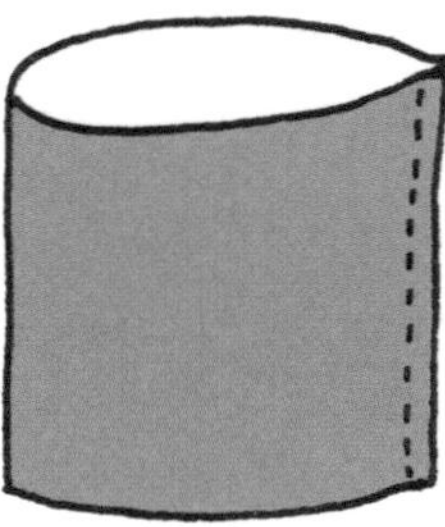

15 Insert the main bucket piece into the lining RIGHT sides together. Stitch ½ inch from the top edge around the perimeter, leaving about a 4-inch opening and slowing down when stitching over the handles to prevent fabric shifting due to the bulk.

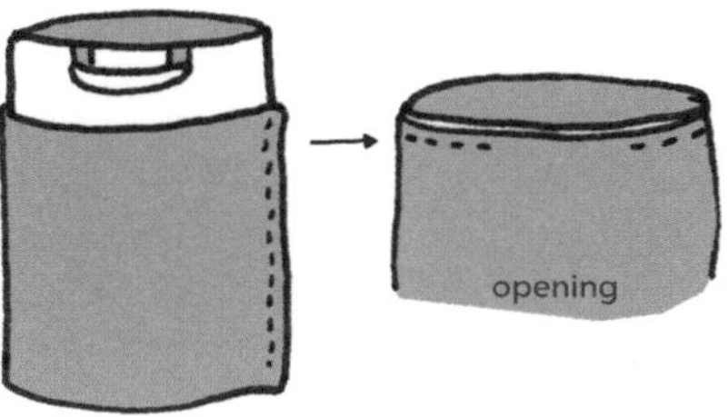

16 Turn the bucket RIGHT side out through the opening, adjusting the lining to fit inside. Press. If you made canvas handles, lift them up and sew the perimeter of the bag ¼ inch from the top to close the opening and finish off the bag. Done!

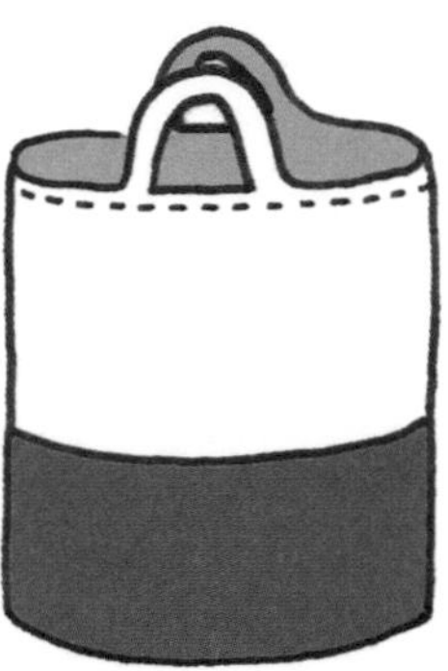

LEATHER HANDLES VARIATION

For leather handles, measure the desired positions first. Using an awl, poke a hole on both ends of the handle (I kept about a ½-inch space from each edge). Poke corresponding holes in the main bucket. (I placed mine about 2 inches from the top.) Make sure the holes go all the way through the main fabric *and* the lining, and are big enough for the screws. Line up the holes, and screw in the rivets. Repeat for the other handle.

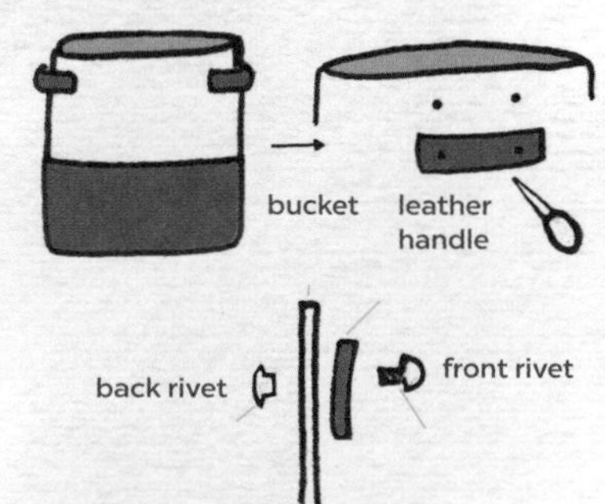

SASHIKO TRIVET

WHEN I LIVED IN JAPAN, friends often invited me into their homes, and invariably they served me tea and a snack. As I sipped my green tea and munched on rice crackers or sweet bean paste treats, like *yokan* or *manju*, I noticed that many of my friends used humble yet beautiful fabric trivets for the teaware, most often made out of patched-together linen or cotton, but I especially admired the Sashiko embroidered ones. To remain faithful to the Sashiko tradition, use white thread on indigo fabric. Don't feel tied to tradition, though—experiment away!

The main thing to keep in mind when creating a trivet is that you need to use natural fibers like cottons, wools, and linens, since most synthetic textiles will burn. And that would defeat the purpose. For that same reason, I recommend wool or bamboo batting instead of the synthetic stuff. Polyester thread should be fine, though. Photo on pages 76 and 77.

SUPPLIES + MATERIALS

½ yard total woven fabric (in at least two different colors)

¼ yard batting

Coordinating thread

Carbon or Chacopy paper to trace design (optional)

Chalk or soluble marker (optional)

Sashiko or long needle (optional)

Sashiko or cotton embroidery floss such as Pearl (optional)

Thimble (optional)

FABRIC RECOMMENDATIONS

For optimal results, stick with fabric made out of natural fibers: sturdy cottons, wools, and linens. Make sure to prep the fabric by washing, drying, and pressing. For the batting, cotton, wool, or bamboo batting works well. Or, if you choose a synthetic heat-resistant batting, be sure to layer a natural fiber batting around it.

FINISHED DIMENSIONS

12 inches wide by 8 inches high

FABRIC PIECES: Front (2), Back (1), Batting (1)

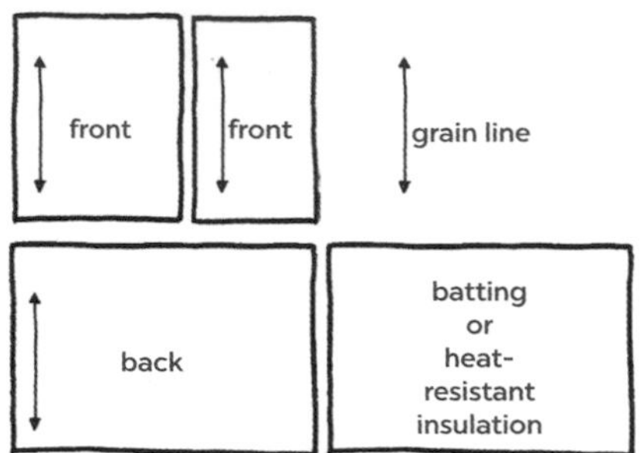

CONSTRUCTION STEPS

1. Cut one 13-by-9-inch piece of main fabric for the back—this includes a ½-inch seam allowance all around. Then, cut a piece of batting the same size. For extra padding, cut out two layers.

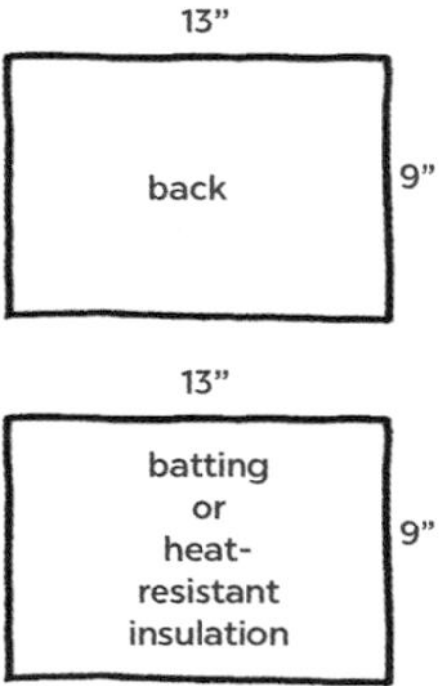

2. Cut two front pieces that will equal 14 by 9 inches (to account for seam allowances). The ratio is up to you, but I made the larger piece 8 by 9 inches and the darker piece, which will be embroidered, 6 by 9 inches

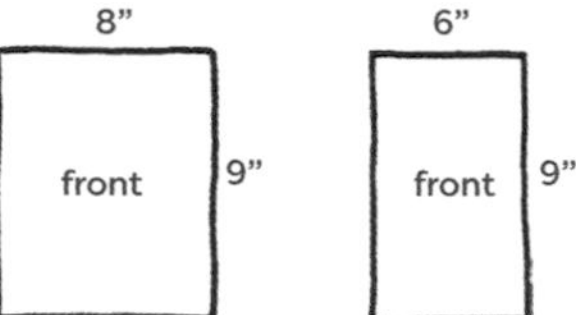

3. With the RIGHT sides facing, sew the two front pieces together and press open the seam. They should now equal 13 by 9 inches.

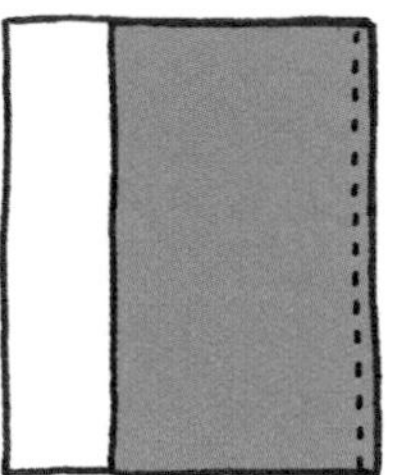

4. Using a marking tool, test a scrap to make sure the marks come out of the fabric. Sketch or trace a Sashiko design of your choosing, leaving a ½-inch space all around the design, unless you don't mind the design getting cut off a little around the edges. See The Mini Sashiko Primer templates (page 118). Place a sheet of carbon (also known as Chacopy) paper between the template and the RIGHT side of the fabric. You can also come up with your own design!

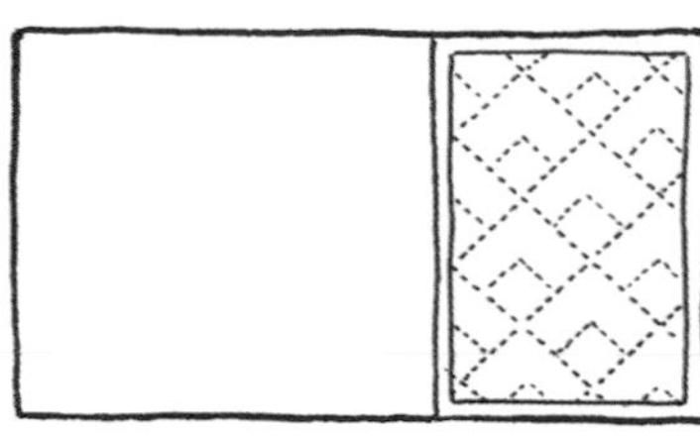

5 Thread your needle with Sashiko thread or embroidery floss. Note: Sashiko thread tends to be thicker and more twisted than embroidery floss—it also has no sheen.

If you are unable to get Sashiko thread, Pearl cotton embroidery floss works just fine. I often like to use just three or four strands of cotton embroidery floss for thinner stitches, but this is up to you!

6 Since the underside stitches will be hidden, insert the needle so the knot is on the WRONG side of the fabric to start your Sashiko stitches, but don't pull the needle all the way through. Using a gathering method, create running stitches. Try to create the stitches with a 3:2 ratio; this means that the stitches on the RIGHT side of the fabric will be slightly longer than the stitches on the WRONG side. Confession: My stitches often end up the same length or with the longer stitches on the bottom and the shorter ones on top. Perfection is overrated. It's all good.

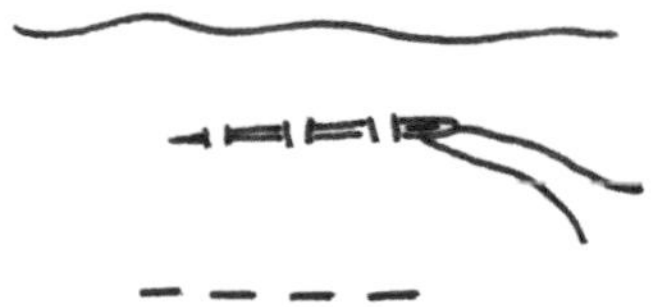

7 Feel free to stitch in any order that feels comfortable for you, but in case you're interested in traditional methodology: Create the horizontal and vertical lines first, then the diagonal lines. Fill in the details last. Try to leave a tiny little loop or slack in the thread at corners so that the stitches don't pucker. It you run out of thread, always knot a new thread on the WRONG side of the fabric.

Once you've completed the design, tie off the thread with a knot on the WRONG side of the fabric, and trim the thread. Note: The reason we are embroidering before adding the batting is because the batting will often "bleed" or poke through with the stitches as you pull the needle, resulting in small white tufts in your design. It's also easier to embroider without the batting in the way.

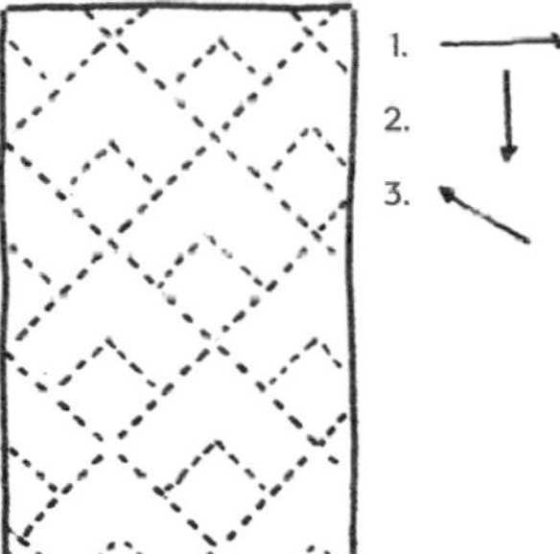

8 Baste the batting layer ¼ inch from the edge to the WRONG side of the back piece. Though this isn't strictly necessary, I find that it helps avoid the shifting of the batting when all the pieces are assembled later. Feel free to simply pin the batting if you want to skip the basting.

9 Flip the back piece with batting, and from the RIGHT side, sew a decorative grid formation to secure the batting to the back piece. Or, if you prefer, you can simply sew rows only or columns only, or even diagonal lines. The important thing is to have even coverage to secure the batting in place.

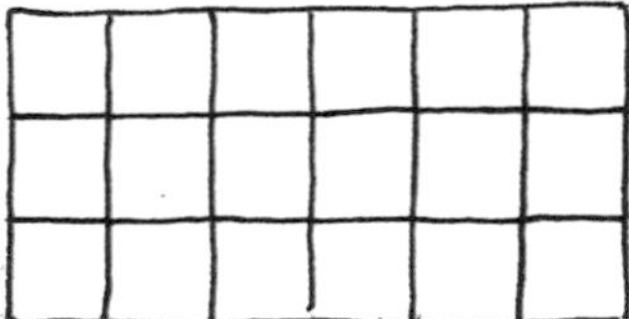

10 Place the front piece with the embroidery onto the back piece with the RIGHT sides facing. Sew ½ inch from the edge all the way around, leaving a 4-inch opening at the bottom.

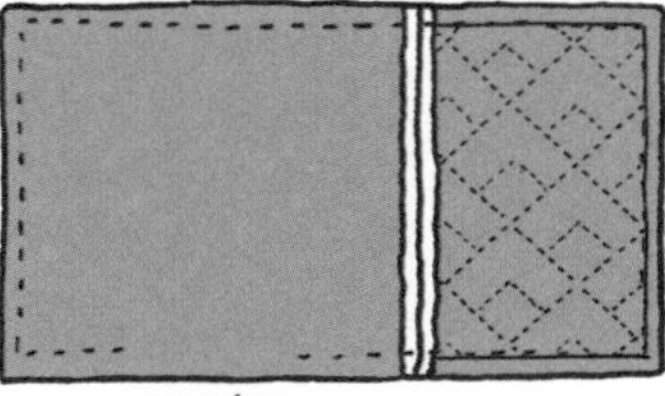

11 Clip the corners and turn the piece RIGHT side out. Push out the corners with a point turner. Be careful not to poke holes through the seam. Press.

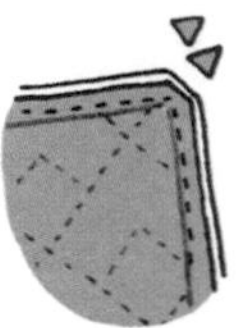

12 To secure the top to the quilted bottom, bartack four sections on the non-embroidered side with coordinating thread. Bartacking is a type of stitch used for reinforcing areas of high stress points (often for jeans) and is created with a zigzag stitched several times in the same place. By widening your stitch to about 3 and reducing your length to 0, you can create a bartack.

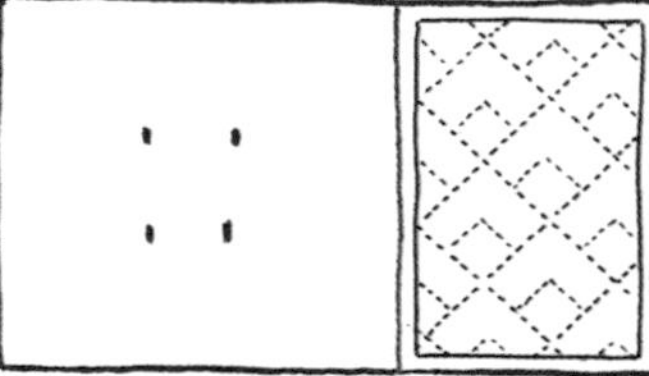

Slip stitch the bottom opening closed and you're finished.

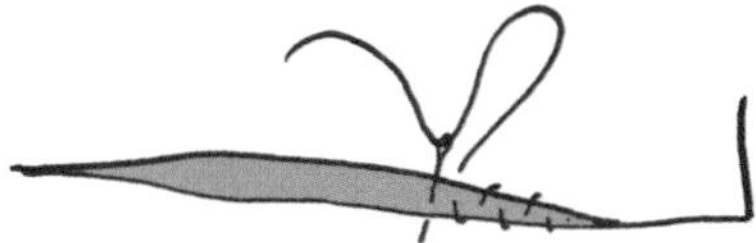

VERSATILE KNIT DRESS

THIS IS ONE OF THOSE workhorse garments that you'll reach for time and time again. With a little nip and tuck and snip and extension here and there, the possibilities are really endless for this beginner-friendly, versatile knit dress. Now, I know that there's a visceral fear of knits out there, but take heart: the stretchy stuff is incredibly forgiving.

I've created a couple versions of this dress using different skirt lengths, which is an easy way to alter the entire look of the dress. All you need is a tank top that you already own to get started on the drafting process. Make sure that the stretchiness of the tank top is comparable to the fabric you're using to get similar fit. For example, if your tank top is super stretchy but your fabric is not (some knits like interlock don't stretch a lot), the bodice of your dress will be too tight. And vice versa. It's always a good idea to first test this out on inexpensive knit jersey before cutting into the nice stuff, just in case. Drafting a dress may seem daunting, and it's quite possible that your first attempt won't look exactly the way you'd hoped. If that happens, I urge you to soldier on and try it again with tweaks because oftentimes repetition is the greatest teacher. I've done my best to include detailed instructions, and I know that with some practice, your result will be a keeper. Photos on pages 78 and 79.

SUPPLIES + MATERIALS

2 to 3 yards knit fabric

Coordinating thread

Ballpoint or stretch sewing machine needles

Drafting kit (see The Drafting Kit, page 96)

A favorite tank top or sleeveless knit dress

Rotary cutter (optional)

Serger or overlock machine (optional)

FABRIC RECOMMENDATIONS

Knit jersey is the required fabric for this project, but keep in mind not all knit jerseys are created equal. Try to find stretchy fabric that isn't too thin (you'll thank me) or prone to curling at the edges. A touch of spandex or lycra—just a touch: you're not auditioning for *So You Think You Can Dance*—will make the sewing experience much nicer. Organic bamboo or hemp cotton knit is absolutely lovely, but quite pricey, or you can actually find some beautiful drapey polyester-blend knits if you don't mind polyester. Make sure to prep the fabric by washing, drying, and pressing.

FINISHED DIMENSIONS

Modifiable to your size and desired length

FABRIC PIECES: Front Bodice (1), Back Bodice (1), Skirt (2), Neckband (1), Armhole Bands (2)

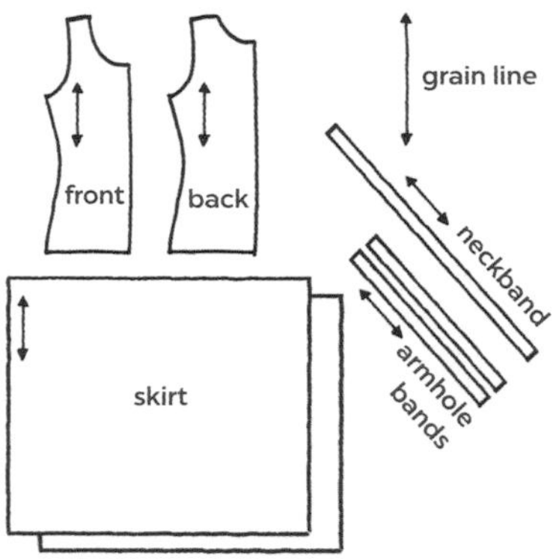

CONSTRUCTION STEPS

1. Did you find a favorite tank top or sleeveless knit dress? This will form the basis of your pattern piece. Put it on, and with a pin or a marking tool that won't leave a permanent mark, decide where you would like your waist to be at the side. Mark or pin that spot.

From that waist point, measure how far down you'd like the skirt portion of the dress to fall. Make a note of that dimension.

2. On a flat surface, lay a large piece of pattern paper. Fold your tank top or dress in half so that your mark/pin is visible. Lay the folded garment on top of the paper. With weights or soup cans or whatever you have on hand, hold down the garment and trace the bodice up to the point of the mark/pin. Remove the garment and clean up your traced lines where they may look uneven or crooked.

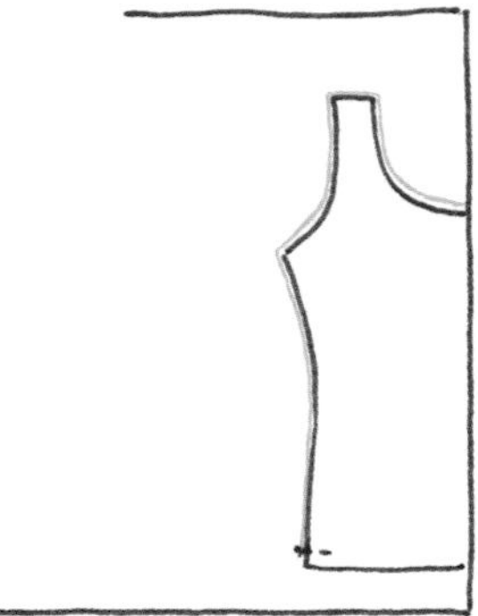

3. Make sure that you have right angles at the following sections: neckline at center fold, neckline corner where shoulder begins, corner under the arms, the corner at the waist, the waistline that meets at the center. Cut out your front bodice pattern piece and label it "Versatile Knit Dress—FRONT—cut 1 on fold."

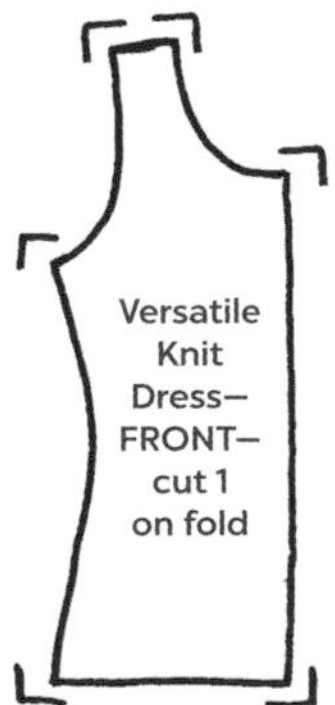

Drape this bodice pattern piece against your body to see if it's hitting mostly in the places that look good to you, but keep in mind that knit jersey stretches so this doesn't require meticulous precision. I usually don't need to add a seam allowance because the knit jerseys I buy at fabric stores seem to always have way more stretch than retail-wear knits. However, the fit really depends on the type of fabric you use, so you might need to tweak this bodice pattern piece a bit before you get just the right fit.

4. Lay the front bodice piece onto the pattern paper and trace. You're going to raise the neckline a little for the back, and my highly technical method of doing this is eyeballing what looks good, and then drawing the new neckline. You could also determine an exact measurement and use a curved ruler to make this neckline. Either works. The only thing to keep in mind is that just like the front neckline, the line that meets at the center fold should be perpendicular (or a right angle) or you will end up with either a peak or divot in the center back. Cut out and label this piece "Versatile Knit Dress—BACK—Cut 1 on fold."

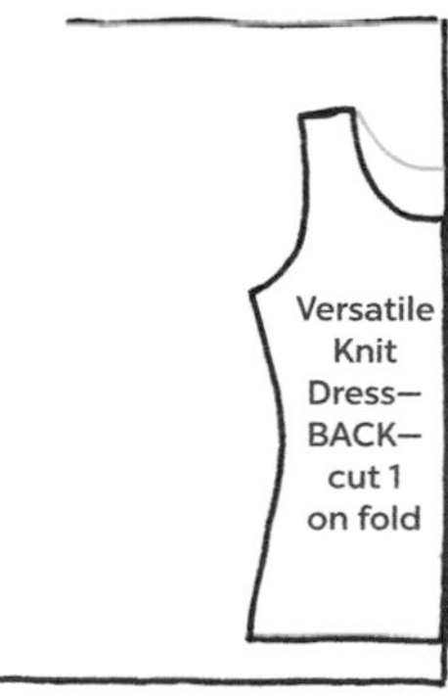

5. The skirt is a simple rectangle. Using the measurement you calculated in step 1, add 1½ total inches for the hem and waist seam allowances. This is your skirt pattern height. Make a note of this number.

For the width, take your pattern piece bodice waist measurement, double it (remember, the pattern piece is for only half the body) and add 4 inches. Keep in mind that the skirt will be gathered at the waist and you might need to adjust after making your muslin version, which is always a good idea. Make a note of this width.

I like to measure the skirt dimensions directly on the fabric, but if you prefer to have a pattern piece, first draw out the rectangle on your pattern paper. If you choose to create a pattern piece, label with "Versatile Knit Dress—Skirt—Cut 2."

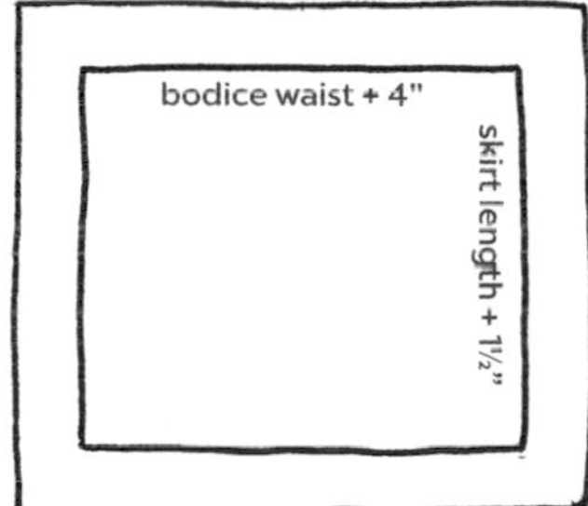

6 Time for some cutting action. Wrangle your knit fabric onto your cutting surface. Unless it's become horribly wrinkled in the prepping process, you shouldn't need to iron it. For the bodice pieces, I like to find the center point of the fabric, and then fold the two edges inward toward the middle (like double doors) with the RIGHT sides facing.

Pin or use weights to hold the pattern pieces in place. Trace with a marking tool, and cut out.

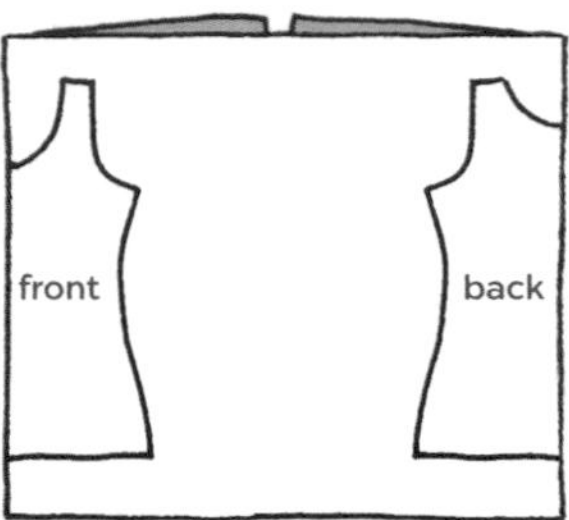

A note about using striped fabric, which is often my go-to for knits. If you don't want terribly mismatched stripes, try this method. The easiest way I've found to match up stripes is cutting the pieces as a single layer (instead of on the fold), aligning the stripes at underarm sections, corners, bottom edges, etc. So I trace the one half pattern piece, and then flip it around to trace the other half, keeping my eye on stripes placement. This will add a little extra time, but the professional finish, in my opinion, is worth it. This method is applicable to all prints you want to make appear seamless.

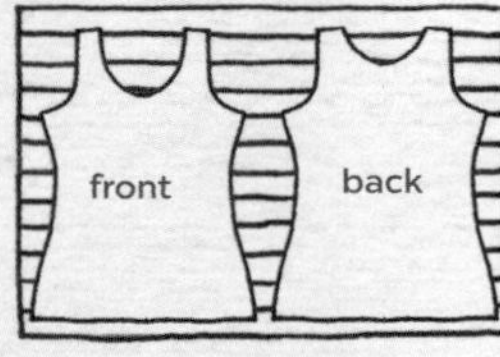

7 Once you've cut out the bodices, fold the remaining fabric in half, and measure out the skirt dimensions. You should have two skirt pieces. If you're using stripes or a print that you want to match up, cut out the skirt pieces from a single layer.

You can place all the pattern pieces and measure out the skirt at the same time as the bodice pieces, but I don't have a large enough surface to do so. I always try to maximize the fabric whenever possible by cutting pieces close together.

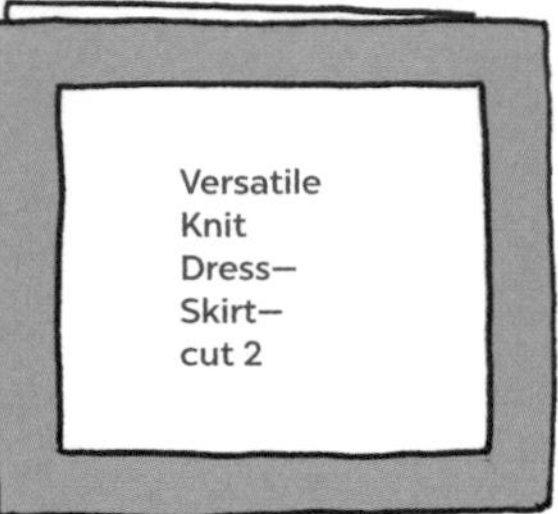

8 To make the neckband and armhole band bindings, I use yet another highly technical method. I simply cut across the length of the fabric (which is usually about 60 inches) at a 1½-inch height. A rotary cutter and large quilter's ruler is extremely handy for this. One 60-inch length is sufficient for both neckline and armhole bindings for me, but if it doesn't look like enough, cut two. Extra binding is always great to have. Note: Unlike wovens, knit fabrics are sufficiently stretchy from selvage to selvage, so you don't need to cut binding on the bias (for wovens, the fabric stretches more on the bias).

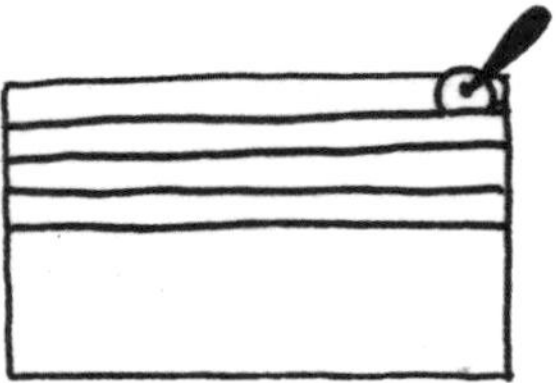

9 OK, you're set with all the pieces you need, minus exact neckband and armhole binding measurements, but we'll work on those later. At this point you should have cut out following:

- Front bodice
- Back bodice
- Skirt pieces (front and back)
- Binding strips for neck and armhole bands

10 VERY IMPORTANT: Change your sewing machine needle to a ballpoint or stretch needle. You will be happier for it since these needles are specifically designed for knit fabrics. Some people recommend a walking foot, but I've never used one and have sewn dozens and dozens of knit projects successfully. There are several stitch style options for knit fabrics (see Sewing Knits, page 105). A regular straight stitch isn't ideal because it doesn't have enough elasticity or stretch, and will break easily.

11 Pin the front and back bodices to each other at the shoulders with the RIGHT sides facing. I use extra fine pins (wonder clips are fantastic for knits too) since regular pins may leave holes in the fabric. Using your choice of one of the knit-friendly stitches, sew ⅜ inch from the edge.

Feel free to leave the raw edges as is since knit fabrics don't fray. I usually use an overlocking stitch to finish the raw edges, but this is purely out of habit. Press the seams open, or if you overlocked the edges, press overlocked edges toward the back.

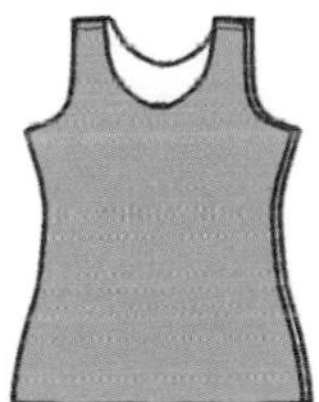

12 Pin or the clip sides together with the RIGHT sides facing. If your fabric has stripes or a print that needs to match up, pay attention to aligning these elements as you pin/clip. Sew ⅜ inch from the edges. Finish (or not) the raw edges. Press the seams in the same way you did for the shoulders.

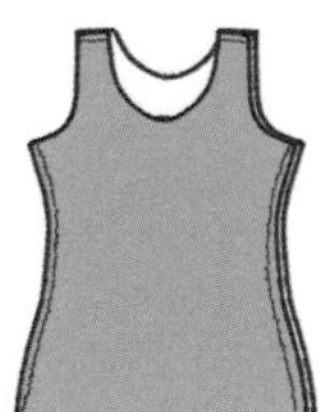

13 Pin or clip the skirt pieces together (again, paying attention to match up stripes or prints), RIGHT sides facing. Sew ⅜ inch from edge. You know the drill with raw edges now.

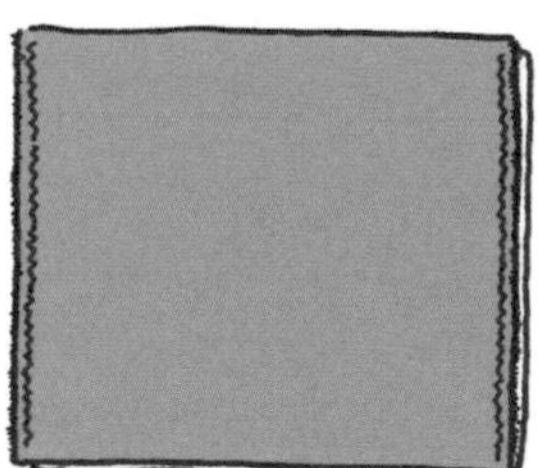

14 Lay your sewn bodice piece on a flat surface, front facing up. Loop the binding strip around the neckline—don't stretch the binding if you can help it—and cut a length that exactly matches the neckline circumference. Use pins or clips if it helps.

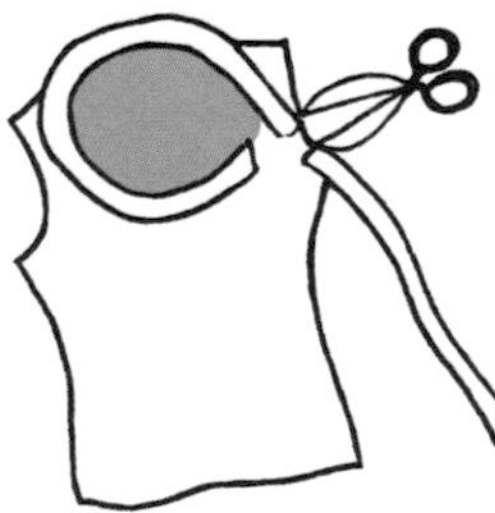

15 With the RIGHT sides facing, sew the short ends of the binding together with a knit-appropriate stitch, about ⅜ inch from the edges. Press the seam open. Then, fold the neckband in half lengthwise, WRONG sides facing, and press.

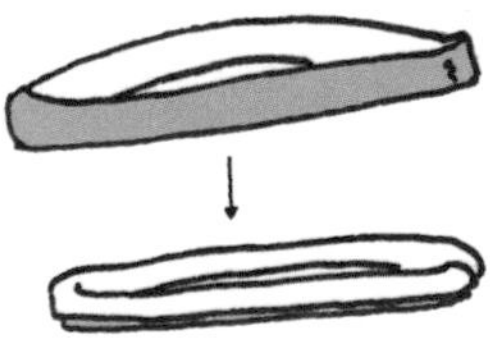

16 With the seam placed at the center back, pin the neckband to the bodice neckline with raw edges matching and the folded side at the bottom. You may have to stretch the neckband ever so slightly to get it to fit evenly around the neckline.

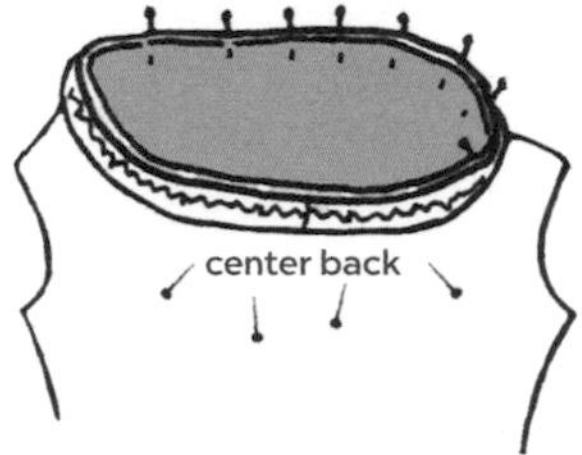

17 Place your machine foot aligned to the left edge of the folded side of the neckband. Sew ¼ inch from the folded edge.

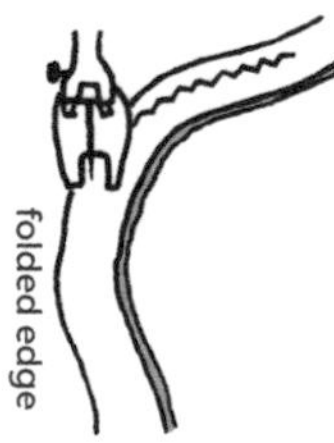

18 Finish the raw edge (or not) and press it toward the bodice. This next step is something that I wouldn't normally recommend, but I've done this on countless necklines and have never had a problem. Change to a straight stitch with a length of about 3½. Working from the center back on the RIGHT side of the bodice, stitch ¼ inch from the edge where the neckband meets the bodice. This holds the seam allowance in place, and gives the neckline a more finished appearance.

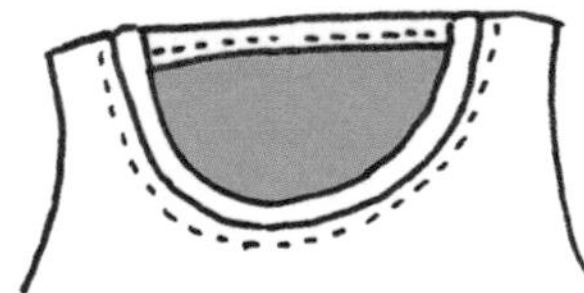

19 Repeat steps 14 to 18 to create and attach the armhole bindings to the dress. Make sure to line up the binding seam to the arm hole seam as you pin the binding to the arm hole.

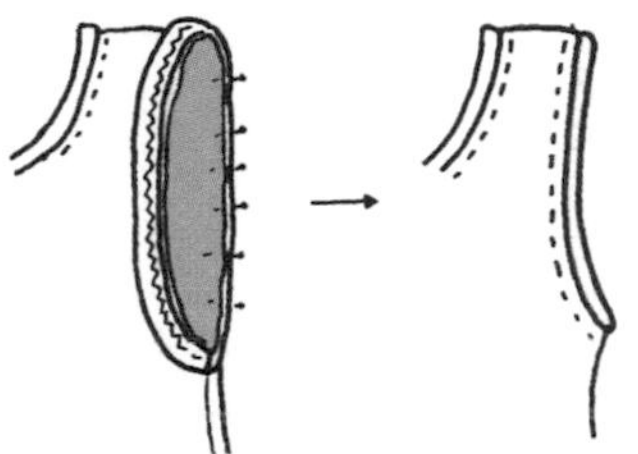

20 To gather the skirt, change your stitch style to a straight stitch, and increase your machine stitch length to the maximum. Without backstitching at the beginning or the end, sew one row about ¼ inch from the top edge, leaving a tail of about 3 inches at the beginning and the end of the row. Then sew a second row (again without backstitching) about ⅜ inch from the top row (again leaving 3-inch tails on either end). Now pull on the two threads that are on the same side. Leave the threads on the other side alone for now. Pull on the threads to gather the fabric, alternating between the left and right sides to get the gathers going.

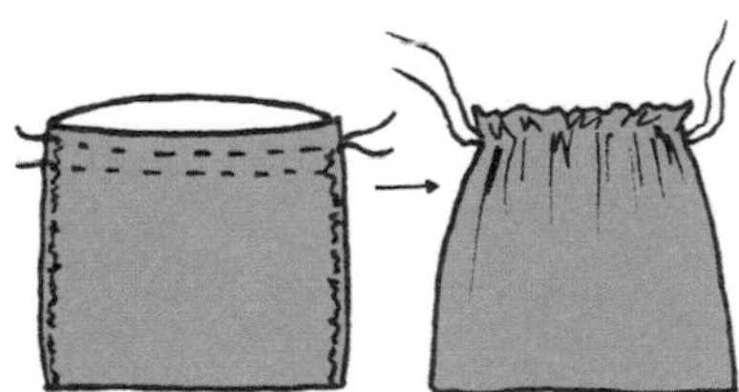

21 With the WRONG side of the skirt facing out and the gathers at the top, insert the bodice RIGHT side out and upside down. Pin or clip at the side seams and adjust so the gathers are spaced evenly. Change your stitch back to a knit-appropriate one and sew ⅜ inch from edge. Tip: Sew with the gathered side up and use a pin to gently adjust the gathers as you sew.

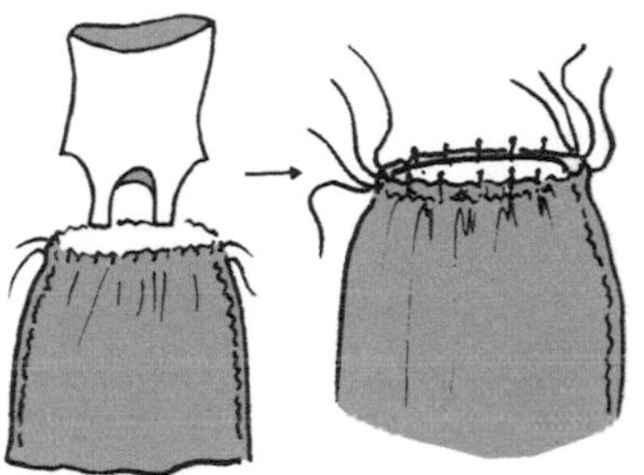

22 Hem the skirt. My preferred method is to overlock/serge the hem, then fold up ½ inch, press, and zigzag stitch close to the edge. However, there are a number of other methods:

- Skip the overlocking step, fold up ½ inch, press, and edgestitch.
- Fold once by ½ inch and fold again by ½ inch, press, and edgestitch (this will shorten the hem by 1 inch).
- Single fold by ½ inch and use a double-needle to mimic a professional finish.

Whatever method you choose, once you've sewn the hem, you're all done! Enjoy your new lovely dress!

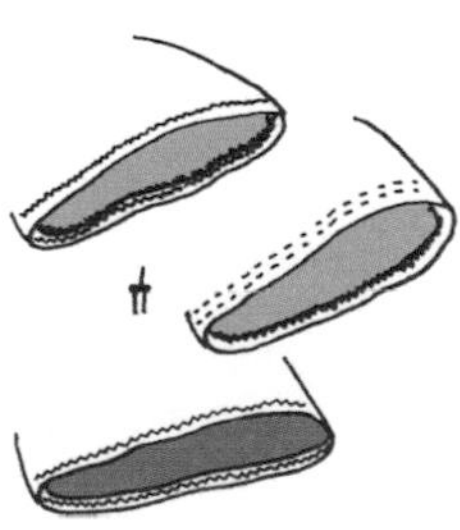

resources

SEWING BOOKS

I've been collecting sewing books for years, and these are invaluable to me:

1, 2, 3 Sew by Ellen Luckett Baker

The Colette Sewing Handbook by Sarai Mitnick

The Colette Guide to Sewing Knits by Alyson Clair

The Complete Photo Guide to Clothing Construction by Christine Haynes

The Complete Photo Guide to Perfect Fitting by Sarah Veblen

Design-It-Yourself Clothes by Cal Patch

Oliver + S Little Things to Sew by Liesl Gibson

Patternmaking by Dennic Chunman Lo

Pattern Cutting Made Easy by Gillian Holman

The Pattern Making Primer by Jo Barnfield and Andrew Richards

Sashiko Style by Joie Staff

Simple Sewing with a French Twist by Celine Dupuy

The Ultimate Sashiko Sourcebook by Susan Briscoe

SEATTLE FABRIC SHOPS + HABERDASHERIES

In recent years, the online resources for sewing have exploded. A quick search will yield everything you need at the tip of your fingers, but for this section, I opted to include my go-to stores in Seattle, where I currently reside. I try to shop local and in person whenever possible for all fabric and notions, although many of the following have online shops as well.

District Fabric (DistrictFabric.com)

Drygoods Design (DrygoodsDesignOnline.com)

Nancy's Sewing Basket (NancysSewingBasket.com)

Pacific Fabrics & Crafts (PacificFabrics.com)

Stitches (StitchesSeattle.com)

JAPANESE SHOP

This amazing shop requires special mention, not only because the owner, Frances, has become a dear friend (I have a bit of a fabric shopping problem now, though I'm learning how to reign it in). The quality of Japanese fabrics is unmatched and I can't recommend this shop enough.

Miss Matatabi (MissMatatabi.com)

SASHIKO SUPPLIES

There seems to be an uptick in the Sashiko stitching trend, with many independent fabric stores carrying specialized needles and threads. In general, Sashiko needles have larger eyes for the thicker Sashiko thread. Here are a couple of resources that I'm aware of, and Amazon is always an option as well—just search for "Sashiko needles" or "Sashiko thread."

Drygoods Design (DrygoodsDesignOnline.com)

Purl Soho (search for "Sashiko") (PurlSoho.com)

acknowledgments

I ALMOST ALWAYS READ THE acknowledgments section of every book I dive into. Partly it's to see if I recognize anyone (it's happened on several occasions), but also I like to see how the author expresses his or her appreciation—I believe you can tell a lot about a person by the way they thank people.

I have learned through this enormous process that it takes more than a village to write a book. I've had to enlist the help of the entire globe, or at least it seems that way. I know I'm going to be guilty of oversight and will forget to mention key people. If I have, I'm so sorry and I promise to sew you something.

A huge thank-you to my editor Hannah Elnan, who tirelessly cheered me on and gave me so many extensions, even before I asked for them. I'm convinced she's clairvoyant. I couldn't have done this without you, Hannah.

Special thanks to my other lovely editor Tegan Tigani, who set into motion this new phase of the book world for me. Anna Goldstein, your impeccable sense of style is a boon to the aesthetic of *Sewing Happiness*. And to the entire staff at Sasquatch Books, it's an honor and a privilege to work with you. Nancy Cortelyou, what a treat to have two of my non-human babies graciously and gently cared for by you.

Many incalculable thanks to the readers of my blog. If it weren't for your constant support and encouragement, I would have stopped yammering on about myself online a long time ago, and I might not have had this chance to yammer on about myself in print. I am deeply indebted. In particular, I'd like to extend a grateful high five to my pattern testers and project reviewers. You've made the book better with your eagle eyes (though all errors are my own). In no particular order: Ute, Lucinda, Kristin, An, Gail, Cherie, Erin, Rachel, Morgan, Robin, Tara, Frances, Elizabeth, Kelly, Brienne, Nicole, Jess, Bridget, Meghan, Alana, Angela, Chandra, Meagan, Holly, Marisa, Katie, Idoia, Lynda, Ailsa, Michaela, Bronwyn, Karina, Lynn, Maria, Nina, Tessa, Dena, Melissa, Heather, Daniela, Crys, Amber, Claire, Julie, Jaime, Sarah, Teri, Jana, Jill, Shelley, Karen, Angela, Asmita, Denise, Sydney, Marta, SarahKeith, Kelley, Brienne, Ana Sofia, Sara, Amy, Kristi, Jessie, Teresa, and Neal.

To the dynamic duo Tristan Brando and Michelle Porter, thank you for your photography/styling magic that resulted in the cover. Who knew that bull clips would give me the waist I never had? I owe you a linen shirt, T. You two *are* magic.

Allie Hsiao, it was manna from heaven that plopped you in Seattle the moment I needed you. Our photo session together made me realize how much I miss aimlessly chatting with you. Thank you for your styling expertise and for connecting me with good people.

George Barberis, you've elevated the photography in the book, and you know how to make a photo shoot feel like a party.

Malia Keene, I can't thank you enough for your pattern drafting advice.

Extra thanks to Morgan Nomura for modeling help. You gorgeous thing, you.

Thanks to Sean at Anytime Fitness for letting me take over the yoga studio for photos. We put everything away just the way it was, I promise. And a shout-out to Andrew of Milstead Coffee, where the beginnings of this book emerged. You arguably serve the best latte in Seattle. And Aran of Cannelle et Vanille, your studio space has sublime light, and I'm now motivated to save up my pennies to build my own studio one day.

Keli Faw of Drygoods Design, you're my sewing fairy godmother, and you make excellent things happen for everyone.

Frances Arikawa of Miss Matatabi, you're making the world a better place, one Japanese fabric at a time. xoxo

Thank you so much Hallie for letting adorable Jago rock the kimono top and bloomers!

Rachel Billings Grunig, stylist extraordinaire, how did I get so lucky? I've found an amazing friend and teammate in you. Thank you, thank you, thank you for everything.

To my dearest friends local and far-flung—you know who you are, thank you for all the coffee dates and listening ears and bear hugs. I don't have enough words to express my appreciation.

To my family in Los Angeles, *arigatou gozaimasu—kansha bakaridesu.* To my family in Indianapolis, your support has been literally lifesaving. To my family on the "compound," as we call it, I have no idea how I could have survived without you all. Viva la neighbors.

To M and K . . . you've been so patient. I love you.

And a final thanks for the sweet poems my little girl writes for me. She asked, "Mama, will you put this one in your book?" Of course, my love:

sewing, the loud rumble rumble it makes that is very distracting
but it's worth it 'cause soon,
sitting in your closet or on your bed is a brand-new outfit
or pillow in the shape of a heart or a moon

writing a book is a challenging thing
you don't know what kind of feelings it will bring
and it might not make any cha-ching
but . . .
it's a very, very happy
and you might start feeling snappy
or even slaphappy or sappy

index

Q

R

S

T

conversions

SEAM ALLOWANCES

⅛ inch = 3 mm	⅝ inch = 1.6 cm
¼ inch = 6 mm	¾ inch = 2 cm
⅜ inch = 1 cm	⅞ inch = 2.3 cm
½ inch = 1.3 cm	1 inch = 2.5 cm

YARDAGE

¼ yard = 23 cm	1¼ yard = 1.2 m	2¼ yards = 2.1 m
½ yard = 45 cm	1½ yard = 1.4 m	2½ yards = 2.3 m
¾ yard = 70 cm	1¾ yards = 1.6 m	2¾ yards = 2.5 m
1 yard = 90 cm	2 yards = 1.8 m	3 yards = 2.7 m

Note: These conversions are rounded approximations. For more accurate conversions, use the Conversion Guide that follows.

CONVERSION GUIDE

FROM	TO	MULTIPLY BY
Inches	Centimeters	2.54
Feet	Meters	0.305
Yards	Meters	0.915

MERCHANT & MILLS

about the author

SANAE ISHIDA writes, sews, draws, and takes photos almost every day. She lives with her husband and daughter in Seattle, Washington. She also wrote and illustrated a children's book, *Little Kunoichi: The Ninja Girl*. Both she and her daughter have too many handmade clothes.

Find more of her work at **SanaeIshida.com**.